M000197895

SCRIPTURE, SKEPTICISM,
AND THE CHARACTER OF GOD

Scripture, Skepticism, and the Character of God

The Theology of Henry Mansel

DANE NEUFELD

McGill-Queen's University Press
Montreal & Kingston • London • Chicago

© McGill-Queen's University Press 2019

ISBN 978-0-7735-5750-5 (cloth)
ISBN 978-0-7735-5825-0 (ePDF)
ISBN 978-0-7735-5826-7 (ePUB)

Legal deposit second quarter 2019
Bibliothèque nationale du Québec

Printed in Canada on acid-free paper that is 100% ancient forest free
(100% post-consumer recycled), processed chlorine free

This book has been published with the help of a grant from the Canadian
Federation for the Humanities and Social Sciences, through the Awards to
Scholarly Publications Program, using funds provided by the Social Sciences
and Humanities Research Council of Canada.

Funded by the   Financé par le   Canada Council   Conseil des arts
Government   gouvernement   for the Arts   du Canada
of Canada   du Canada   Canada

We acknowledge the support of the Canada Council for the Arts.

Nous remercions le Conseil des arts du Canada de son soutien.

Library and Archives Canada Cataloguing in Publication

Title: Scripture, skepticism, and the character of God: the theology of Henry
    Mansel/Dane Neufeld.

Other titles: Theology of Henry Mansel

Names: Neufeld, Dane, 1983– author.

Description: Includes bibliographical references and index.

Identifiers: Canadiana (print) 20190074876 | Canadiana (ebook)
    20190074965 | ISBN 9780773557505 (hardcover) |
    ISBN 9780773558250 (ePDF) | ISBN 9780773558267 (ePUB)

Subjects: LCSH: Mansel, Henry Longueville, 1820-1871. | LCSH: Religion—
    Philosophy—History—19th century.

Classification: LCC BL51 .N48 2019 | DDC 210—dc23

This book was typeset by Marquis Interscript in 10.5/13 Sabon.

Contents

Acknowledgments

This book originated as a doctoral dissertation written during my time at Wycliffe College in Toronto. Like all dissertations, it would not have been possible without the wonderful support of college staff and students and the many friends who made my time there such a rich and memorable experience. I am grateful especially for the supervision of Dr Ephraim Radner whose incredible gifts as a professor, supervisor, and theologian have been a great light to a whole generation of young and aspiring theologians and pastors.

The main portion of this book was written in Fort McMurray, Alberta, where I continue to serve as the rector of All Saints'. I am so deeply grateful for the people of this parish who provided me with their time, support, and friendship as I struggled to bring this work to completion. Likewise, I am grateful for our Bishop Fraser, who was very supportive of my writing and frequently checked in to ensure that I was devoting enough time to my studies.

I am very thankful for the very skilled editorial team at McGill-Queen's University Press and for their commitment to this book. It has been both a pleasure and an honour to work together toward publication.

Most of all, I am grateful to my family: to my parents who nurtured both my faith and love of reading; to my dear children who never failed to lighten my mood and keep my feet grounded in reality; and to my wonderful wife who has supported me every step of the way and believed in me with a confidence that far exceeded my own.

My hope and prayer is that this book can make a small contribution toward contemporary discussions around faith and belief, and toward the self-understanding of the Christian tradition in which I serve as a minister of the gospel.

SCRIPTURE, SKEPTICISM,
AND THE CHARACTER OF GOD

Introduction

The following pages are concerned with the retrieval and illumination of the writings of Henry Mansel, a now long forgotten figure in the Victorian Church. There are of course reasons that figures become overshadowed within any one particular intellectual tradition, and the reasons are fairly evident in the case of Mansel. Mansel's career was cut short by a relatively early death that deprived him of the time to formalize and restate his views to his critics; his opponents were prominent and powerful writers who eventually won the sympathy of the embattled and distracted theological circles of the Church of England; and perhaps more importantly, Mansel's brief moment of renown was quickly overwhelmed by the now classic and historic controversies surrounding Darwin, John William Parker's *Essays and Reviews*, and the Colenso affair. Even still, for all the clamour and confusion that defined the theological climate in which Mansel lived, it must be acknowledged that his ideas simply failed to persuade the majority of his contemporaries, even those who were sympathetic with his cause. Why this was the case will be the subject of this book, along with the argument that Mansel, despite certain shortcomings, perceived an approaching danger for Christian theology and practice in England that would not fully arrive until the next century. Mansel was one of only a few Christian philosophers who attempted to make use of modern philosophical strategies to defend a traditional and in some sense, precritical form of Christian belief and piety. Rowan Strong has written: "In 1800 theologian and parishioner shared a common outlook – the historical accuracy of the Bible, its literal veracity, the timelessness of doctrine, and a culture largely permeated by Christianity. By 1900 Christian clergy and many educated laity were more aware than their forebears that these beliefs were difficult to sustain."[1] Mansel perceived this emerging crisis and lived through the most critical years of upheaval in English Christianity, where the faith of many people was either starved or shattered to an unprecedented degree. This loss of faith among many of his contemporaries was the single greatest motivating factor in Mansel's work.

The theological and spiritual difficulties that confronted the Victorian Church remain largely unchanged among modern Christians, though today these difficulties no longer grip the public life of an entire society. Debates and discussions around faith and reason, the nature of religious knowledge and character of Christian scripture are very much alive at present in theological circles that no longer occupy the public eye. In 2019, Henry Mansel could have said everything he did in the nineteenth century with very little public disturbance. No doubt some theologians would take issue, others would agree, but it is unlikely that disagreement over his ideas would escape the relative obscurity of theological journals and blogs. But this was far from the case in the 1850s and 1860s when Mansel's "Bampton Lectures" exploded in the public life of Victorian England and exposed deep divisions and insecurities in the emerging sense of what it meant to believe in God. His arguments were not entirely new, he insisted, as many writers had before him, that we do not know as much about God as we think, and for this reason we must rely on the Christian scriptures for our understanding of what it means to live and think as God's creatures. For this conviction, and for the language with which he advanced it, Mansel was branded a hopeless Fideist by the free thinkers and a dangerous skeptic by high, broad, and evangelical churchmen alike.

What is now commonly referred to as the crisis of faith in Victorian England, at the time had less do with the existence of God and supernatural realities. The crisis of faith that confronted many Victorian Christians concerned more directly the character of God as it had been revealed in the scriptures and communicated in the tradition. The "honest doubt" of Tennyson or the "withdrawing roar" of Arnold's "Sea of Faith" was concerned less with the existence of God than with the demise of the whole moral, theological, and scriptural apparatus that sustained such a vision. In this light, I believe Francis Newman's sentiments to be broadly representative of his generation: "If I admitted morals to rest on an independent basis, it was dishonest to shut my eyes to any apparent collisions of morality with the

Scriptures."[2] Though Newman could appeal to ideas of moral progress to explain difficult portions in the Bible, "it was hard to deny that God is represented as giving an actual sanction to that which we now call sinful."[3] This question alone troubled the faith of many and today its difficulty has only increased. The question of God's character was the issue to which Mansel devoted himself, not strictly in the form of theodicy, but as a matter that pertained to the entire order of theological knowledge and understanding. The God of the scriptures is the Christian God, Mansel argued, regardless of whatever moral or intellectual dissonance this reality may produce in one generation or another. The method by which Mansel made this argument and the obstacles and reactions it produced among his contemporary and future readers is the subject of this book.

The career of Mansel's ideas, subsequent to his "Bampton Lectures" in 1858, marks a puzzling sequence in modern intellectual history. His lectures went through five editions and were enormously popular for well over a decade. One early critic complained that "the hurried procession of the religious critics, one after another, rushing into print and into praise, by all the world, was like nothing so much as, a flock of sheep escaping over a fence, through some gap they had just discovered."[4] Indeed, some early critics resented this "furious current of popular enthusiasm"[5] because Mansel's lectures, they argued, were seized upon peremptorily as a salve to the deepening concerns about the state of Christian orthodoxy. Initially regarded as a hero of orthodoxy, Mansel eventually found himself entangled in a number of debates with powerful contemporary figures. Mansel's debate with F.D. Maurice was celebrated as one of the great religious controversy of the nineteenth century,[6] and he drew fire and recognition from some of most prominent intellectual figures of his day, such as J.S. Mill, Herbert Spencer, and John Henry Newman. The philosophical idealism that took hold of Oxford after Mansel's death, represented by figures like F.H. Bradley and T.H. Green, grounded its constructions on the repudiation of Mansel's ideas.[7] Yet aside from some initial applause and intensely negative reactions, the positive influence of Mansel's ideas on the Anglican theology of his own generation or that of later generations is difficult to trace. Despite Mansel's fierce loyalty to the Church of England and her articles of faith, some of his most adamant opponents were fellow clergymen who saw in his lectures a dangerous and threatening theological method. In many ways Mansel cut across the grain of his theological climate by offering what seemed to be a narrow scriptural view of reality. His theology lacked the comprehensive ambition that characterized the aspirations of the later *Lux Mundi* writers who sought to provide a theological vision that could incorporate modern developments in science and philosophy. For this reason, Mansel's contemporaries were not pleased to recognize themselves in his writings, and this, in part, accounts for his marginalization in the history of Anglican theology. But I will argue throughout this book that Mansel's seeming lack of ambition is a fundamental oversight. Mansel's hope was not to articulate a defensive or regressive theological vision, but rather his aim was to allow the scriptures "to absorb the universe,"[8] to use George Lindbeck's now well-known phrase. The limitations of human thought, or theological skepticism, were simply a method of ensuring that the Church apprehended itself and its God within the narrative of the Bible.

I argue that Mansel's skeptical philosophy is derived from his basic axiom that people "learn to pray before they learn to reason."[9] His skepticism is used to examine the foundations and logic of varying forms of human thought that seek to reconfigure, augment, or obscure what Mansel understands to be the scriptural account of God's relation to his people. The person of Christ and the language of scripture are regulatively true, in that they do not present God in his essence but as he chooses to be known within his creation: God cannot be thought of under any terms that transcend the structure of human thought and the Divine appeal to us is formed in a manner that appeals to our humanity. For Mansel, the canon of scripture, read through the figure of Jesus, reveals a truthful account of God's character and the created world. This truthful account necessarily includes the strange, difficult, and, at times, seemingly contradictory aspects of scripture. The scriptures, Mansel argued, formed an "incomplete system" that described God's revealed character in contrasting, fragmented, and sometimes antinomous anthropomorphic language.[10] But it is within this form of divinely inspired but humanly rendered language that God is revealed and efforts to complete or fill out this language, or to construct an ideal portrait of God's being, often distort the scriptural images under which God has chosen to represent and reveal himself within the constraints of time. While the language of scripture can create speculative difficulties, Mansel urged that the portrait of God that scripture renders must be accepted in faith, or not at all.

Mansel's contemporary and later critics suggested that his account of epistemological skepticism and revelation ultimately render God unknowable and distant. One writer in the *Eclectic Review* questioned "but what if the hero himself also has perished, and if his mangled and lifeless body be found under the heaps of his slain enemies?"[11] The perception among many fellow churchmen was that Mansel's skepticism, in an effort to protect a certain form of theological orthodoxy, actually sacrificed the immediate knowledge of God: the real God remained hidden behind the regulative God. Likewise, critics suggested that Mansel's theology authorized the immoral and violent acts of God, especially in the Old Testament, with little attempt to mitigate the collision between modern moral sentiments and the scriptural account of God's character. This criticism was most famously captured by Mill's memorable words: "I will call no being good, who is not what I mean when I apply that epithet to my fellow creatures."[12] At a time when the moral character of God revealed in the Bible was becoming increasingly difficult for Victorian intellectuals to accept, Mansel's affirmation of the whole range of scripture struck an emphatic and dissonant note. But I argue, in contrast to these criticisms, that Mansel's skepticism and theory of regulative truth do not alienate God from the created world but rather they allow the scriptures to speak truthfully of God: God can in fact be known and encountered throughout the entire canon of scripture. The strength of Mansel's skepticism is that the revelation of God in scripture does not require a metaphysical or ontological framework in order to make sense or perform its task: there is no broader or deeper framework to describe the reality of God than the language of the Bible itself. For this reason Mansel resisted philosophical, theological, and moral presuppositions that sought to streamline portions of scripture in order to fit it into a larger vision. While critics saw in the Bampton lecturer's theology a haphazard scripturalism, for Mansel the scriptures came alive with the presence of God when the whole array of Biblical texts were allowed to reveal God in a dizzying but ultimately unified witness. The main argument of this book is that Mansel's skepticism places the continually evolving life of the Church within the narrative and language of scripture. This language is on one hand solid and concrete in its ability to reveal and refer to God. But on the other hand, Mansel's account of the limitations of the human mind grants the Spirit-inspired language of scripture a depth that is capable of expanding around and describing a constantly changing world.

THE LIFE AND CAREER OF HENRY MANSEL

Henry Mansel was born in 1820 in the village of Cosgrove. He studied at St John's, Oxford, where he read logic and mathematics. In 1844 he was ordained a deacon and the following year, a priest, but he would spend the next twenty-four years at Oxford in various teaching posts.[13] In 1855 he was elected to the readership in moral and metaphysical philosophy in Magdalen College, a position that allowed him to get married the same year to Charlotte Augusta.[14] Several years later he was named the Waynflete Professor of Metaphysics at Magdalen, a position he would hold until his appointment as the Regius Professor of Ecclesiastical History in 1866. This appointment was a surprise to many, given Mansel's background philosophy and logic, and it was one he accepted with some hesitation. In the end he accepted the post to secure "sound teaching at the University of Oxford" and to afford himself more opportunity to pursue his writing.[15] However, only two years later, in 1868, Mansel was appointed the dean of St Paul's Cathedral. In this appointment he undertook the commuting of the estates of the cathedral, a task that was nearly complete upon his sudden death in 1871.[16]

Mansel was known as a High Tory and a descendant of the Oxford Movement. In his later years at Oxford, he corresponded frequently with E.B. Pusey about university affairs and different scholarly topics. Mansel was a close friend of H.P. Liddon, and upon Mansel's death Liddon wrote to inform Pusey: "His death was instantaneous. It was occasioned by the bursting of a blood vessel at the back of the brain just as he was getting into bed at night. He had been complaining of fatigue – mental fatigue ... In him the cause of positive truth has had a great champion: whether he was right or wrong in his use of the Hamiltonian philosophy in his bampton lectures. And we have lost here a great deal which no one is likely to replace."[17] Liddon's brief retrospective is a telling statement of Mansel's position within High Church Anglicanism. Though even his closest allies were not always sure what to do with his specific arguments concerning theological knowledge, Mansel remained an important figure and friend within the movement. Mansel's many books and articles bear little explicit reference to the Tractarian authors, and in this way he was perhaps more typical of the second generation of the Oxford Movement, which was concerned about the divisive character of the movement and its weighted appeal to antiquity.[18] Mansel's biographer, Dean John

Burgon, expressed the concern that the Oxford Movement, despite its conservatism, neglected the classic Anglican focus upon the scriptures: "It is a memorable fact that throughout this period (1830 to 1850) holy scripture itself experienced marked neglect."[19] Mansel was well read in Patristics and Anglican divinity, but it was his focus upon the defense of scripture that inspired his writings. Despite his obvious devotion to the Church of England, he wrote very little that might be called ecclesiology, but his theology, as I will argue, can be understood as an articulation of the space in which the Church reads, responds, and lives within the scriptures. He certainly inherited the Tractarian concern that the Church of England was becoming increasingly marginalized in public life; he worried about the steady stream of constitutional changes that began in 1829 and which gradually reformed and altered the Church of England's position of privilege and dramatically altered the fabric of the nation.[20] His satirical poem *The Phrontisterion*, which describes the increasingly secular attitudes of Oxford's intellectual life, is a testament to this anxiety.[21] But he was most energized and motivated to preserve the place of the Bible in the Church of England's common life and worship.

While the Oxford Movement quickly diverged in a number of directions Mansel's writing shows no traces of a desire to follow Newman or the many others who left the Church of England for Rome. Nor did he express any sympathy with the ritualism that came to define the movement's later generations. Perhaps like Pusey, who Timothy Larsen argues "surveyed the challenges of the Victorian age and decided that the right response was to invite people to listen to Holy Scripture," Mansel turned to scripture as the central place of contestation and resolution in the Church's commons life.

CONTEMPORARY SCHOLARSHIP ON MANSEL

The Victorian era was characterized by massive intellectual and theological disturbances that provoked considerable confusion within the Church. Mansel's career and the controversy that surrounded him offer a unique lens into this confusion over the status of the Church's scriptures and the intelligibility of its central claims. Charles Taylor has written that in this period "belief and unbelief exist in contrast and tension with each other" in a manner that was largely unprecedented in England.[22] As the traditional metaphysical frameworks in which Christian claims had been rooted began to disintegrate, theologians were pressed with the task of articulating new spaces within which Christian teaching could flourish. Even more, theological writers were searching for frameworks within which to describe the relationship between God and his people. In nineteenth-century England this meant making alliances with the continental philosophy of Immanuel Kant and his successors, while attempting to make sense of the empirical bent within English philosophy and, to some extent, within Anglican theology. Kant seemed to offer a rational structure for the mediation of theological knowledge, even if this form of mediation carried threatening demands.[23]

Thus Mansel has been largely read in the twentieth and twenty-first centuries as a Kantian religious philosopher. While it is true that Mansel engaged Kant's philosophy, there were limits to which he could appropriate Kant's views. This was most apparent in his theology of scripture, the aspect of Mansel's thought that has surprisingly not been engaged by the vast majority of scholars who have written about him in recent years. From the publication of the "Bampton Lectures" until recently, it has been customary among Mansel's readers and critics to overlook or ignore any integral connection between his philosophical skepticism and his theological and scriptural orthodoxy. This is merely to say that the majority of writers to have taken up Mansel's ideas have separated these aspects and in most cases dismissed the latter as an outdated or even desperate attempt by the Victorian philosopher to hold onto his religion in the grips of a disintegrating agnosticism. On account of this assumption, two general approaches to Mansel's philosophy can be traced.

The first approach is characterized by a scholar like Bernard Lightman who views Mansel as a creative and interesting thinker, who nevertheless failed to come to terms with the shifting intellectual patterns of German idealistic philosophy. Lightman's book *The Origins of Agnosticism* has convincingly shown how Mansel's ideas on the unknowability of the absolute and the infinite, derived in part from Kant, were adopted and altered by the early English Agnostics, most notably Herbert Spencer.[24] What made this transferal of Mansel's ideas into an alien context possible, Lightman argues, was Mansel's failure to come to terms with Kant's resolution of faith and reason: "Mansel's selective use of Kant, and his additions, warped Kant's delicate epistemological viewpoints so that, in Mansel's hands, reason was divorced entirely from faith. Only through such a process could Kant's brand of agnosticism be transformed into the basis for what was to become Huxley's agnostic position."[25] Mansel's explicit rejection of Kant's practical reason meant that he was left standing awkwardly with the two incommensurate commitments of epistemological skepticism and orthodox religious faith, which, in effect, symbolized the general fate of Victorian theology. Lightman's approach finds correspondence in other works on Mansel with its portrayal of him as a thinker who failed to synthesize the increasingly disparate aspects of nineteenth-century scientific and philosophical thought.[26]

A second way of approaching Mansel's thought has been to characterize him as a proleptic thinker who was entirely ahead of his times, which accounts for the apparent failure of his ideas to take hold within his contemporary context. While the approach is obviously more sympathetic toward Mansel as a whole, it typically retains the stark separation of his philosophical skepticism and his views of Christian scripture. Christopher Herbert's book *Victorian Relativity* provides a particularly startling instance of this interpretation. Herbert explores some of the fascinating tendencies in Victorian thought, which seem to anticipate Einstein's theory of relativity and postmodern modern notions of difference and the relative or constructed character of knowledge. In particular, Mansel's idea, following William Hamilton, that all knowledge is conditioned by relations, a contingency of the mind which makes the absolute inconceivable, Herbert writes, "is an unmistakably revolutionary act"[27] within the discipline of philosophy. Yet Herbert maintains that Mansel shrinks back from the revolutionary character of his thinking into a conservative orthodoxy that "is very much a system of rigid practical control appealing to an expressly authoritarian and absolutist ideology."[28] Presumably, Herbert is referring here to Mansel's theory of the regulative truth of scripture. Mansel's theory might be characterized otherwise than "authoritarian" or "absolutist" but presently it is sufficient to simply note the incongruence Herbert perceives between his radical philosophical skepticism and his high view of scripture: the latter simply does not keep pace with the former. This is characteristic of the second approach I have described which applauds Mansel for his unusually postmodern philosophical views, though these views have been torn out of the context of his understanding of scripture.[29]

While figures like Lightman and Herbert have provided important insights into the character of Mansel's thought and, even more, his perplexing place in intellectual history, it is fair to say that neither scholar has made an effort to understand the relationship between his skepticism and scripturalism. Granted, this was not their intention, but it will be the purpose of this book to stress this very relationship and to argue that his skepticism can only be understood as an extension of his traditional commitments to scripture. The common accusations that Mansel separates faith and reason, that he truncates the human search for knowledge – as true as these may be – in the end, merely underline the general crisis of theological thinking in nineteenth-century England. By his own admission, Mansel was not trying to build a new synthetic system; rather, his philosophy was critical and sought to chastise human reason in order to make space for Christian faith, founded on the entire scriptures and the creeds. In his own words, "A writer who is content with the humbler task of confuting objections will be satisfied to find his 'positive side,' not in his own confutations, but in that Catholic faith which exists independently of the objections and of the answers to them."[30] It is true that in order to do this he engaged Kant and the philosophy of his day, but given his general aims, I believe it is more important to assess his thought in the tradition of the eighteenth-century Anglican apologist Joseph Butler, who Mansel admired greatly and quoted abundantly. In this sense, it is possible to argue that for Mansel Christian orthodoxy – scripture and the creeds – was not an isolated set of beliefs asserted in a skeptical void, but, in the Butlerian sense, the "scheme of salvation" was literally written into the created world. Mansel pursues this conviction through the examination of human consciousness and the corresponding character of divine revelation in scripture which accommodates itself to the contours and strictures of the human mind. In order to demonstrate the manner in which scripture adjusts and responds to human reality, Mansel made use of typological, allegorical, and figural methods of reading. In this respect he truly was ahead of his time, though not perhaps quite in the way that Herbert imagined.[31]

To read Mansel in light of Butler is, in essence, to read him theologically, the context where he naturally belongs. And yet, ironically, this is the context in which he has seldom been read except, perhaps, during his own life. The fact that Mansel has been primarily remembered as the unlikely progenitor of English agnosticism is unfortunate given his own devotion to the Church of England and the integrity of the Christian faith. For this reason, I believe the time is ripe for a reconsideration of his work, especially as the pressures of unbelief and secularism that he perceived in his own era have only deepened and expanded their influence in the contemporary Church. Mansel believed that certain metaphysical and philosophical schemes, when pushed beyond the limits of human conception and capacity, risked subjecting the scriptures to a deforming criterion unable to render the Bible as a unified whole. The consequence of violating these limits, for Mansel, is that the portrait of God's presence in the world witnessed to in scripture becomes increasingly difficult to apprehend. Contrary to the conception that his skepticism described a remote and unknowable God, the limits of religious thought, for Mansel, were designed to make the God of scripture available and present in a world that was growing impatient of the difficulties and complexities of the scriptural account. Of course, for Mansel the stakes concerned not only the status of the Bible but also the character of God as he is revealed and described in its witness.

SUMMARY

In what follows, I explore the influence of Kant and German idealism in England and I argue that Mansel, far from being a Kantian, actually linked the new philosophy of the continent with the deist tradition in eighteenth-century England. In many ways, the deeper antecedents of Mansel's theology can be found in the eighteenth-century debates between figures like George Berkeley, John Toland, Peter Browne, and Joseph Butler. In particular, I contrast the figures of Coleridge and Joseph Butler to illuminate the various uses of theological skepticism in relation to the reading of scripture. Mansel was indebted primarily to Butler, as his contemporaries all understood, and it in this light that I describe and defend his theory of the regulative truth of scripture. Butler's analogy of religion and the correspondences between the scheme of salvation and the natural world formed a framework for Mansel, who pursued this analogy within the context of the human mind and personality. Although Mansel is best known for his skeptical approach to theological knowledge, the fourth chapter focuses upon his more explicitly theological writings, sermons, and letters in order to understand how his theory of regulative truth functioned in a scriptural and theological context.

The final chapters engage Mansel's reception in the late nineteenth century and the twentiety century. Here I argue that while Mansel's ideas were rejected by idealist theologians and philosophers in England, his reception can function as a lens into the place of scripture in the modern Church of England. In effect, the inability of Anglican theologians to come to terms with Mansel's central concern for the integrity of the entire scriptures has contributed to the perplexity and conflict within modern Anglicanism with respect to the scriptural witness and the God it reveals. This reception history begins with T.H. Green and the *Lux Mundi* theologians and closes with a discussion of Don Cupitt, Mansel's best-known twentieth-century interpreter.

Rowan Williams has argued that a certain form of theological skepticism or agnosticism has been one of the primary virtues of Anglican theology because it has created a broad and inclusive Christian tradition that is not organized around tightly defined confessional and disputed doctrinal commitments.[32] If this is indeed the case – I would argue that it is – then an exploration of Mansel's thought is highly valuable in clarifying the nature of this claim and its relation to the reading and interpretation of the scriptures.

Kant and Anglican Theology in the Nineteenth Century

The philosophy of Kant and those he influenced was welcomed by nineteenth-century English intellectuals with great excitement, anxiety, and confusion. Thomas Carlyle's characterization of English reactions to German culture in particular is telling:

> That the Germans, with much natural susceptibility, are still in a rather coarse and uncultivated state of mind; displaying, with the energy and other virtues of a rude people, many of their vices also; in particular, a certain wild and headlong temper, which seizes on all things too hastily and impetuously; weeps, storms, loves, hates, too fiercely and vociferously; delighting in coarse excitements, such as flaring contrasts, vulgar horrors, and all sorts of showy exaggeration.[1]

Carlyle's devotion to Goethe, an embodiment of at least a few of these susceptibilities, reveals the author's own preferences and what would be expressed more generally in early-nineteenth-century England as an emerging dissatisfaction with the flattened and shallow reality bequeathed by the philosophical traditions of empiricism and rationalism. It is precisely for these "exaggerations" that German thinking gained a hearing in England, and yet the ways in which German idealistic philosophy was received on English soil differ wildly. This is especially so in such seminal figures as S.T. Coleridge, William Hamilton, and Henry Mansel, whose diverging interpretations of Kant and his successors exercised a striking influence on the thinking of the Oxford Movement, the Broad Church, Romantic literature, and Victorian agnosticism. The disparate and yet overlapping nature of all these movements is enough to show that German philosophy was immediately taken up into inherited and particular English concerns, and, thus, the accusation has commonly been made that the English never really understood Kant. Rather, figures such as Kant, Schelling, and Hegel were simply merged into historic discussions, which revolved around the place of natural theology, empiricism, and Platonism in English thought, without being heard on their own terms.

While this may true, the introduction of Kant's philosophy in England undoubtedly helped to crystallize and, to some degree, extend the intimate relationship between epistemology and religious knowledge of God. Questions about the nature of individual consciousness, perception of the external world, and the limits of religious knowledge, as articulated by Kant, in many ways framed the discussions of belief and unbelief in nineteenth-century England. In particular, Kant's unknowable things-in-themselves, somewhat paradoxically, lent a certain depth to reality, which tumbled out in varying directions in the minds of his English readers. His resolution of the incapacities of pure reason – the practical postulates of God, freedom and immorality – ascribed a moral and spiritual quality to knowing that many felt had been lost in the empiricist writings of someone like Paley, whom Coleridge and others regarded as the troubling epitome of Lockean epistemology. Whether with Coleridge or Carlyle, there was a desire in many English readers of Kant to move beyond the empiricist notion of the mind as a passive receiver of external impressions, toward a more holistic understanding of reality in which there are powerful correspondences between the mind, world, and God. They did this with the help of Schelling and other post-Kantians and indeed surpassed many of the limitations that Kant himself had placed on reason.

But others like William Hamilton and Henry Mansel and, in very different ways, agnostics such as Spencer and Huxley leaned toward the more negative aspects of Kant's philosophy.[2] In some sense, many English readers never got far beyond Kant's initial skepticism concerning the powers of reason, and certainly Hamilton and even more so Mansel, in the tradition of Scottish Common Sense philosophy, employed the Kantian antinomies as a device to hold back rationalist objections to the credibility of the Christian faith: what reason cannot be sure of, it cannot possibly criticize. This cleared the ground for something that resembles what Richard Popkin describes as "sceptical fideism," the deconstruction of reason to make room for faith.[3] In others like Spencer, Huxley, and Stephen it simply led to outright skepticism about religious claims.

These, then, are the two most significant ways in which Kant was received in the first half of the nineteenth century in England.[4] Mansel has primarily been remembered as an interpreter of Kant who failed to follow through on the furthest implications of Kant's philosophy. But I would argue that Mansel should be primarily regarded as a critic of Kant – a critic who understood him, appropriated aspects of his thought but ultimately discerned that Kant's philosophy presented insurmountable difficulties for traditional Christian belief. If Mansel's central goal was to create a space in which the scriptures could reliably and powerfully reveal God in a rapidly changing intellectual and cultural landscape, the theological implications of Kant's philosophy became one of the greatest threats to this goal in nineteenth-century England. Though Kant himself was critical of English deism, Mansel regarded his philosophy as an extension of eighteenth-century deistic attempts to shape and mould the contents of Christian belief by the standards of human reasoning.[5] In fact, Mansel identified John Locke as the English originator of this particular transgression of the limits of religious knowledge, and in so doing he grouped philosophers as diverse as Locke and Kant into the rationalist tradition in English thought.

The purpose of this chapter is to outline Mansel's criticism of Kant and to then explore the greater influence and reception of Kant's philosophy on religious and theological thinking in nineteenth-century England. I give special attention to the figures of S.T. Coleridge and Thomas Carlyle, who both seized upon Kant's philosophy as an opportunity to move beyond the entrenched philosophical and theological heritage of the eighteenth-century theological controversies. Coleridge attempted to appropriate Kant's distinction between reason and understanding into a renewed and orthodox theological synthesis. Though, as I will argue in this chapter and the next, this endeavour placed considerable pressure on Coleridge's theology and reading of scripture. Carlyle, on the other hand, also made use of Kant's distinction but moved in a more overtly agnostic position in which the particular scriptural and doctrinal claims of the Christian faith began to wither. Mansel understood and reacted against the difficulties in both of these trajectories and for that reason an account of Kant's influence on English writers and their reading of scripture is essential for understanding Mansel's own thought. In pursuing this topic I will also engage a few representative scholars in order to show that Kant, even in the twentieth and twenty-first centuries, has continued to function as a benchmark for assessing the religious thought of the nineteenth century. While this is a testament to the profound influence of Kant's philosophy in England, I also hope to show that the writings of Mansel, among other theological writers of the period, are better assessed by more explicitly theological standards.

RATIONALISM AND SCRIPTURE
IN THE NINETEENTH CENTURY

Mansel and Rationalism

Henry Mansel was concerned for the integrity and coherence of the entire scriptures. This concern emerged from tensions and criticisms of the Bible that had deep roots in England. David Friedrich Strauss's *Das Leben Jesu* and his investigation of the contradictions within scripture and the mythical character of biblical miracles did not represent a novel thesis but was the product of long-standing streams of thought that received popular expression in eighteenth-century England by deist writers.[6] John Toland's *Christianity Not Mysterious* embodies the classic rationalist statement that anything within scripture that is not easily comprehended by reason cannot be required of Christian belief.[7] To be sure, this was an extension, or perhaps distortion, of Locke's claim that "God, out of the infiniteness of his mercy … gave him [man] reason, and with it a law, that could not be otherwise than what reason should dictate, unless we should think, that a reasonable creature, should have an unreasonable law."[8] In Mansel's view, this already dangerous position of Locke's was amplified by Toland and others and used to run roughshod over the scriptures by separating reasonable and unreasonable portions within the text … Thus, while books like *Das Leben Jesu* were shaped in a particular Kantian form of philosophical idealism, Mansel's claim that the philosophy of Kant and Hegel represented a renovated or renewed form of deism is true insofar as it placed tremendous pressure on the coherence and integrity of scripture.[9] Thus, while Mansel acknowledged that his arguments for the regulative truth of scripture carried a skeptical strain, he tried to distinguish this skepticism from both Locke and Kant and their respective followers.

In an essay on "freethinking," Mansel chronicles the slippage of the mysterious aspects of Christian doctrine, from Locke's initial indifference down to the deist's outright hostility toward any notion of an incomprehensible reality.[10] Locke, Mansel argues, treated the attributes of God as if they were similar in kind to the attributes of a stone, and as a result he forfeited the analogical relation – circumscribed by an inherent imperfection – between language about God and language about created reality.[11] The inevitable result was that distinctive Christian doctrines that did not conform to human notions of reality would become increasingly irrelevant or even absurd. So while Mansel, in some sense, was a descendant of the English empirical tradition, his empiricism, if it can be called that, was theologically altered in order to avoid what he saw as the natural outcome of Lockean philosophy.[12]

Likewise, for Mansel, German idealism – the philosophy of Kant, Schelling, and Hegel – was little more than an extension of this form of reasoning.[13] Kant's distinction between the phenomenal and noumenal realms was one that Mansel made use of, but he rejected Kant's mediating faculty of practical reason. Kant argued that, while we cannot perceive the noumenal – the real or the spiritual aspect of reality – it was necessary for moral living that our practical reason posit the existence of God, freedom, and immortality.[14] These postulates are not known as transcendent realities but as regulative ideas that are necessary for the moral life. At least this was how Mansel read Kant, and his criticism of Kant relates precisely to my initial statement:

> Let us hear then the philosopher's (Kant's) *rational* explanation, upon this assumption, of the duty of Prayer. It is a mere superstitious delusion, he tells us, to consider prayer as service addressed to God, and as a means of obtaining his favor. The true purpose of the act is not to alter or affect in anyway God's relation towards us; but only to quicken our own moral sentiments.[15]

Mansel's worry with Kant is that his rational description or account of God cannot permit basic scriptural notions such as petitioning prayer because this form of prayer does not cohere within Kant's constructed framework of knowledge, a framework that extends its boundaries to God's character.

While Mansel followed Kant in his limiting of speculative knowledge, Mansel felt as though Kant left the door open for Schelling and Hegel to construct a purely rational theology:

> Kant neither absolutely accepted the unconditioned as a product of Reason, nor absolutely rejected it; but assigned to it a kind of shadowy existence on the confines of light and darkness, speculatively unknown and unknowable, regulatively present and in operation.[16]

Because Kant left this speculative door open, his followers constructed rational accounts of God based on principles such as the infinite and the absolute. And though Mansel was severely critical of what he regarded as the pantheism of Hegel, he at least applauded Hegel for carrying the implications of such a philosophy to its logical conclusion: "That which is conceived as absolute and infinite must be conceived as containing within itself the sum, not only of all actual, but of all possible, modes of being."[17] Hegel's dialectic was in Mansel's eyes the most thorough and consistent attempt to pursue this mode of reasoning.[18]

Mansel's criticism of Kant in particular was based upon the Scottish philosopher Sir William Hamilton. Hamilton argued in *The Philosophy of the Unconditioned* that "consciousness is only possible under the antithesis of a subject and object of thought, known only in correlation and mutually limiting each other."[19] In this respect, Hamilton argued that all knowledge of the world exists within conditions of distinction, and for this reason nothing can be known of the world beyond sense aside from what is revealed:

> Consciousness is to the philosopher what the bible is to the theologian. Both are professedly revelations of divine truth; both exclusively supply the constitutive principles of knowledge, and the regulative principles of its construction ... Each may be disproved, but disproved only by itself.[20]

To argue beyond the realm of consciousness is to argue toward "zero," against the very conditions of thinking at all. Likewise, Mansel took from Hamilton the notion that the scriptures contain their own logic and must be understood from within the character of their own narrative. In this way, Kant's philosophy was dangerous because it threatened to subject the scriptures to the constraints of practical reason.

This is a sketch of Mansel's criticisms of "rationalism" – whether German idealism or English empiricism. In both systems the tendency is to describe and characterize God according to humanly constructed accounts of God's character and our ability to perceive his character. Staying with the theme of prayer, Mansel writes,

> They may not, forsooth, think of the unchangeable God as if He were their fellow man, influenced by human motives, and moved by human supplications. They want a truer, a juster idea of the Deity as He is, than that under which He has been pleased to reveal Himself; and they call on their reason to furnish it.[21]

It is the conflict between what people think God ought to be like and how he actually appears in scripture that leads into Mansel's skeptical epistemology. In other words, his skepticism is an attempt to examine the modes of thinking that various philosophical positions employ that inhibit them from affirming basic and intelligible scriptural realities.

Kant in England

However, unlike Mansel, other English theologians did not see in Kant an extension of English deism but an opportunity to move beyond shallow empiricism of men like Toland and his orthodox opponents and the restrictions they placed on the capacity of reason.[22] S.T. Coleridge and Thomas Carlyle are perhaps the most profound examples of people who wholeheartedly moved away from Locke's limitation of reason to the sensible world in favour of Kant's epistemology, which seemed to promise reasonable access to spiritual realities.

The delayed influence of German thought, and the philosophy of Kant in particular, in nineteenth-century England is related to a number of complex historical factors, not least the national isolationism that the French Revolution provoked on English soil.[23] English intellectuals were leery of German philosophical writings, not only for their seemingly dangerous political implications but also because they employed a language and form of reasoning that seemed abstract, obscure and remote from the common-sense tendencies within the English philosophical and theological tradition.[24] Yet it was the metaphysical character of Kant's writings that at the same time made his philosophy appealing to English writers who were weary of the empirical restrictions operating within English theology and philosophy.[25]

A.O. Dyson, for example, has argued that the decline of deism in England, and what seemed like an orthodox consensus, concealed the enduring weaknesses in the orthodox conception of reason and faith.[26] This would come to a crisis, for orthodox and deist alike, in the criticisms of David Hume, represented in Demea and Cleanthes. So long as the criteria for a rational religion lay in the external evidences either side could muster, one way or the other, the balance tipped in favour of the deists, though neither side could cope with Hume.[27] Dyson goes on to say,

> The orthodox believed that in practice totally satisfying proof could be found. The deists believed that totally satisfying disproof could be found. If the debate is couched in these terms, then the deists were victorious ... A very different approach of this kind could not be broached without a far richer concept of reason than that provided by Locke and without the help of the kind of historical sensibility which the 18th century English theology never knew.[28]

What was needed, Dyson claims, was a more searching and profound understanding of reason as rooted in the subject or religion "that has its roots in man."[29] The unproductive oscillations between revealed and natural religion that characterized English thought stalled any progress in this regard and ultimately left English theology more vulnerable to the threats of modern science that arose in the nineteenth century.[30] England lacked both the intellectual climate and the "creative theological figures"[31] that could have inspired the necessary innovation. According to Stephen Sykes, theologians weary of the natural-law tendency in English divinity were attracted to German philosophies that regarded the world and history as "subject to mysterious forces which from time to time mould out of individuals a 'spiritual whole.'"[32]

Dyson's view of the impoverishment of English theology is not entirely uncommon. One thinks of Paul Tillich's straight-faced remark that the "contribution of the established church in Great Britain to systematic theology is almost nonexistent."[33] His reasons are similar to Dyson's and, for that matter, Ward's, in that the national Church in England provided a conservative liturgical shelter that did not necessitate vigorous engagement with the issues emerging in the culture; rather, theology and philosophy developed like two parallel paths that never met. Whether true or not, it is hard to avoid the conclusion that this was a common impression in the minds of many in early nineteenth-century England. As a result, figures as diverse as Coleridge, Carlyle, Hamilton, and Pusey turned to German idealism with mixed feelings of hope, trepidation, and some sense of national humiliation as they struggled to reconfigure and articulate their belief in God and his presence in the world.

Coleridge and Kant

Of all early nineteenth-century theological writers in England, Coleridge is regarded as one of the few who took up this "creative" theological task. Coleridge provides the most spectacular attempt to translate Kant and the later German idealists into an orthodox Christian idiom. Yet many critics have argued that this unusual and prolific attempt at a synthesis proved too difficult for Coleridge to accomplish, and it represents the sort of synthesis that Mansel suspected might be dangerous.

Rene Wellek is the classic example of this approach, and his book *Immanuel Kant in England*, written in 1931, is still an essential touchstone on the topic. Coleridge's failure to understand Kant, according to Wellek, stems from his indiscriminate endorsement of the *Critique of Pure Reason* without confining himself to the narrow escape from the problems of reason that Kant articulated.[34] For example, Coleridge makes the distinction between reason and understanding central to his own religious thinking, but he immediately extends the sphere of reason beyond the limits the distinction was meant to preserve for Kant.[35] In *Aids to Reflection*, Coleridge writes, "Reason is then the Spirit of the regenerated man, whereby the Person is capable of a quickening intercommunion with the Divine Spirit."[36] Wellek sees this dualism in Coleridge as a fideistic attempt to circumvent the oppositions that Kant sets up between form and matter, perception and things. In this regard, Coleridge follows Schelling, Wellek argues, though he ends up in a very different place:

> Schelling – like Coleridge – wholeheartedly adopts "intellectual intuition" as the solution of the dilemma, as it means for him the concrete unity of intuition and thought, of action, and insight … Both of them recognize the deficiencies of a Kantian dualism, but they never succeeded in carrying out this synthesis speculatively. Coleridge fled into a deeper and more pernicious dualism, Schelling merely showed Hegel the way to solve it.[37]

Clearly, in Wellek's mind, Coleridge's flight into a "pernicious dualism" secured his position outside of the philosophical mainstream, as he was unable to extend the discussion that Kant inaugurated in any sort of intelligible manner. To this end, Coleridge simply used Kant's distinction between reason and understanding to ensure that the faculty of understanding could not be applied to spiritual concerns; this was the disaster of deism and evidential theology in the eighteenth century. But rather than abandon Kant at this point, Coleridge was inclined to search the philosopher for some kind of concealed intention that would lead in this direction:

> In spite therefore of his own declarations, I could never believe, that it was possible for him to have meant no more by his Noumenon, or Thing in itself, than his mere words express; or that in his own conception he confined the whole plastic power to the forms of the intellect, leaving for the external cause, for the material of our sensations, a matter without form, which doubtless is inconceivable.[38]

While Wellek can admit that Kant may have left such a door open, the direction in which Coleridge proceeds veers further and further from any of the positive aspects of the German philosopher's thinking.[39]

In the end, Wellek portrays Coleridge as a "struggling spirit" caught up in currents of thought that ultimately overwhelmed him, and the conservatism that would emerge in his later life was little more than a desperate solace, sought out when it became clear that there was nowhere left to hide. This does not stop Wellek from describing Coleridge as the great inspiration for romanticism in England, but his spectacular struggle with Kant and the philosophy of the age can only be described as a failure.[40] Thus Coleridge, much like Mansel, has often been remembered as another incurably religious Englishman who could not fully appreciate the genius of Kant's philosophical revolution.

However, more recently, scholars have begun to look more sympathetically on Coleridge's philosophy of religion. Ward's comments seem to be indicative of this shift: "What Coleridge valued in the Germans, in other words, was not the critical achievement, but the possibilities of metaphysical construction he perceived in them."[41] Coleridge thought that Kant's and Schelling's philosophies represented a novel initiative toward a revival or retrieval of metaphysical thinking, which provided structure for his sense of spiritual communion with a living God. Douglas Hedley argues that for Coleridge, the eclipse of Cudworth and the speculative thinking of the seventeenth century by empiricism was where it all went wrong. Hedley suggests that both Coleridge and Paley agreed that the world spoke of God and to this extent they stood against Hume. The issue, Hedley writes, has more to do with the content:

> Dr Paley is not attacked because of his rationalism but because he diverts Christianity away from its centre: the indwelling Logos. Paley's *Natural Theology*, as much as the deists', constitutes "the utter rejection of all present and living communion with universal Spirit." In order to experience this Logos, mankind must turn within.[42]

It is this "turn within" that marks both Coleridge's affinity with idealism and his departure from its strictures. He writes of speculative and practical reason, in the manner of Kant, but, Hedley argues, what he really means is "immanent reason" through which humans can contemplate, in a limited fashion, reality, by the very thoughts of God that reason can attain to.[43]

While Mansel, with the help of Hamilton, denied the existence of a higher faculty by which human reason could perceive and know, even partially, spiritual realities beyond the constraints of the visible world, Coleridge turned to Kant to articulate and defend this capacity. Yet Coleridge's use of the reason-and-understanding distinction does, as Wellek suggests, create a certain kind of dualism, especially with respect to the scriptures. In chapter 2 I argue that the structure of spiritual communion, mediated by the faculty of reason, created difficulties for Coleridge in reading the whole Bible as a coherent witness to God's character in history.

Carlyle and Kantian Agnosticism

While Coleridge shared Mansel's concern that Kant's practical reason might be used to shape and control theological beliefs and scriptural imagery, he nevertheless found the distinction between understanding and reason to be an opportunity for a theory of spiritual illumination facilitated by the elevated faculty of reason. Thomas Carlyle, like Coleridge, also seized upon Kant's distinction between reason and understanding, but he used the distinction for more overtly agnostic purposes. In this way Carlyle more fully represents Mansel's concern that Kant's philosophy created profound difficulties for Christian belief. For example, in his essay "The State of German Literature," Carlyle writes,

> Reason, the Kantists say, is of a higher nature than
> Understanding; it works by more subtle methods, on higher
> objects, and requires a far finer culture for its development,
> indeed in many men it is never developed at all; but its results
> are no less certain, nay rather, they are much more so; for Reason
> discerns Truth itself, the absolutely and primitively True; while
> Understanding discerns only relations, and cannot decide with-
> out it.[44]

While "British Philosophy, since the time of Hume, appears to them [Germans] nothing more than a 'laborious and unsuccessful striving to build dike after dike in front of our churches,'" Carlyle argues that the philosophy of Kant represented an elevated purpose that bypassed the defensive and narrowed ambitions of English philosophers and theologians.[45]

However, for Carlyle, the higher aims of reason did not function to penetrate deeper into scriptural mysteries, but instead reason seemed to move beyond scriptural particularities. Though Wellek argues that Carlyle was yet another Englishman who failed to understand Kant,[46] Frank Turner has shown that Carlyle had an enormous influence in providing the spiritual energy and rationale for a new generation of English agnostics. Turner describes Carlyle as an agnostic whose "idealist concepts and moral doctrines eased the transition from a religious apprehension of the universe to a scientific and secular one."[47] This was done through ascribing powers and forces to nature that were unhindered by traditional and dogmatic definitions, while retaining a place for the religious within the hearts of the people, astonished and overwhelmed by the mysterious world around them. Carlyle's influence on the Victorian agnostics has been frequently noted, and Turner suggests it was his imprecise notion of force, or natural supernaturalism, that animated and inspired the research of the new class of English scientists. Coupled with this was a personal ethic of industriousness and passionate engagement provoked by a wonderful and awful encounter with the forces of nature.[48] In *Heroes and Hero Worship* Carlyle exclaims,

> This Universe, ah me! – what could the wild man know of it? What can we yet know? That it is a Force, and thousandfold Complexity of Forces; a Force which is not we. That is all; not we, it is altogether different from us. Force, Force, everywhere Force; we ourselves a mysterious force in the centre of that.[49]

This force is beyond comprehension, unknowable in Spencer's terms, and yet it undergirds all of reality with its powerful and indefinite energy.[50] In a like manner, Herbert Spencer described the progress of this conception of an incomprehensible force: "While this process seems to those who effect, and those who undergo it, an anti-religious one, it is really the reverse. Instead of the specific comprehensible agency before assigned, there is substituted a less specific and less comprehensible agency."[51]

Carlyle's views of nature may be closer to Goethe's or Schelling's than Kant's, but the overall impression of an unknowable world that is yet received and penetrated by the powers of reason provides a setting for an elevated sense of human agency within a quasi-religious world that is ultimately more interesting than the law-governed rationalistic universe of English deism. Turner writes, "More than any other popular writer during the first half of the century, Carlyle had conceptually separated religion and spirituality from their contemporary institutional and dogmatic incarnations. Religion for Carlyle was wonder, humility, and work amidst the eternities and silences. The true realm of religion and the spirit was the inner man; all else was unessential externality."[52] While Coleridge's romanticism led him toward a defense of the national Church, in a somewhat idiosyncratic sense, Carlyle moved toward an antidogmatic view of religion that tried to retain and renew religious vitality without inhibiting ecclesial structures. This vision was characterized by a profound and moral sense of the individual situated within a mysterious, immanent world, along with an agnostic posture toward defined metaphysical theological doctrines. Thus Carlyle's Kantian skepticism, unlike Mansel's, promised a certain kind of spiritual knowledge through the faculty of reason, but this came at the cost of particular scriptural and doctrinal claims.

METAPHYSICS, SCRIPTURE, AND MORALITY

Mansel and Mill

In Carlyle and Coleridge, scholars have found two figures who represent the early and eager appropriation of German idealism and the struggles and conflicts that this reception initiated. If German idealism represents the search for a new holistic and still Christian view of the world, as the inherited "great chain of being" was passing away, it is not clear that this was actually achieved on English terms. Timothy Gouldstone writes in his book on Anglican idealism, "the tradition of Kant and Hegel provided for those in the Christian tradition who inherited a belief in the unity of the created order and the destiny of mankind a possible means of reconciling the moral law with the material world."[53] And yet the tensions within these means were apparent from the outset and most demonstrably in someone like Coleridge.[54] For Gouldstone, German idealism represents an uneasy resting place for the Church of England in the nineteenth century.[55]

Gouldstone's suggestion that idealism promised a reconciliation between the moral law and changing conceptions of the material world is echoed by Charles Taylor. Speaking of Matthew Arnold's turn to culture, Taylor writes, "It is an aspiration towards wholeness, towards a fullness of joy where desire is fused with our sense of the deepest significance."[56] As I argue throughout this book, this aspiration was pursued by many Victorian philosophers and writers outside of any intelligible scriptural context, and in turn it created a space in which the scriptures began to flounder. The assumption that the scriptures, without serious augmentation and revision, could not meet the moral and spiritual needs of modern people was already pervasive in Mansel's England, and it is a theme that is often repeated in the more contemporary scholarship on the period.[57]

For Victorian intellectuals this conflict was brought to a point of profound clarity in J.S. Mill's response to Mansel's lectures and the philosophy of Hamilton. Shortly after these lectures, both Mansel and Hamilton were subjected to a long critique from Mill. Alan Ryan writes that Mill had two main critical points:

> The first is Mill's claim that the majority of cases of inconceivability can be explained by our experience of inseparable associations between attributes, and the other his claim that most of the things that Hamilton claims to be inconceivable are not difficult, let alone impossible, to conceive.[58]

Mill's concern seems to have been that Hamilton's skepticism was based on false alternatives within the sphere of consciousness and that the effect was to allow back through faith what had been eliminated through philosophy. It seems Mill regarded Hamilton and Mansel as a "halfway house" between the relativity of knowledge in Kant and his own empiricism.[59] In this regard, Ryan argues, Mill was still operating from a basically empiricist position:

> Mill thinks it is an empirical conviction, implanted by experience, reflecting the way the world actually is, but telling us nothing about how it has to be. The opposition have no common doctrine; the Kantian members of it think that since "the world" is a phenomenal product of our minds working upon unknown and unknowable data it must obey the laws of our own minds.[60]

There is no relation between knowing something and conceiving something entirely. The relative part of our knowledge is what originates in our minds, and the inconceivable or absolute is that which eludes us. This is Mill's caricature of Hamilton, and he wishes that he had simply gone all the way to the Kantian position.[61] According to Mill, because Hamilton permits an alien aspect to our knowledge, that which is inconceivable, he leaves open the option of revelatory truths that in fact contradict the very structure of human perception and cognizance. This becomes most apparent in the work of Mansel, who argues strongly that human conceptions of goodness have a complicated and sometimes opaque relation to divine goodness. It is this consequence of Hamilton's thought that provoked Mill's well-known words "I will call no being good, who is not what I mean when I apply that epithet to my fellow creatures."[62] In other words, human understanding of morality, in a manner that is different than Kant's, still must in some sense correspond to our understanding of divine morality.

F.D. Maurice and Mark Pattison, among other churchmen, gladly received Mill's critique of Hamilton and Mansel, as they sensed that this skeptical philosophy was a threat to their own theological understandings, which were heavily influenced by the Coleridgean "holistic" tradition.[63] The resulting impression of this conflict is one in which two different forms of Christian theology, both influenced by Kant, came into collision and were to some degree arbitrated by an agnostic like Mill.

Bernard Lightman has convincingly shown how the philosophy of Hamilton and Mansel exercised a strong influence on Victorian agnosticism and people like Spencer, Stephen, and Huxley.[64] Lightman argues that Mansel's failure in part was due to his unnecessary opposition between faith and reason: "Where Mansel grouped knowing, thinking and reason together in opposition to faith, Kant conceived of thinking and reason as an integral part of the realm of faith."[65] This statement, as I argue, is not quite true of Mansel. However, the simplistic surmise of the conflict of faith and reason symbolizes the vying trajectories that signify the age, where theologians and philosophers alike were reaching out for a new understanding of knowledge and faith but at once with a mixture of hesitation, urgency, and perplexity. This is the picture that often emerges from contemporary scholarship on the topic of the reception of Kant and German idealism in nineteenth-century England: Kant was never really understood, and his most notable interpreters were bound by theological commitments that did not allow them to follow Kant's positive philosophy. However, while the philosophical rigor of Kant has been employed as a criterion for assessing the writings of various theologians and philosophers in the nineteenth century, it is often the case that certain moral and theological presuppositions undergird this standard. Mansel was one of the few philosophical theologians in nineteenth-century England to perceive that two distinct theological visions of God and reality were beginning to emerge and conflict with each other.

Kant and Theology

J.S. Mill was obviously not a Kantian, and yet despite all the concerns for philosophical rigor that surround Kant's reception, Mill's moral concern about the scriptural depiction of God were shared deeply by Kant. For example, Donald Mackinnon's comment on Kant's influence on English theology is telling:

> It was from Kant that theologians were enabled to see that the universalism of the Enlightenment was no facile optimism, but an expression of the need for the devout to submit their aspirations to judgment at the bar of a common humanity – lest indeed they failed to see the Son of Man in the least of his brethren and, failing, forfeited the very faith by which they claimed to live.[66]

However, it is this very notion of the "common bar of humanity" that seems confused in contemporary scholarship on the issue in question. Wellek's assessment is based upon the ability of Kant's interpreters to understand the philosopher and to integrate his conclusions in a coherent philosophical manner. Certainly in Mansel's eyes, while the method of figures like Mill and Kant differed, they shared, in some sense, "the bar of common humanity." Or in other words, they shared a common moral perspective that concealed a considerable danger for scriptural interpretation.

From a contemporary theological perspective it is now becoming clear that Kant's philosophy, as a representative of modern trends, is not necessarily hospitable for the articulation of a Christian understanding of the world.[67] Kant's own comments on the status of Christian claims are well known:

> Reason does not dispute the possibility or the reality of the objects of these ideas [grace, miracles, mysteries]; she simply cannot adopt them into her maxims of though and action ... for dogmatic faith which proclaims itself as a form of knowledge, appears to her dishonest or presumptuous.[68]

Kant's distinctions between the phenomenal and noumenal, the understanding and reason, lent the possibility of greater depth to the created order and a higher mode of knowledge that was flattened out by the deists. Yet in a way, concrete scriptural claims about the reality of

God's presence in the world become obscure, and, even worse, they become matters of potential indifference because they do not relate to the central experience of the moral life. Kant asks, "Do you really trust yourself to assert the truth of these dogmas in the sight of Him who knows the heart and at the risk of losing all that is valuable and holy to you?"[69] Such creedal-ecclesiastical theology Kant calls "fetish worship."[70] These particularities will one day disappear as man takes his autonomous place in the world, and "God is all in all."[71]

This specific notion that theological and scriptural particulars stand in opposition to or even destroy the genuine moral life represents one of the great themes of Mansel's period. Whether in Kant's philosophy of the subject, Spencer's philosophy of the unknown, Arnold's theory of culture or Mill's memorable rebuke of an immoral God, the common unifying claim is that the specificity of scripture's reference to the life of God is no longer capable of guiding human life in the modern world. Much less is the scriptural narrative able to describe the reality of the changing and progressive historical developments of modernity.

Thus, while Mansel made use of Kant's criticisms of reason, in the end Mansel's theology, in its core themes, was ultimately critical of Kant or any philosophy where "the law of human morality must be regarded as the measure and adequate representative of the moral nature of God."[72] Charles Taylor's point about the Victorian era is that while the rise of science undoubtedly created problems for religious belief, it was the emergence of a new moral idea that was most dangerous to traditional Christian faith. First, "We have an obligation to make up our own minds on the evidence without bowing to any authority. The second is a kind of heroism of unbelief, the deep spiritual satisfaction of knowing that one has confronted the truth of things, however bleak and unconsoling."[73] Francis Newman's *Phases of Faith* offers a perfect example of this emerging attitude. After struggling with the scriptures, Newman confesses, "At last it pressed on me, that if I allowed morals to rest on an independent basis, it was dishonest to shut my eyes to any apparent collisions of morality with the Scriptures."[74] Mansel was keenly aware of this burgeoning moral awareness, and in response to one of his lectures' critics, Goldwin Smith, he writes, "You have adopted a historical theory, which virtually divides the thinking part of the world into two classes, the friends and enemies of Progress."[75] It is within this moral framework that the theological conception of God and the scriptures were increasingly entangled.

Contemporary Theological Critiques of Kant

While, as I have argued, it has been common to assess Mansel and nineteenth-century English theologians like Coleridge according to standards of Kant's philosophy, it has become increasingly common among theologians today to criticize the influence of Kant on modern theology. However, it is not always the case that these criticisms focus in upon the general philosophical and moral sentiment that provoked Kant to relegate scriptural realities to secondary considerations. John Milbank, for example, in *The Word Made Strange*, argues that "The metaphysics of Kant, which is totally agnostic as concerns God-in-himself, but in a way dogmatic as concerns his relationship to finite beings, and the metaphysics of Aquinas, which is less agnostic concerning God-in-himself, is also more agnostic concerning the conditions of our relationship to God."[76] Kant, for Milbank, represents the modern culmination of Dun Scotus's separation of the finite and infinite; in the case of Kant, the infinite can only impinge upon the finite as an "empty formality" devoid of any participatory dynamic between the realms.[77] Unlike many of the scholars mentioned earlier, Milbank's argument is not that nineteenth-century theology in England was insufficiently Kantian but that it was too much so: the medieval and patristic notion of a participationist ontology had been replaced by a barren and sterile epistemology of religion. Thus Milbank's argument, in the face of modern secularism, is to reassert this classical vision as an ontology in which Christian claims, and all truth claims, can be intelligibly made:

> Between one unknown and the other there is here no representational knowledge, no "metaphysics," but only a mode of ascent which receives something of the infinite source so long as it goes on receiving it, so constituting, not a once and for all theory (or account of the ontological difference) but an endlessly repeated as always different theoretical claim which is nothing other than all the biographies of every ascent, and the history of human ascent as such.[78]

This account of the dynamics of knowledge represents for Milbank theology's "evacuation" of metaphysics, or rather, it is a way of incorporating all of reality within a theological vision that is all embracing. Thus if theology "wishes to think again God's love, and think creation as the manifestation of that love, then it must entirely evacuate philosophy, which is metaphysics."[79]

Milbank offers a powerful alternative to many of the confused and entangled theological visions of the modern era that seek to integrate progressive and developmental schemes into theological or providential terms. It stands in stark contrast to the scholarly readings of the period that argue that theologians faced the dilemma of either keeping up with developments in modern philosophical thought or falling desperately behind. For Milbank, modern secularism and unbelief don't stem from the Church's inability to keep pace with philosophical and scientific developments, but rather they are the result of the Church's fatal assimilation of forms of theological thinking that eclipse the ontological framework in which Christian claims have always flourished. Like Mansel, Milbank has argued that Kant's philosophy can have destructive consequences for Christian belief if it becomes the standard by which Christian doctrines are measured. Still, the question that concerned Mansel was how particular metaphysical or ontological schemes can make sense of the entire scriptural account and its witness to the character and life of God within the world. This question can be asked of Kant or Milbank as it can be asked of any theological system and its author. It is the purpose of this book to explore this question under the terms in which Mansel posed it.

CONCLUSION

This paradigmatic conflict between the emerging moral sensibilities and the morality or character of scripture's representation of God made any discussion of the "common bar of humanity" fraught with complications in nineteenth-century England. While Coleridge, for example, struggled deeply to articulate the Christian faith within the general philosophical terms of his era, he was forced to resist the philosophy of Kant and the idealists in a manner that, despite its confusion, made space for a scriptural understanding of God. Yet, as I argue in the second chapter, Coleridge too carried some ambivalence toward the whole scriptural witness, especially the Old Testament portrayal of God's actions in history. Mansel's goal was to defend the whole scriptures and the character of God embedded within them, but in doing this he did not disregard the "common bar of humanity." He argued that the scriptures' presentation of a personal God, with all of its complication, difficulties, and contradictions, was in fact a profoundly fitting address within the strictures of human personality in general.

But Mansel's account of human personality was simply one among many, and the idea that it should "fit" with a scriptural account of the world may seem too good to be true. The reality for Mansel, however, was that the Church's understanding of the world or human nature and the character of God is located primarily and sufficiently within the scriptural account. However, if readers bring certain controlling moral and metaphysical assumptions to the text of scripture, it will be difficult for them to discover the character of this "fittingness" that Mansel described. For this reason Mansel's "Bampton Lectures" argued that the scope of rational criticism extends only to created realities, and for apologetic purposes he begins his arguments with a description of human thought and personality. But his skeptical conclusions about the capacity of human reason, as I will argue in the following chapters, emerged from a deeper commitment to the internal coherence of the entire scriptures, represented in the twentieth article of religion in the prayer book: no portion of scripture should be interpreted as repugnant to another. While Mansel, in his sermons and theological writings, attempted to build and illustrate this coherence through typological readings of the Bible, his theological skepticism was a simple admission that this coherence may not always be perceivable. Or, in other words, believers may not always understand the purposes and actions of God in the world, but the scriptures provide a particular and comprehensive account of God's character that is centered and interpreted through the life and death of Jesus Christ.

Mansel was one of the few philosophical theologians in nineteenth-century England to perceive that Kant's philosophy posed serious dangers to the articulation of the Christian faith. Though it is has been argued that Mansel separated faith and reason, the deeper nature of his argument was that faith had a form of reasoning that was particular to Christian scripture and tradition. I explore this form of reasoning more fully in chapters 3 and 4.

2

Anglican Apologetics and the Limits
of Religious Thought

It is likely that at the time of Mansel's "Bampton Lectures" there were still many English clergymen who would have wanted to affirm Aquinas's distilled notion that "contempt in the will causes dissent in the intellect, by which the act of unfaithfulness is completed."[1] While Aquinas could divide and integrate subtly diverse concepts like unbelief (unfaithfulness), heresy, blasphemy, and apostasy, the Victorian Church was beset by a crisis where the traditional claims of Christian orthodoxy were exposed to the escalating threats of skepticism and revision. What some called unbelief, others called the progress or "phases of faith,"[2] the purification of historic theological notions such as the divinity of Christ, or the inspiration of scripture. The long litany of public controversies in the nineteenth century – the repeal of the Tests and Corporations Act, The University Reform Act, *Essays and Reviews*, and the controversy over the Athanasian Creed[3] – not only challenged the status of the Church in England but also questioned the theological bearings that upheld its core articles of faith. In addition, the high profile "loss of faith" narratives,[4] coupled with the defection of prominent churchmen like Newman and Manning to Rome, pressured Anglican theologians to defend their positions on a number of varying and opposing fronts.

The story of Victorian unbelief has been frequently and well told, so it is not my intention to offer another genealogical account in this chapter.[5] Instead I focus on the nature of the problem confronting Anglican theology in the nineteenth century and the theological context that Mansel drew from and reacted against. Not only did Anglican theologians have to defend the reasonableness of the Christian faith in some measure, but even more they had to show that the narrative of scripture could still describe the world they lived in. Most essentially, this narrative included the character of God and his dealings with humanity, which since the time of the eighteenth-century deists had been under criticism in favour of more materialistic or impersonal renderings of the cosmic order. Charles Taylor describes the slide away from the personal, biblical image of God in terms of maturation:

> This stance is part of the modern identity of the buffered self, which thus finds a natural affinity for the impersonal order ... We have to rise above and beyond our particular, narrow, biased view on things, to a view from everywhere, or for everyman, the analogue of the view from nowhere which natural science strives to occupy.[6]

The notions of comprehensiveness and limitation were central for many Anglican theologians in the eighteenth and nineteenth centuries. In particular, these ideas were pursued in relation to orthodox Christian claims – the creeds and scripture – and the degree to which the authorized words of the Church closed off or opened up conceptions of reality and of God's identity. What drove the quest for a more comprehensive worldview – "a view from everywhere, and for everyman" – was something upon which theologians disagreed. It was not always clear that writers who argued for this more comprehensive view at the cost of orthodox particularities were motivated by a "contempt in the will." But the stance that varying theologians took toward this motivation in many ways characterized the manner in which they articulated their respective understandings of the limits of human knowledge and the limits or domain of the scriptures and the creeds. Or, in other words, theological writers generally agreed that it was essential to discuss the limitation and constitution of the mind, but they differed sharply over the degree to which these accounts of human knowledge were allowed to shape or control the contents of revelation.

The purpose of this chapter is to explore the context and background of Mansel's skeptical philosophy and theory of regulative truth. I briefly look at the status of philosophical and theological skepticism in eighteenth-century England and the manner in which skeptical arguments were used to both buttress and redefine orthodox Christian claims. The debate between George Berkeley and Peter Browne in particular provides an illuminating lens into the nature of such arguments. Then I examine more closely the theology of Joseph Butler – Mansel's closest spiritual and theological mentor – and his understanding of human ignorance and the knowledge of God's providence. Finally, as a partial contrast to Butler and as a development of philosophical skepticism and its idealistic cure, it is important to discuss S.T. Coleridge and his attempt at a chastened though relatively comprehensive Anglican theological vision.

In looking at Butler and Coleridge, alongside writers who influenced them, I outline two differing though not entirely dissimilar tendencies in English theology that were available to Mansel when he approached the topic of human knowledge and the character of God revealed in the scriptures. Both Butler and Coleridge were concerned to protect the integrity of Christian revelation, while at the same establishing continuity and coherence between that revelation and human knowledge and experience. The degree to which Coleridge extended this coherence beyond particular scriptural accounts toward a more comprehensive theological vision will be the central question in contrasting the two figures.

SKEPTICISM IN CONTEXT

The earliest reactions to Mansel's lectures contained worries and criticisms that his skeptical epistemology, which circumscribed the range and extent of human knowledge of God, risked making the very contents of revelation themselves obscure or, worse, unknowable. Speaking of Mansel's ostensible victory over his rationalist opponents in the lectures, an anonymous writer in the *Eclectic Review* questioned "but what if the hero himself also has perished, and if his mangled and lifeless body be found under the heaps of his slain enemies?"[7] The lurid image was to some degree insightful, and the work of Bernard Lightman has traced the steps by which Mansel's own ideas were turned against him by figures like Herbert Spencer and Thomas Huxley.[8] The suggestion of these critics is that an attempt to safeguard Christian truth claims by restricting or diminishing the scope of human reason only serves to drive these truth claims beyond the field of recognizable human experience, rendering them unbelievable or, as it turns out, irrelevant.

In fact, this contention raised by Lightman and others directed toward the use of skepticism in the realm of theological knowledge is far from new, and it is important to place the issues in some context.[9]

Richard Popkin's work on skepticism has opened a whole field of study that undoubtedly pertains to Mansel's position. Popkin's thesis, simply put, is that the revival of skeptical texts in the Renaissance period provided tools for religious controversialists of the Reformation to undermine opponents' arguments.[10] While Protestants attacked the tradition of the Catholic Church and its spurious role in the establishment of truth, Catholics replied by questioning the ability of individuals to interpret the Bible outside of an established and traditional framework. Over the succeeding centuries, Popkin argues, these mutual recriminations stirred a search for new dogmatic systems of knowledge that would close Luther's "Pandora's box."[11] However, "the gradual failure of these monumental efforts was to see the quest for certainty lead to two other searches, the quest for faith – pure fideism – and the quest for reasonableness – or a 'mitigated scepticism.'"[12]

Popkin provided a context in which to place the varying functions of skeptical reasoning in modern theology, and to be sure, Mansel, in some measure, belongs to this stream. Popkin discusses a range of figures whom he describes as "sceptical fideists," Montaigne perhaps being the paradigmatic example. Popkin quotes from Montaigne to illustrate the skeptical fideistic position:

> There is nothing in human invention that carries so great a show of likelihood and utility as this; this presents man, naked and empty, confessing his natural weakness, fit to receive some foreign force from above, unfurnished of human and therefore more apt to receive into him the divine knowledge, making nought of his own judgment, to give more room to faith.[13]

The extent and manner of this skepticism as it pertains to reality and revelation varies from figure to figure, but I would argue that Mansel's particular form of skepticism stands loosely within this fideistic context that Popkin traces from the Reformation. Furthermore, Popkin's description of the dangers of this position sounds very much like an echo of Mansel's critic in the *Eclectic Review*: "The new machine of war appeared to have a peculiar recoil mechanism that had the odd effect of engulfing the target and the gunner in a common catastrophe."[14] In other words, Catholic and Protestant polemicists devoured each other at the cost of their own positions; skepticism, in this sense, which was intended to buttress certain theological positions, actually ended up corroding their foundations.

Iain Hampsher-Monk pursues this insight in the context of Anglican theology in a fascinating article on Edmund Burke's skepticism. Hampsher-Monk argues that Anglican divines had to finesse a middle position between their fundamentally anti-Catholic and antideistic commitments. For example, he writes, "The success of their position hinged on certain epistemological and hermeneutical issues having to do with the limits of reason in religious matters and the need to maintain the integrity of the sensory and textual evidence on which Christianity or Christian dogma was based."[15] The emphasis on sensory and textual evidence is much in the tradition of Locke, who regarded the senses – unlike, perhaps, Montaigne[16] – as generally reliable for the basic purposes of life. However, Locke's distinction between real and nominal essences places a limit on the depth of human understanding regarding revealed truths.[17] This trajectory in English theology – the appeal to common sense, or accessibility to the "vulgar"[18] – was derived in part from an aversion to "extravagant" and "speculative" Roman Catholic reasoning in their defense of transubstantiation. But, Hampsher-Monk claims, this moderated skepticism had its own recoil effect:

> Extravagant claims about the application of rational standards to matters of religious belief rebounded on them, threatening their own position which involved adherence to what their nonconformist critics saw as unreasonable theological tenets. For as Catholic opponents realized, the stress on the evidence of the sense and common reason as criteria of the admissibility of articles of faith, as well as undermining transubstantiation, rendered vulnerable that other crucial touchstone of orthodoxy of rationalist Deism – namely the Trinity ... And so, however incautious Anglicans grew in pursuit of their Catholic adversaries, they had always to retreat to a position which enabled them to combine their attacks on the unreasonableness of transubstantiation with a defence of the Trinity.[19]

This tension between two rival positions forced Anglican theologians to constantly shift from one ground of authority to another, from reason to scripture to tradition, and then around again. But as the threat of Catholicism began to wane and the public pressures of the deists increased, fideistic positions that more closely resembled that of Montaigne began to emerge.

Thus, while the empirical bent of Anglican theology was very much formalized and influenced by Locke, there also needed to be a way to limit the encroachment of his mitigated skepticism into the realm of revelation. So, Hampsher-Monk writes, "Anglicans deployed a range of skeptical arguments against the extension of Lockian 'understanding' to the realms of religion and morality."[20] In this way, the empirical strictures of the human mind were regarded as adequate to receive the necessary content of revelation, but they were not capable of forming or revising these contents according to any larger framework, which is to say that the reception of revelation was to some degree passive. Passivity here need not mean irrational or unreasonable but more indicates a certain posture to tradition and theological authority wherein the articles of the faith are regarded as sufficient for salvation, if not exhaustive explanations of reality.

So the Church of England very much experienced the skeptical crisis that Popkin describes, even though many of these issues would not be fully exposed until the nineteenth century. However, the empirical or "textual" base of English theology ensured that these topics were not pursued purely in the abstract apart from particular scriptural claims. For writers like Butler and Mansel, revelation was not a bulk of propositions to be merely received on skeptical or epistemological grounds; rather, revelation was in the form of the scriptures, an articulate and particular witness. And however much they might have used skeptical arguments or appeals to ignorance as a ground for their acceptance, because the scriptures were writings embedded in the empirical or visible world some accounting of the coherence between the world of the scriptures and the present was imperative. In this way, Mansel is not quite at home in the skeptical fideist tradition, though his arguments often bear a surface, and at times deeper, resemblance: the inadequacy of reason to judge matters of faith and the reception of doctrines that cannot be accounted for by reason are among the obvious. Yet, as we will see, he inherited from Butler not just a stress upon the ignorance of man but, further, a complex and subtle notion of God's character and purposes both revealed and concealed in the scriptures.

DEISM AND ANGLICAN APOLOGETICS

Mansel's comments in his essay on freethinkers clearly demonstrated the continuity that he perceived between the eighteenth and the nineteenth centuries: "The English Deism of the last century, like the English gentlemen of the same period, has made the grand tour of Europe, and come home with the fruits of its travels."[21] The "grand tour of Europe" refers, of course, to the inroads of German idealistic philosophy in England in the nineteenth century, which Mansel saw as nothing more than a more sophisticated form of deism. If this is true, it is no small wonder that Mansel's arguments bear strong affinities with his Anglican predecessors of the eighteenth century, however altered to suit his circumstances. While orthodox writers such Joseph Butler, Peter Browne, and George Berkeley employed strategies similar to Mansel's in their defence of Christian particularities, the differences between these respective authors clearly suggest that the presence of a lurking fear that theological skepticism might undermine the entire theological enterprise was already making itself felt. But despite this fear, it is equally evident that some of the greatest figures in eighteenth-century Anglican theology felt it was necessary to negotiate the limitations of human thought in order to retain the doctrinal core of the Christian faith.

Toland and the Limits of Scripture

As in the Victorian Church, eighteenth-century churchmen disagreed sharply about how the Christian faith should be articulated and defended against rational criticism. This was nowhere more evident than in the debate that took place between Peter Browne and George Berkeley, both writing in some measure against Toland's already well-known *Christianity Not Mysterious*. The debate took place between 1728 and 1735,[22] though the longtime Irish bishop of Cork, Browne, had expressed the main points of his thought many years earlier in a short letter responding to Toland's major work.[23]

In *Christianity Not Mysterious* Toland famously made use of Locke's basic epistemology to argue that the statements of scripture must be understood in a clear and distinct sense or not understood at all:

> No Christian doctrine, no more than any ordinary piece of nature, can be reputed a mystery, because we have not an adequate or complete idea of whatever belongs to it ... what is revealed in religion, as it is most useful and necessary, so it must and may be as easily comprehended, and found as consistent with our common notions, as what we know of wood or stone.[24]

As with Locke, Toland argues that all objects of sense have properties that render adequate, though not exhaustive, knowledge for the perceiver, and much in the same manner, scripture teaches what people need to know about God for practical living.[25] What scripture does teach can be clearly known and requires no recourse to a greater depth or mystery. Toland's ostensible purpose in making this claim was to allow the literal words of scripture to stand plainly without "being wrapped in mystery or garnished with a figure."[26]

The promise of the plain sense, in Toland's mind, was the potential to surpass what he regarded as the deforming effects of party-driven theological controversy. He makes this clear in the introduction and argues that the divines of the Church "prove the authority and perfection before they teach the contents of Scripture. Whereas the first is in great measure known by the last."[27] To this end, Toland anticipated strains of Mansel's own thinking, and he lashed out against what he regarded as the evident consequences: "The very supposition, that reason might authorize one thing, and the Spirit of God another, throws us into inevitable Scepticism; for we shall be at a perpetual uncertainty which to obey."[28] Toland's concern for certainty in this case seems to be what drove him to take such a strong position against the idea of scriptural mysteries. If the words of scripture are merely the foreground for an illimitable depth that extends beyond the definite and plain sense of the words, there is no limit to what theologians might import into their meaning.

Toland, unlike deist writers after him, made a strong appeal to the scriptures and in particular to their plain sense.[29] But this plain sense was rooted in an epistemology that clearly extended its controlling reach into scripture's meaning. This allowed Toland to sever the connection between certain doctrinal claims and the appeal to natural analogies, or, in other words, the supposed mysteries of the scriptures were entirely alien to the created world and the proper mode of human reasoning within it. Toland writes,

> we knew nothing of things, but such of their properties as were necessary and useful. We may say the same of God; every act of religion is directed by the consideration of some of his attributes, without ever thinking of his essence.[30]

Strangely, Mansel – and Berkeley and Browne as well – would say remarkably similar things but with the opposite intent. They had to show not only that it was possible to believe in something that could not be conceived in thought but also that it was useful or beneficial to do this. Toland's view was clear: the insistence on various mysterious aspects of scripture simply reflected the prejudices of interested theological parties.

Berkeley and Browne: A Divided Response

Both Berkeley and Browne considered deeply the arguments of Toland and the other deists and mounted responses that turn on highly similar themes. So it was with some surprise that Browne read Berkeley's criticism of his position in the *Alciphron*. Berkeley had likely read Browne's *Procedure, Extent, and Limits of Human Understanding*, which was a fuller statement of Browne's already established rebuttal against Toland in a much earlier letter.[31] In this letter Browne lays down his skeptical position about the knowledge of God, which he would never depart from:

> We have no proper ideas of the things of another world, but frame to ourselves conceptions of them, from those things in this world whereof we have clear and distinct ideas ... there are but two ways of God's revealing anything to us; either by giving us new faculties, or by adapting his revelations to those we have, which are our senses and our reason.[32]

Here Browne's argument about God's manner of revelation anticipates Mansel's theory of regulative truth, and it is based on a similar analysis of the concept of infinity.[33] In contrast to Toland's argument that something without recognizable empirical properties is inconceivable, Browne suggests that inconceivable realities are represented in revelation within the realm of human sense and reason. In some sense, Toland and Browne are agreed that knowledge requires clear and distinct ideas, but Browne does not want this concept of knowledge to deform or shape God's revelation. For example Browne argues that we cannot form an idea of the infinite by simply accumulating instances; God is infinite but the human mind cannot represent this attribute in any meaningful manner.[34] Thus, Browne concludes,

> Therefore it is that the Spirit of God in all his revelations, hath made use, not only of the words and phrases commonly received and understood; but likewise of those common notions in the minds of men, of things in this world, to represent truths, which

are in respect of us now unconceivable; and for which there are as yet no capacities in our nature.[35]

So Browne's skepticism is not so much about the senses but rather about the limitation of the senses and their proper domain or use. And his skeptical arguments are not used to sow distrust in common knowledge but to show how reason cannot be the judge of revelation, however successful he might have been. This position inevitably led Browne into a discussion of analogy as the question was put to him by Berkeley, among others, of just what connection pertained between the phrases employed in revelation and the realities that they refer to.

In response to this question, Browne drew a sharp distinction between analogy and metaphor. Metaphor, he claims, "has no real foundation in the nature of things compared,"[36] and scriptural descriptions of God as light or discussions of his breath, the strength of his arm, and so on are merely intended as figures for moral instruction. This is because ideas of sense have no analogical relation to the immaterial world.[37] But because humanity is created in the image of God, Browne claims that the more complex ideas of the mind can relate analogically to the immaterial because the mind, operating at a certain level, is combined of matter and spirit.[38] For Browne, created reality referred analogically to God on a graduated Platonic scale: "All the perfections of intelligent beings must be greater or less, as they make nearer or more distant approaches in their kind to a resemblance of Him, who is the only source and fountain of all perfection."[39] While these analogies could never reach full conception, they approached varying degrees of certainty based on their proximity to or combination with the Spirit.[40] While this is a brief summary, it is enough to establish the grounds of Berkeley's criticism against Browne, which focused on this very partitioning of knowledge.[41]

In the *Alciphron* Berkeley does not mention Browne by name, but the references are quite clear, and his criticisms of Browne's position reveal the division within orthodox responses to the deist onslaught. Berkeley's reply to deist objections against the mysterious aspects of Christian belief hinged upon his understanding of abstract ideas and his criticism of Locke's clear and distinct ideas. In the dialogue, Euphanor explains to Alciphron,

I do not see Alciphron, i.e. that individual thinking thing, but only such visible signs and tokens as suggest and infer the being of that invisible thinking principle or soul. Even so, in the self-same manner, it seems to me that, though I cannot with eyes of flesh behold the invisible God, yet I do in the strictest sense behold and perceive by all my senses such signs and tokens, such effects and operations, as suggest, indicate, and demonstrate an invisible God, as certainly, and with the same evidence, at least, as any other signs, perceived by sense, do suggest to me the existence of your soul, spirit, or thinking principle.[42]

This method of argument Berkeley calls the parity of reason; in other words, the same standards of reasoning applied to God apply in some sense to the natural world. In relation to Alciphron, Euphanor argues that we see only the effects and activity of a thinking subject but not the subject himself, which is to say that we have no abstract idea of the subject. Language, or individual words and phrases, do not necessarily correspond to clear ideas, but "the mind overlooks them, so as to carry its attention immediately on to the things signified."[43] This is the character of language for Berkeley, and he expands this theory into the theological realm:

Since you cannot deny that the great Mover and Author of nature constantly explaineth Himself to the eyes of men by the sensible intervention of arbitrary signs, which have no similitude or connexion with the things signified; so as, by compounding and disposing them, to suggest and exhibit an endless variety of objects, differing in nature, time, and place; thereby informing and directing men how to act with respect to things distant and future, as well as near and present.[44]

Based on this notion of language, Berkeley famously claimed that the human mind can no more form a clear idea of divine grace than it can of gravity.[45] Both are known by their effects, not by their essence. Michael Hooker describes Berkeley's theory of divine language as follows: "In the case of spoken language it is the speaker's intention that ensures the reference relationship, and in the case of the language of nature it is the theophonic deity, always speaking to us through our senses, who ensures the reference of our sense experience."[46] This makes sense of the preceding passage from Berkeley, and, unlike with Browne, it is the divine intention that ensures the accuracy of revelatory and natural language, which operate in the same created realm and retain the same powers of signification.

Berkeley's concern with Browne's theory was that the language of revelation – the clear and distinct depictions of God in scripture – did not actually refer to a reality in any way that was recognizable. So Berkeley puts Browne's argument in the mouth of the freethinking Lysicles, who suggests that nothing can be drawn or inferred from a God whose attributes, in the end, cannot be known: "Since, therefore, nothing can be inferred from such an account of God, about conscience, or worship, or religion, you may even make the best of it. And, not to be singular, we will use the name too, and so at once there is an end of atheism."[47] But Berkeley responds with a long disquisition on the nature of analogy in the theological tradition, appealing to Cajetan, Suarez, and Aquinas, in order to argue for an analogy of proportionality.[48] At first glance, Berkeley's view of analogy is scarcely distinguishable from Browne's: he too draws a distinction between metaphorical language about God – the finger or breath of God – and proper analogical referents such as knowledge or wisdom.[49] But Berkeley perhaps preserves a greater stress on the likeness of these latter analogies. For instance, on knowledge he writes,

Knowledge, therefore, in the proper formal meaning of the word, may be attributed to God proportionably, that is, preserving a proportion to the infinite nature of God. We may say, therefore, that as God is infinitely above man, so is the knowledge of God infinitely above the knowledge of man, and this is what Cajetan calls *analogia proprie facta*.[50]

Proportion in this case simply intends to guard the distinction between God and humanity; that is, the perfections in humanity exist in God in an eminent manner.

In a later letter to Browne, Berkeley tries to clear up the point of analogy by speaking of divine wisdom:

This, methinks, brings the controversy to a point, and I call upon your Lordship to speak out, and either own to the glory of your Maker, that he is properly and literally wise, or plainly tell mankind, that the Being they adore does not design good ends, nor use consistent methods to attain them. Between these, there is no medium, God has ends in view, or he has not; if he has, they are either good, or otherwise suitably pursued, or improperly attempted.[51]

Wisdom, in this case divine, must have a recognizable form, even if God's activities and purposes cannot be discerned. The form that is common in human and divine wisdom is the establishment of desired ends and the corresponding means to attain these ends. In other words, it is one thing to deny any abstract conception of divine wisdom – both Berkeley and Browne were agreed on this point – but it is another thing to claim that God's wisdom bears no common features to humanity's. This is the conclusion that Berkeley drew from the analogy of proportionality, which allowed for both agreement and disagreement.

Browne was incensed at Berkeley's criticism in the *Alciphron* and responded with a large volume on the topic of divine analogy and a chapter devoted to Berkeley. Browne argued that Berkeley had misread his opponents because it was not that Toland and company demanded abstract ideas of God but any ideas at all, abstract or particular. To this end, Berkeley's argument had not accomplished anything because it still could not prove that there was a God who produced these visible signs. Browne writes,

> But what they demand is, any ideas of them as different from all the ideas and conceptions of things sensible and human, as these are from things imperceptible and divine: and accordingly they tell you that when they look inward for such ideas to annex to the terms, their mind is an empty void; and therefore they look no farther than the strictly proper and formal and literal acceptation of those words … [Thus]their fatal error is, that upon their principle they must necessarily reject the truth and reality of everything that is thus inconceivable to us as it is in itself, and of whatever is not otherwise conceivable than by analogy with things natural and human; even the attributes of God included.[52]

Just as Berkeley worried that Browne had given in to the deists by rendering God unknowable, Browne now worried that Berkeley had removed the special province of faith to assent to theological realities that could not be conceived in the mind through reason or observation. In Berkeley's case, according to Browne, faith is placed on the same ground as science and the natural order. So Browne concludes,

> You may confess indeed to believe in father, son, and spirit; in the grace of God; and in the mediation and intercession of

Christ; but yet it is not always necessary or possible for you
to acquire, or exhibit to your mind, any ideas, conceptions or
notions of the things marked out by those words: tho' by this
rule you may as well be said to have faith in the noise of sound-
ing brass or a tinkling cymbal. Nay your believing a God would
be very useful; tho' upon his scheme it may be no more than
faith in a monosyllable.[53]

This conclusion is striking because Browne accuses Berkeley of
employing language about God that is meaningless or, in Berkeley's
sense, intended primarily for a person's emotive and practical living
– "influencing his life and actions."[54] For Browne, this was the cost
of relinquishing clear and distinct ideas of God.

The irony here is great; Browne's own clear ideas of God were
themselves considered quite opaque. As Berkeley pointed out, the
attributes of God in scripture, for Browne, might not bear any resemblance to anything recognizable in human experience, but still they
were related as clear and plain. And furthermore, much like with
Berkeley and Toland, the primary purpose of scriptural language was
to teach moral and practical duties, not metaphysics.

Admittedly, the difference between Berkeley and Browne is quite
slight, despite the mutual fear that each other's skeptical approach
somehow risked the perspicuity and immediacy of the Christian's
knowledge of God.[55] But the difference is still important: For Berkeley
God's revelation in scripture is immersed within the complicated and
dynamic field of natural and human language. His parallel between
gravity, or force, and grace demonstrates the manner in which these
realities, while different, perhaps, in agency still operate within the
same realm and are experienced empirically with all of the attendant
difficulties of any human experience. The essence or truth of force
and grace alike are inaccessible to human perception and cognition.

Whereas for Browne, this is not quite true. Like Berkeley, he agrees
that the contents of revelation should not be conformed to Locke's
clear and distinct ideas, but rather than question Locke's basic epistemology, he simply pushes revelatory claims beyond the field of
Lockean application. To be sure, scripture represents God in a clear
and understandable manner, but these representations bear only a
slight resemblance to the realities that they refer to. So in Browne's
case, the limits of human knowledge do not really alter Toland's view
of reality or the experienced world; instead he stakes his case on the

argument that human reason can credibly assent to truths that are inconceivable, though represented in conceivable terms. This is an important point because though Browne accused Berkeley of not addressing Toland's true concern that no idea of God could be formed in the mind, whether abstract or particular, Browne created a scheme of analogy that in a certain sense divided up the world – and the scriptures as well – into objects with varying referential power. The scriptures, then, are grafted on to this description of reality and derive their intelligibility from the extent to which certain referents approach the spiritual or immaterial realm. This is the danger of accommodation theories of revelation: that, in effect, they leave the created world to some degree unaltered by the gospel. This is what Alan Sell calls the "natural-theology-supplemented-by-revealed-approach," so characteristic of Locke's influence on eighteenth-century theology.[56] The result for Browne is that while he laboured exhaustively to show how scriptural statements might be true, in one sense or another, the scriptures themselves are treated almost piecemeal and pulled painstakingly back and forth between his two domains of knowledge. In this respect, Browne's employment of the limitations of human thought, despite his specific efforts, struggled to show how the scriptures might encompass or describe an overarching theological vision of both God and the created world.[57]

Berkeley at least tried to demonstrate that the limits of human thought pertained analogously to both natural and revealed knowledge. In this case, his skepticism linked the mystery of the world with the mystery of God, which allows God to be known empirically by his effects and actions, without compromising his otherness. Though, as Browne noted, God's otherness then became equated with the otherness of empirical forces and objects, most notably gravity. To this end, it might be said that Berkeley's appeal to analogy sits uncomfortably within his theory of emotive language, or at least the connection is not clear. The analogy of proportionality is predicated entirely upon the distinction between God and creation.

The criticism made here against Browne's theory of revelation and human knowledge comes close to hitting at the heart of Mansel's theology, though, I argue, in the end it misses the mark.[58] Still, Browne's ideas are not without merit in this discussion, though historically he was interpreted in the same manner as Mansel would be a century later, somewhat unjustly. Still, as much as Mansel was influenced by Browne, he also drew from Berkeley[59] and even more from Butler, so it is important to get a sense of Butler's position within this contested circle of Anglican apologetics.

BUTLER AND THE SCHEME OF SALVATION

Despite being an established work within the Oxford curriculum for more than a century, Butler's *Analogy* is a curious book that stands aloof in some senses from the theological and philosophical world that he inhabited, even while it continually circles many of the great themes of the age. Terence Penelhum suggests that Butler's skepticism has no known origin, or, at the very least, his sources are unclear.[60] Scholars have traced the influence of Locke and the similarity to Pascal, among others, but Butler rarely registers in the skeptical literature about the period, and despite writing his great work on the topic of analogy, he is not easy to place within the theological tradition. Aside from this anomaly, Butler's work is intensely theological as it represents the patient and still pressing search for a coherent worldview that is ordered and formed by the narrative of scripture.[61]

At first, to draw a parallel between Mansel and Butler may seem like a stretch. Though Mansel quotes Butler frequently, their respective styles differ considerably: Mansel was a polemicist and a rigorous philosopher who pursued definitions to their bare bones, while Butler concealed his opponents and preferred to hesitate before drawing sharp conclusions; he traced trajectories and probabilities while remaining understated about his deepest commitments. Butler did not see the world quite like Mansel and was adverse to highly analytical accounts of the human person or mind: "We know little more of ourselves, than we do of the world about us: how we were made, how our being is continued and preserved, what the faculties of our minds are, and upon what the power of exercising them depends."[62] For Butler, an overly determined account of reality obscured rather than clarified the world around,[63] whereas for Mansel a lack of precision risked the disordering of human knowledge of both the world and God.[64] Yet for all of these apparent differences, Mansel was a Butlerian, and it is important to stress the sense in which this was true.[65] I will spell out more fully in the third and fourth chapters Mansel's own indebtedness to Butler, but here I will focus more singularly on Butler's own thinking on the Christian scriptures and their place in the created world.

Butler was very much a contemporary of Browne and Berkeley and wrote in response to the same crisis posed by the English deists. On the surface, to be sure, it appears that Butler had little interest in the questions concerning the status of human knowledge and the mediation between the human and divine spheres. At the least, he did not approach these questions in a manner that had much in common with many of his contemporaries. But as an orthodox theologian and apologist he was faced with the same task of rendering the claims of scripture intelligible and credible, which he did by using an informal and empirical form of reasoning that make his larger theological commitments, at times, more difficult to sort out.

In this sense, Butler seems to have assumed a basic theological and doctrinal consensus and instead devoted his energy to illustrating and depicting the manner in which scriptural claims cohere or fit with the human experience of reality. So Butler introduces his argument in the *Analogy* with a well-known endorsement of Origen's observation that "He who believes Scripture to have proceeded from him who is the author of nature, may well expect to find the same sort of difficulties in it, as are found in the constitution of nature."[66] Berkeley made a similar claim, but Butler pursued this idea into a deeper theological insight about the character of reality and the lived Christian experience. Both Browne and Berkeley seemed to agree that the purpose of theological knowledge was for practical living, and the veracity of scripture was ordered around this concern. And while this is true for Butler as well, scripture's function is not simply its ability to teach clear and plain truths, but, in addition, even its obscurity and difficulty may be essential to its formative character. Ignorance of the world and God, according to Butler, is somehow integral to the probationary aspect of human life.[67] Bob Tennant makes the distinction as follows:

> In opposition to a whole climate of intellectual opinion, he wishes to demonstrate that the limits of human knowledge are to be discussed not in terms of adequacy (approximation to truth) but sufficiency for the purposes set out in the Christian revelation: an apparently drastic narrowing of intellectual ambition.[68]

This is a narrowing perhaps in the sense that Butler did not pursue questions of knowledge and truth outside of the context of scriptural claims, or, in other words, he attempted to measure the internal coherence of the Christian worldview and its ability to achieve its own desired outcomes. But in another sense, this represented an expansion or escalation of intellectual ambition, to stay with the phrase. Butler writes, "But the thing here insisted upon is, that the state of trial which religion teaches us we are in, is rendered credible, by its being throughout uniform and of a piece with the general conduct of providence towards us, in all other respects within the compass of our knowledge."[69]

Thus, Butler's response to the various criticisms that deist authors brought against the scriptures – its lack of universality and historical veracity, among others – was not to rebuff the criticisms outright but to show that these problems are rooted in all of created life. To use the example of universality, Butler writes, "Indeed he appears to bestow all his gifts with the most promiscuous variety, among creatures of the same species: health and strength, capacities of prudence and of knowledge, means of improvement, riches and all external advantages."[70] Of course, Butler's point is not that scripture is just as bad as nature but that scripture shares in the created character of the world – in many cases beyond human comprehension. But given this, the revelatory claims of the Bible emerge from within the historical and created context of human and natural life. Again, he claims,

A system of constitution, in its notion, implies variety; and so complicated a one as this world, very great variety. So that were revelation universal, yet from men's different capacities of understanding, from the different lengths of their lives, their different educations and other external circumstances, and from their difference of temper and bodily constitution, their religious situations would be widely different.[71]

The whole idea of a purely universal revelation, for Butler, does not make any sense within the endless and unfathomable variety of created life. The reason for this condition, he admits, is beyond human understanding, though he offers the familiar explanation of moral probation: regardless of the proximity with which one stands to the light revelation, every human location provides the possibility for the exercise of prudence, moral examination and free will.[72]

Even more, these endlessly diverse and particular human situations are rooted in natural providential tendency, and the meaning of this tendency is deepened and extended through the scriptures. For example, Butler acknowledges that in the ordinary course of things, vice is not always punished or virtue rewarded. However, there is a tendency in the world, despite some appearances, that this might be so: "And these tendencies are to be considered as intimations, as implicit promises and threatenings, from the author of nature, of much greater rewards and punishments to follow virtue and vice, than do at present."[73] The appeal to probability is rooted in Butler's belief that the general course of progress is necessarily beyond our comprehension: "So that we are placed, as one may speak, in the middle of a scheme, not a fixed, but a progressive one, every way incomprehensible; incomprehensible in a manner equally with respect to what has been, what now is, and what shall be hereafter."[74] There are traces of this tendency or scheme in nature, and Butler draws on these – analogies of judgment and mercy, growth and maturation – though they exist in a set of relations that are only perceived in part.[75]

Scripture, then, for Butler is not rooted in a larger philosophical framework or in an architectural account of human understanding or knowledge. Rather, scripture itself is an authorized account of the world, its natural tendencies and God's redemptive activity within his creation. Butler suggests, in his typically subdued fashion, that scripture serves "First as a republication and external institution of natural or essential or essential religion, adapted to the present circumstances of mankind, and intended to promote natural piety and virtue; and secondly, as containing an account of a dispensation of things, not discoverable by reason."[76] In the first sense, scripture confirms the already apparent, though fragmented, intuition that nature, in general, tends toward the good, the just, and the harmonious. In the second sense, scripture reveals a new set of relations that the world finds itself engaged with, namely, the Spirit and the Son, who are revealed for "the recovery and salvation of mankind, who are represented in Scripture, to be in a state of ruin."[77] And while nature demonstrates the continual need for improvement and growth by "immediate means," nature itself cannot provide these means.[78] Thus, despite the natural coherence of revelation and nature, this is discovered almost retrospectively, following the sustained engagement with the scriptures:

> The account now given of Christianity most strongly shews and enforces upon us the obligation of searching the scriptures, in order to see what the scheme of revelation really is instead of determining beforehand, from reason, what the scheme of it must be.[79]

The scriptures inform people about the world and the natural analogies that Butler pursues in such painstaking detail are only evident in the light of revelation. This is not to say that they emerge clearly and without obscurity but only that they are fitted into the scheme of salvation, as always, imperfectly understood.

From a theological point of view, there is nothing remarkable about Butler's positive affirmations. He believes in the mediation of Christ, the sanctification of the Spirit, and the Church as the place where people experience God and serve him in the world. These facts alone are obvious and barely worth explication aside from the manner in which they are situated and fitted within the Christian scheme. And like the world in which they are revealed, the teachings of scripture are likewise not fully understood; their meaning is explored, much as in the natural world, "by the continuance and progress of learning and of liberty, and by particular person, attending to, comparing and pursuing, intimations scattered up and down it, which are overlooked and disregarded by the generality of the world."[80] In this way, the particularities of scriptural teaching, while being irreducible beyond their revealed meaning, still contain a further depth that extends beyond their immediate explication. This "further depth" is both historically rooted and inexhaustible in light of humanity's enduring ignorance, but for Butler, the particular claims of scripture run through the depths of the created world, even if they cannot be followed at every step.

In an essay on Butler's theology of the incarnation, Gordon Kendal writes that for Butler

> particular events embody meaning prior to our launching our-selves upon them, and the content of any particular event has ramifications stretching far beyond itself; it may stand for more than it shows. The world is such that moral agents not only must but can emerge and grow in it.[81]

However, this depth or something more is articulated and circum-scribed by the language of scripture, which creates a patchwork of boundaries that describe the basic Christian mysteries. For example, when Butler speaks about the sacrifice of Christ, he quotes a long list of passages from the Old Testament law and prophets that speak to and foretell the nature of sacrifice.[82] Much as in his accounting of natural instances of sacrifice, these references are intended to denote a tendency and pattern, the full extent of which remains elusive. Butler writes,

If the scripture has ... left this matter of the satisfaction of Christ mysterious, left somewhat in it unrevealed, all conjecture about it must be, if not evidently absurd, yet at least uncertain ... Some have endeavored to explain the efficacy of what Christ had done and suffered for us, beyond what the scripture has authorized; others, probably because they could not explain it, have been for taking it away ... [but] it is our wisdom thankfully to accept the benefit, by performing the conditions upon which it is offered, on our part, without disputing how it was procured for us.[83]

Butler's defence against the charge of fideism here is that this is the manner in which reason normally proceeds, by pursuing patterns and probabilities, allowing them to accumulate, and then drawing inferences about general laws and conclusions. In the case of the sacrifice of Christ, the patterns exist clearly in scripture and in nature, and for that reason there are compelling reasons to believe, even if the evidence is not conclusive. The meaning of the event of Christ's sacrifice is marked off by the revealed words of scripture, but the practical experience of this event can be lived into, deepened, and more fully understood without altering the arrangement of words in scripture that make it known. This is primarily what Butler intends with his notions of progress and tendency in theological knowledge.

In light of this conviction, it is no surprise to read Butler's overarching summary of the scriptures:

For prophecy is nothing but the history of events before they come to pass: doctrines also are matters of fact; and precepts come under the same notion. And the general design of scripture, which contains in it this revelation, thus considered as historical, may be said to be, to give us an account of the world, in this one single view, as God's world.[84]

Or, as he also says, scripture is an "abridgement of history," though one that he admits is open to the "largest scope of criticism," given the range and diversity of its material.[85] This is the area where modern scholars seem to think that Butler is most dated in light of modern biblical and historical criticism.[86] But Butler is not worried that the Bible might contain historical errors or problems of transmission; these may even have a morally probationary role to play in the life of the Church.[87] Further still, the narrative of scripture, the pattern of prophecy and fulfillment, the propagation of the gospel – all admittedly circumstantial evidence – bear continuities with the present world. The existence of the Jews alone, Butler thinks, ought to incline an unbiased observer to taking the claims of scripture seriously.[88] The important point is that scripture provides a picture of the world as God's, and its rough outlines, porousness, and obscurity, though sufficient for godliness, indicate the manner in which humanity relates to the world and to God.

Certain modern scholars seem to agree that Butler's skepticism, or appeals to human ignorance, do not date well precisely because so much of his skeptical thinking relies on the mysterious aspects of the natural world that, perhaps, have been obviated to some extent by modern science. More sympathetic readers have drawn attention to Butler's subtlety and his patience for particularity and diversity in ethical and theological thinking. Donald Mackinnon, for instance, writes, "Because he is agnostic, Butler is ready to set out the moral life piecemeal, now letting his attention fall on one set of problems, now on another."[89] In other words, Butler's skepticism or agnosticism makes his thought more pliable and amenable in the face of modern complexities and, even more, the contemporary distaste for theory-driven ethics. This seems to be true, but even more, Butler's skilful attention to the particularities and complexities of human life are situated in a world providentially ordered and attended by God. The scriptures describe this world and a God who took on flesh and lived within it, adjusted and surrendered to it, while carrying out his providential plan. As Gordon Kendal writes of Butler, there is a "providential kinship" between humanity and the natural world that is revealed in Christ and accounted for in the scriptures.[90]

In this way, the account of the world offered in scripture – the "abridgement of history" – is a revealed account that, in the end, will be shown to bear a deep and unbreakable coherence with the natural world. However, for Butler, human ignorance is a brute fact that hinders the perception of this full unity, though there are traces in the world – analogies – that draw the Christian into a deeper trust in the God of the Bible. Butler even writes that to love God is not to love an idea wholly imperceptible but to believe that those things that are most loveable in humanity – kindness, love, wisdom – are virtues that reach their perfection in God.[91] Butler's skepticism, in this regard, is not merely an attempt to safeguard Christian truths, but, much more, it is a method of allowing the particularities of scripture to emerge, albeit ambiguously, within the context of the Christian experience.

Butler, then, is probably closer to Berkeley than Browne, but even still, he pursues the idea of scripture as an account of God's world further than Berkeley or in far greater detail, despite the fact that both emphatically agree that every aspect of created life is bound up with God's providential ordering. It is in this sense that Mansel was most deeply influenced by Butler. For Mansel, much as for Butler, the revelation of God in the scriptures is embedded within the course of human history – this is what it means for God to have taken on flesh – and the whole range of scripture, somehow, provides the most truthful account of the world.[92]

COLERIDGE, IDEALISM, AND SCRIPTURE

Despite the wide variety of approaches in the eighteenth century to natural theology and the veracity of scriptural and revelatory truth claims, by the early nineteenth century there emerged an increasing unrest with the whole framework of apologetic theology in England. While Coleridge retained a soft spot for Butler, he turned aggressively against figures like Paley. Others simply lumped Paley and Butler together as representatives of a diminishing age who tried to hold the crumbling traditional views of the Bible together with the new scientific worldview.[93] These perceptions, precipitated by a wide range of theological and social transitions in England, stirred an interest and receptivity to German idealistic philosophy that would in many ways come to characterize nineteenth-century intellectual life in England.[94] By 1857, Mark Pattison was able to state that German theology and philosophy, though not without controversy, was

> no insulated phenomenon. Though generated in Germany, it belongs to Christendom. It is the theological movement of the age. It is only because there is fuller intellectual life in Germany than elsewhere, only because it so happens that, at present, European speculation is transacted by Germans, as our financial affairs are by Jews, that German characteristics are impressed on the substance of the Christian science.[95]

As mentioned in chapter 1, many of these impressions and themes come together most forcefully in Coleridge, by all respects the most influential mediator of German philosophy in early nineteenth-century England. Mansel, too, was one of the early and capable readers of Kant and Hegel, though, despite borrowing, heavily at times, from the *Critique of Pure Reason*, Mansel made little constructive use of Kant or Hegel in his positive articulations of Christian orthodoxy. As Lightman has pointed out, Mansel's borrowing from Kant is somewhat deceptive: "The sporadic borrowing from the critique of pure reason gives Mansel's work a deceptive Kantian quality, and the illusion is only dispelled when their fundamental opposition is perceived."[96] With Coleridge the opposition is not quite as clear, though I will argue that it still exists. However, Coleridge's interpretation and use of Kant still differs from Mansel's, and the contrast with Mansel becomes clear in the third chapter. In this context the struggles of Coleridge's philosophy illustrate the difficulties of framing Christian orthodoxy within a Kantian or idealistic context. Despite these difficulties, Coleridge's views of scripture, as we will see, are still highly influenced by his idealistic inclinations. To this extent, Coleridge's position can be contrasted with Butler's and, later, with Mansel's.

For Coleridge, Kant's distinction between reason and understanding was paramount to stemming the tide of unbelief in England. The application of the understanding to spiritual truths that are not fitted for the faculty inevitably tended toward unbelief or atheism: "Wherever the forms of Reasoning appropriate only to the natural world are applied to spiritual realities, it may be truly said, that the more strictly logical the Reasoning is in all its parts, the more irrational it is as a whole."[97] His appeal to a separate and spiritual form of reasoning was derived, in part, from Kant's practical reason, but as mentioned previously, Coleridge was ill at ease with the constraints this placed on revelation and the scriptures in particular. Much as with Butler, Coleridge was seeking a resonance between Christian truth claims and lived human experience, though he sought this not through scriptural analogy but through the yearnings and intuitions of spiritual reason.

In *Aids to Reflection* Coleridge writes, "The utter rejection of all present and living communion with the Universal Spirit present and living communion with the Universal Spirit impoverishes Deism"[98] and, for that matter, the views of Christians who defend the faith on these terms. So the stated aim of his most well-known work is to reinterpret those aspects of the Christian faith, those parts of the scriptures that do not fit with this faculty of reason:

> It is only where the belief required of them jars with their moral feelings; where a doctrine in the sense, in which they have been taught to receive it, appears to contradict their clear notions of right and wrong, or to be at variance with the divine attributes of goodness and justice; that these men are surprised, perplexed and alas! Not seldom offended and alienated.[99]

Coleridge goes on to list these various doctrines: arbitrary election, hell, substitutionary atonement, the wrath of God.

In pursuing this task Coleridge sounds initially much like Butler: "the purpose of Scripture was to teach us our duty, not to enable us to sit in judgment on the souls of our fellow creatures."[100] Later on he states, "How can I comprehend this? How is this to be proved? To the first question I should answer: Christianity is not a Theory, or a Speculation; but a Life. Not a Philosophy of Life, but a Life and a living Process. To the second: TRY IT."[101] As Butler did, Coleridge employs a form of skepticism to put forward the essential lived quality of the Christian faith, and the doctrines and teachings of the Church are primarily purposed toward this end. This is exactly why he seeks to reinterpret those aspects of Christian teaching that offend or distract from this goal. But for Butler the difficult and potentially offensive aspects of the scriptures were situated within a set of relations and a providential scheme that are beyond human searching. Yet they are still integral to Christian truth claims and, just as much, · essential to the moral and probationary aspect of Christian living. Butler argued that the scriptures in their entirety reveal the most comprehensive perspective on God's world, and he sought to establish a resonance between their overall character and the human experience of the world.

For Coleridge this is not quite the case. Jeffrey Barbeau is surely right in claiming that Coleridge's emphasis on scripture has been neglected: he was an experienced exegete and was deeply concerned in articulating his views within a scriptural context.[102] The biblical theme of redemption for Coleridge, Barbeau claims, is at the heart of his theology. But given this fact, Coleridge's method of reading the scriptures is not immediately obvious. Much like Browne before him and Mansel after, Coleridge expresses a view of scriptural language that is mediated through human conceptions and terms. For example, he writes,

> The truths that are given to us ... are spiritual things which must be spiritually discerned. Such, however, being the means of the effects of our redemption, well might the fervent Apostle associate it with whatever was eminently dear and precious to erring and afflicted mortals, and seek from similitude of effect to describe the superlative boon by successively transferring to it, as by a superior claim, the name of each several act and ordinance, habitually connected in the minds of all his hearers with feelings of joy, confidence and gratitude.[103]

In some sense, Coleridge is using here an accommodation theory of scriptural language: biblical writers speak in terms that readers can understand. But the language itself, it would seem, or the events that it speaks explicitly about are not the mediating lens through which the truth is perceived but rather the associations that they call to mind and provoke in the heart. The words in this sense frame the inward conception, the spiritual meaning, of the particular text.

However, Coleridge was not lighthearted about the historical character of the Bible. As he said, the Bible "is a History, a series of Facts and Events related or announced. These do indeed, involve, or rather I should say they at the same time are, most important doctrinal Truths; but still Facts and Declaration of Facts."[104] Even more, in the *Confessions of an Inquiring Spirit* he writes, "all history must be providential, and this a providence, a preparation, and a looking forward to Christ."[105] Yet despite this, Coleridge, in the same work, speaks disparagingly about typological attempts to underline this providential character of the world that scripture speaks about:

> Of minor importance, yet not to be overlooked, are the forced and fantastic interpretations, the arbitrary allegories and mystic expansions of proper names, to which this indiscriminate Bibliolatry furnished fuel, spark, and wind ... add to all these the strange – in all other writings unexampled – practice of bringing together into logical dependency detached sentences from books composed at the distances of centuries ... under different dispensations.[106]

In *The Confessions of the Inquiring Spirit* Coleridge's own voice is obscured somewhat by the severe caricature he provides of his opponent's theory of verbal inspiration. He might here be referring to extreme instances of this method. Yet it does seem that for Coleridge, the words of the Bible, at least in certain places, derive their power from the inward images and sentiments they provoke and not from their surface or plain referents. And this, in part, is also an apologetic strategy for Coleridge:

> But let a man be once fully persuaded that there is no difference between the two positions – "The Bible contains the religion revealed by God" – and "Whatever is contained in the Bible is religion, and was revealed by God," – and that whatever can be said of the Bible, collectively taken, may and must be said of each and every sentence of the Bible, taken for and by itself, – and I no longer wonder at these paradoxes. I only object to the inconsistency of those who profess the same belief, and yet affect to look down with a contemptuous or compassionate smile on John Wesley for rejecting the Copernican system as incompatible therewith.[107]

Wesley, it would seem to Coleridge, was simply following this logic to its absurd conclusion. Coleridge's answer to the problem is that the Bible contains Christianity but not every last sentence or word; the truth needs to be sifted according to some criteria. He alludes at one point to Irenaeus and the rule of faith but in a peculiar manner:

> Is it not a fact that the Books of the New Testament were tried by their consonance with the rule, and according to the analogy of Faith. Does not the universally admitted canon – that each part of Scripture must be interpreted by the spirit of the whole – lead to the same practical conclusion as that for which I am now contending; – namely, that it is the spirit of the Bible, and not the detached words and sentences, that is infallible and absolute?[108]

While this distinction between the "words" and the "spirit" of the Bible is somewhat confusing, or unnecessarily polarizing, it allows Coleridge to root the scriptures in a larger framework of spiritual communion. In the end, he writes, "Revealed Religion is in its highest contemplation the unity, that is, the identity or co-inherence, of Subjective and Objective. It is in itself ... at once inward Life and

Truth, and outward Fact and Luminary."[109] The subjective experience of the believer must cohere with the spirit of the scriptures in the spiritual drive toward unity and comprehensiveness. For this reason, a patient and nonliteral reading of the Bible will eventually render the reader's life objectively:

> I say that no Christian probationer ... can find his own state brought before him and, as it were, antedated, in writings reverend even for their antiquity and enduring permanence, and far more, and more abundantly, consecrated by the reverence, love, and grateful testimonies of good men through the long succession of ages, in every generation, and under all states of minds and circumstances of fortune, – that no man, I say, can recognize his own inward experiences in such Writings, and not find an objectiveness, a confirming and assuring outwardness.[110]

It seems that the inward experience of conscience and the struggle of reason to follow its inclinations finds in scripture a history of human experience that is "antedated." Furthermore, the errors and inconsistencies of the scriptural account are a human and necessary part of this history: "how could these Writings be or become the history?"[111] In statements like these, Coleridge veers toward Butler's own conception of scripture: the narrative of scripture in its full arc describes the experience of people as they live their lives before God. Even errors and inconsistencies are a part of this providential rendering, though for Butler, the full comprehension of this description is hidden from human eyes and grasped through faith.

But for Coleridge, scripture's ability to locate an individual's life, to objectify it, is rooted largely in those places where the person is able to recognize it:

> In the Bible there is more that finds me than I have experienced in all other books put together; that the words of the Bible find me at greater depths of my being; and that whatever finds me brings with it an irresistible evidence of its having proceeded from the Holy Spirit. But the Doctrine in question requires me to believe, that not only what finds me, but that all that exists in the sacred volume, and which I am bound to find therein, was ... dictated by an Infallible Intelligence; – that the writers, each and all, were divinely informed as well as inspired.[112]

In some ways this is the heart of Coleridge's hermeneutic: scripture is read through the criteria of interior coherence or resonance. While this interior experience is theologically understood, and the inner person is redeemed by the mediation of Christ, scripture's intelligibility rests upon the subject-object recognition, the identification of a person's experience with the objectified form.

One might say that Coleridge's attempt to relate scriptural claims to the faltering faith of his generation risked streamlining the scriptures into a subjective groove, while the already difficult portions of the Bible were driven further into obscurity. In addition, it provided a method for further revision of scriptural claims along subjective or experiential lines. But to make this claim, I would have to show that this in fact took place, with this writer or that. However, it is more to my point to simply show the way in which Coleridge attempted to establish a coherence between the scriptures – their central teachings – and the life of the individual. In this way, Coleridge's task was much like Butler's, but whereas Butler employed a form of skepticism to demonstrate that the narrative of scripture provided the most faithful account of the world and God's providential scheme, Coleridge's skepticism allowed him to separate those aspects of scripture that applied to the understanding and reason. In other words, Coleridge gave a particular status to the moral inclinations of his generation through a theological variation of Kant's categorical imperative, realized in the practical reason, and he allowed this faculty, lifted from a temporal or contextual origin, to operate as a cipher for scriptural interpretation. Coleridge could still speak severely about "the evil heart of Unbelief."[113] But this "apostasy" included those theologians for whom the "Gospel gave way to speculative Systems, and Religion became a Science of Shadows under the name of Theology, or at best a bare Skeleton of Truth, without life or interest, alike inaccessible and unintelligible to the majority of Christians."[114]

Coleridge might have agreed with Aquinas that unbelief originates in the will, but for Coleridge the will became an emboldened faculty that exercised a formative influence on central Christian truth claims: it demanded realization, expression, and a deeply resonant encounter with its object of faith. He seemed fully convinced that no thinking person could not find this in the gospel, if read through the proper epistemological lens. This is undoubtedly Coleridge's greatest strength and what made him so attractive to Victorian writers. In this way Coleridge managed to set up an antagonistic polarity between orthodox writers who were moved to defend the faith by "that faithless and love less spirit of fear"[115] and those who sought "to rouse and emancipate the Soul from this debasing Slavery to the outward Senses, to awaken the mind to the true Criteria of Reality."[116] This criticism would have applied, in varying degrees, to Browne and Butler, writers whose skepticism was regarded as highly defensive in tenor. And it seems quite certain these were the charges brought against Mansel, who, by his own admission, did not try to "build the fortress" which he defended because "the fortress is built already."[117]

CONCLUSION

By the eighteenth century, and much more in the nineteenth, theology in England was bound to the apologetic mode and was in a constant state of anxiety to show how a Christian scriptural conception of reality could still be maintained as moral while scientific and philosophical trends began to shift. Part of this shift I have explained by Popkin's argument that the Reformation, and ensuing theological controversies, loosened a skeptical crisis in the retreating absence of any agreed upon criterion for consensually establishing Christian claims. Certainly by the time of Toland and the deists, Christianity's lack of universality – the scripture's intense particularity and local character – presented one of greatest difficulties to rational belief. This problem would only be expanded and extended in the philosophies of Kant and Hegel, who invested the subject and reason with incredible, though circumscribed, mediating powers between heaven and earth. Coleridge's theology, I have argued, displays the relative discomforts of articulating Christian orthodoxy within an idealistic framework. Even more, despite his attention to the scriptures, the mediating role between God and humanity shifted slightly away from the scriptural account of Christ and providential history, toward an interior or subjective center. For Coleridge this was a highly self-conscious move, as he struggled to understand how the full range of the scriptures could mediate a God whose character was appropriable and attractive within his account of spiritual communion and reason's ascent to God. The empirically driven apologetic theology of the eighteenth century, Coleridge maintained, pushed God away and impoverished any attempt to describe the communion or encounter between God and humanity.

Mansel seldom referred to Coleridge, but he clearly identified himself with the Browne, Berkeley, and Butler trajectory, if it can be described as such.[118] I have argued that Mansel drew most consistently from

Butler. He could not quite follow Berkeley all the way in his idealism, and Browne's theory of analogy drifted, in some senses, from a scriptural rooting into a somewhat idiosyncratic metaphysical dualism.[119] It must be said, however, that Mansel heartily endorsed Browne's theology, without taking up many of these features for his own purposes. But most importantly, Mansel followed Butler in his insistence that the scriptures – read, as commonly understood, through the first four ecumenical councils – were the primary form of mediation between God and humanity. Like Butler, his skepticism was employed to allow the whole range of scriptural writings to speak truthfully about God and the world, and this conviction was rooted in an incarnational theology wherein God adjusted and accommodated himself to the vast and inscrutable complexity of human life. In many ways, Mansel and Butler are characteristic examples of what Hampsher-Monk calls the "textual" emphasis of Anglican theology.[120]

However, the common criticism, from Coleridge and others, that this style of theology lacks a certain amount of existential import is one that needs to be taken seriously. Coleridge's insistence that only certain portions of the Bible could "find him," or put in reverse, that he could only recognize his experience in certain portions of the Scriptures, was exactly what Mansel feared. This, for Mansel, was a form of spiritual dislocation brought on by rational theological accounts that did not pay heed to the particular claims of the Bible or that reached out for theological accounts of the world that eased this sense of disruption. In a certain way, Mansel risked a further dislocation by claiming that God – in himself unknowable – concealed himself in every aspect of the scriptures. But it was a risk he was willing to take in order to preserve a traditional textually based understanding of God and the world.

To this end, Maurice Cowling's summation of Mansel's theology seems at once to be fairly accurate and yet misleading:

> Mansel's strength, and also his weakness, was that Christian agnosticism reflected the loss of authority which Christianity had suffered at the hands of philosophy and science. Because he knew what he was doing, Mansel was able to be intellectually aggressive but he also reflected the loss. Retreat, doubtless, was essential, if the ramparts were to be manned or an equality of esteem to be established for religion and theology in relation to science

and philosophy ... In leading a retreat, however, he was assisting at the slide which led through "incognoscibility" to the subjective religion of the Aesthetes and the intellectual anarchy of modern Anglicanism.[121]

Cowling is perhaps right to say that Mansel's theology reflects a loss, in some sense, but his skepticism or agnosticism should in no way be associated with the "subjective religion of Aesthetes" and much less the "intellectual anarchy of modern Anglicanism."

On the contrary, Mansel's skeptical theology was an attempt to carve out a space in which the scriptures and the traditions of the Church could function as they more or less always had, but now within a very different environment. It is true that Mansel's and perhaps even Butler's theology might appear like a bare scripturalism, lacking in the intellectual enrichment that it might have needed to survive in the Victorian era. As already noted, Mansel's contemporaries insisted that such a method made God seem more distant, a betrayal of his intention to defend a certain portrait of the biblical God. But my purpose in the following chapters is to show that this accusation need not attend to Mansel's style of theology, and even more, Mansel's theology still holds promise for articulating a Christian worldview in our contemporary pluralistic context.

3

Mansel and the Theology of Skepticism

In the fourth of Screwtape's letters to his nephew Wormwood, the uncle demon commends Coleridge's personal example of prayer: "One of their poets ... has recorded that he did not pray 'with moving lips and bended knees' but merely 'composed his spirit to love' and indulged 'a sense of supplication.' That is exactly the sort of prayer we want."[1] C.S. Lewis's rather severe depiction of Coleridge highlights not only the lingering presence of the latter's influence on English Christianity but also the practical stakes of the theological controversies that concerned Mansel and many other English theological writers. In Mansel's eyes, as in Lewis's, theological frameworks that elevated certain leading principles ran the risk of obscuring or denying certain traditional forms of piety and spiritual action. This was especially the case with prayer, Mansel argued, as the supplicant required a personal God – capable of listening, speaking, and acting – with which to engage. But the very idea of a personal God was becoming an increasingly disputed concept both within and outside the Church, and, in order to retain the idea, Mansel suggested that theologians needed to balance a number of competing scriptural images, and this very act of balancing imposed certain restraints upon theological and philosophical speculation.

Mansel's theological skepticism, as I will argue in this chapter, emerged from this concern that ordinary Christian people and communities might continue to engage in the personal forms of piety. His skepticism and theory of the regulative truth of scripture caused concern among orthodox critics because they seemed to enclose God behind a veil of language that referred only indirectly to God. But for

Mansel, in order for the language of scripture to be meaningful the Church required an epistemology restrained and modest enough to allow all of scripture to be simultaneously true, a prospect which struck many critics as absurd. For this reason Mansel argued that the Bible was intended primarily to show us how God has engaged with creation and how people ought to live in response. The greater speculative difficulties that emerge from the text of scripture can be grappled with and explored but never resolved in ways that distort and unravel the unity of the text itself.

In this particular chapter I describe the features of Mansel's skepticism and theory of the regulative truth of scripture. Mansel's skepticism denied an immediate knowledge of God's being and many critics objected that the regulative truth of scripture drew a veil between God's being and his witness in the world. But far from severing the connection between the language of scripture and the life and character of God, I argue that Mansel's theory of regulative truth actually enabled the language and narrative of the entire scriptures to reliably and consistently reveal God's presence in the world.

Interpreters of Mansel have typically confined their focus to Mansel's "Bampton Lectures" and a handful of other philosophical texts. This is perhaps sufficient to gain a general outline of his views, but these representative texts give only glimpses of how his philosophical position might actually function in engagement with scripture. Part of my purpose in chapter 4 is to look more closely at Mansel's sermons and more intentional theological works, but for now I restrict my focus to the lectures and his other key philosophical works, as these have been the dominant medium through which Mansel's ideas have been encountered. Nevertheless, though Mansel admitted that his lectures were heavily philosophical in their content, *The Limits of Religious Thought* is a work that is suffused with scriptural references. Even more, the stated goal of the entire book is to illuminate and protect the scriptural account of the Triune God.

CONSCIOUSNESS AND THE LIMITS OF RELIGIOUS KNOWLEDGE

Skepticism

To call Mansel a skeptic about religious knowledge is perhaps misleading, unless the term is given further definition. Rowan Williams describes a certain form of skepticism that has been common in the Anglican tradition, a skepticism

> about formulae and dogma that is fundamentally skepticism about the capacities of the human mind. It assumes that we are liable to self-deceit, that our knowledge is affected by our moral and spiritual lack. In this context, to be cautious about herme-neutical or dogmatic closure is not to discard or relativise sanc-tioned words; you occupy the territory marked out by those words, but you will not know where the boundaries are, because the search for definite boundaries suggests that you might be "in possession" of the territory ... And this contrasts with a scepti-cism more obviously generated by Enlightenment suspicion of authority, in which the target of the questioning is the formulae as such and the processes by which they were shaped.[2]

Williams's description of Anglican skepticism is perhaps not far off from Mansel's, but there is a shade of difference that will become clearer throughout this chapter. Mansel as well defines two varying forms of skepticism:

> The one is based on the assumption that the human mind is divided against itself, the testimony of one faculty contradicting that of another, – the reason, for example, being opposed to the senses, and the senses to reason ... The other proceeds on the assumption that the human mind, though at unity with itself, is at variance with some higher truth unattainable by it, things as they see to us being different from things as they are in them-selves. The inference from the latter is, that human conscious-ness, however trustworthy within its own sphere, is trustworthy as regards phenomena only, and is in error from the point of view of a higher intelligence, the nature of the phenomena being different from that of reality.[3]

Clearly, Mansel's preferred form of skepticism is not unlike Williams's as it relates to the limits of the human mind, though there is a philo-sophical underpinning that sets it apart. It seems he is less concerned with the "territory" of sanctioned words and the manner in which they are inhabited – whether in humility or possessiveness – but more so, he wishes to examine the context in which they can be affirmed and the laws under which such affirmations are made. In both forms of skepticism, Mansel is operating within a Kantian realm: in the first instance he is criticizing Kant's antinomies of reason, but in the second he seems to endorse the unknowability of things in themselves, set apart from phenomena. So while Mansel clearly uses Kantian terms to begin his discussion of the limits of the human mind, it is equally clear that his purposes are markedly different.

To some degree, then, it confuses the origins of these ideas. Hamish Swanston speculates along these lines: "It may be, however, that Mansel was not following Kant at all, but had already a notion of man's being confined to the finite, and employed the model of vision because it occurs in the Bible and common speech."[4] Mansel said as much himself: "All that Kant did in relation to these doctrines, was to supply a psychological confirmation of conclusions which had been previously held on metaphysical and theological grounds."[5] However, despite Mansel's own words, it is possible that he was being slightly disingenuous; certainly his early psychological work, *Prolegomena Logica* (1853), displays only minor discomfort with Kantian epistemology, though, as we will see, this discomfort would increase in his later works. Still, regardless of the chronology and order of these concepts, Mansel came to see the psychological interpretation of Kant – an interpretation, however misguided, that was common in nineteenth-century England[6] – as a natural confirmation of revealed truths. In other words, where Butler searched the natural world for corresponding analogies between nature and the scriptural scheme of salvation, Mansel turned to the human mind, where he perceived that the nineteenth-century struggle for truth was being waged.

The Limits of Human Consciousness

Mansel himself stands within a complicated philosophical matrix influenced by a range of figures and traditions, including Kantian idealism, Butlerian probabalism, and commonsense realism represented by William Hamilton. What these figures have in common is the emphasis upon human ignorance and the limits of human reason, however those limits might be configured. It is from Hamilton primarily that Mansel derives his examination of human consciousness, the keystone of his skepticism. For Mansel, as for Hamilton, the examination of human consciousness reveals the conditions under which we are able to know both the world and God. Mansel writes,

Revelation represents the infinite God under finite symbols, in condescension to the finite capacity of man; indicating at the same time the existence of a further reality beyond the symbol, and bidding us look forward in faith to the promise of a more perfect knowledge hereafter. Rationalism, in the hands of these expositors, adopts an opposite view of man's powers and duties. It claims to behold God as He is now: it finds a common object of religion and philosophy in the explanation of God.[7]

The limitations of consciousness that the rationalist violates in ascending to an unmediated conception of God are discovered in the exercising of this very manner of reasoning. The contradictions of reason that Mansel demonstrates parallel the antinomies of Kant in order to show up the limitations of reason, though they are more closely related to the structure of the mind than the transcendental character of reason.[8]

Mansel uses the concepts of the infinite and the absolute as examples, but here I will focus on the infinite. Hamilton's basic proposition was that "to think is to condition"[9] or that all thinking revolves around relations of objects and subjects. To speak of the unconditioned is to speak of something that cannot possibly be conceived; the unconditioned represents the dissolution of thinking altogether.[10] In other words, thinking has no shape unless it has objects or limitations to run up against. Mansel follows Hamilton almost word for word in this regard:

> The very conception of Consciousness, in whatever mode it may be manifested, necessarily implies *distinction between an object and another* ... But distinction is necessarily limitation; for if one object is to be distinguished from another, it must possess some form of existence which the other has not.[11]

If this is true of human consciousness, then a contradiction creeps into our conception of the infinite: "But it is obvious that the Infinite cannot be distinguished, as such, from the Finite, by the absence of any quality which the Finite possesses; for such absence would be a limitation."[12] The infinite, by definition, transcends such distinctions, and yet it is only through distinction that humans can form and distinguish one thought from another. Thoughts, after all, like all human activities, are subject to duration – the succession of moments – that are the precise conditions that cannot be present within the infinite.

Yet the contradiction inherent within reason's conception of the infinite does not banish the idea altogether; rather, the notion of a negative limit, Mansel claims, necessarily implies an existence beyond the boundary that the limit establishes: "it is a duty, enjoined by Reason itself, to believe in that which we are unable to comprehend."[13] Reason drives the human mind toward a collision with its own limits and toward the departure of faith. Thus, Mansel concludes, the infinite must exist even though it cannot be conceived, and human consciousness can reach this point by reason, even if reason exhausts itself in faith. The fate of English empiricism, Mansel claims, is that it had no mechanism for retaining a credible belief in the incomprehensible, or, in other words, it had no concept of a negative limit.[14] This is an important distinction because on the surface Mansel's theology shares a similar tenor to Locke's *The Reasonableness of Christianity*: a moralistic stress, a simplified Christian existence, and an open hostility to religious speculation.[15] Yet a negative limit holds open the possibility of an incomprehensible reality – a reality that is unintelligible to human reason – that still impinges upon human life and is articulated in the wide range of revealed language. Without this notion, even scripture can be sifted along the lines of intelligibility, which, as I have begun to argue, is Mansel's principle worry.

Mansel's notion of a negative limit also related to his critique of Kant. Kant, for instance, argued that

> I cannot infer the magnitude of the regress from the quantity or magnitude of the world, and determine the former by means of the latter; on the contrary, I must first of all form a conception of the quantity or magnitude of the world from the magnitude of the empirical regress. But of this regress I know nothing more than that I ought to proceed from every given member of the series of conditions to one still higher. But the quantity of the universe is not thereby determined, and we cannot affirm that this regress proceeds *in infinitum*."[16]

Kant's distinction between the "*regressus in indefinitum*" and the "*regressus in infinitum*,"[17] for Mansel, confused the nature of a limitation in thought. Mansel writes,

> Kant confesses that we have no intuition of the unconditioned; that we only infer its existence as implied by the conception of

the conditioned. But this admission reduces the former idea to the mere negation of the latter; a negation is as empty regulatively as speculatively, and assuredly not needing a special faculty for its conception, inasmuch as it is never conceived at all.[18]

In other words, Mansel concludes, "He treats an impotence of thought as if it were a faculty. The infinite and the indefinite may be thus distinguished: the former implies an actual conceiving the absence of limits; the latter is a not conceiving the presence of limits."[19] Therefore to distinguish between reason – which tends toward the unconditioned in order to unify our thoughts – and understanding is misleading. The understanding, Mansel suggests, constantly "implies the indefinite" already, and so "Reason does no more."[20]

In effect Mansel denies the distinction between the understanding and reason, especially, as already mentioned above, Kant's use of practical reason. "Kant's head and heart led him in two opposite directions,"[21] Mansel claims: though Kant gives up knowledge of the unconditioned, the infinite, through speculative reason, he in effect claws it back through practical reason.[22] And despite the subtleties of Kant's distinctions between these faculties, Mansel regarded the latter as yet another attempt to surpass the negative limits of consciousness.

While Mansel considered his skepticism to be within the mainstream of Christian theology, his strictures upon the conceivability of the infinite especially provoked visceral rejoinders. He seemed somewhat surprised that fellow theologians would take up the causes of Kantian and idealistic philosophy against him. F.D. Maurice's response is perhaps best known: "He seems to me to crush the search after Truth, all that is expressed in the word philosophy, by crushing at the same time the discovery of Truth, all that is expressed in the word revelation."[23] Maurice was quick to perceive the threat that Mansel's lectures represented to his own theological convictions: the core of Christian belief is that the infinite God has been "manifested in the Eternal Word, and the only begotten son,"[24] which of course, in some manner, implied the transcendence of the limited, finite human situation. To know God required the communion of the finite with the infinite, which was the hallmark of English romantic theology derived from Coleridge and the German idealists.

In some sense, Maurice's outrage and puzzlement seems justified: how can anyone know God if he cannot, by definition, conceive of the infinite? A modern reader might ask, in an age where Christian orthodoxy was being pried apart from every side, why would Mansel risk offending a fellow Anglican on such a fine point of distinction? Hamish Swanston insightfully remarks that this was a period characterized by an "inability to recognize a friend."[25] In a certain way Swanston's remark seems obviously true, and yet Mansel's concerns were derived from a complex set of circumstances, not least of which was the emergence of German biblical criticism. Mansel regarded the new forms of biblical criticism, represented by Strauss and Jowett, among others, as the natural extension of philosophical rationalism into the domain of scripture, with the same inevitable results.

It may be true that Mansel needlessly alienated a potential ally in someone like F.D. Maurice, but the danger he perceived in employing the infinite as a description of God is that it distracts readers of the scriptures from the manner in which God has in fact revealed himself. Mansel believed that God was infinite, but because the term defies human conception, God revealed himself under finite symbols so that his people could know him. The conditions and relations of consciousness – subject to object and the succession of time – are the conditions through which God speaks to humanity through the scriptures. Mansel summarizes these conditions with the term "personality"; that is, humans relate to the world as distinct persons who make choices, perceive objects, and relate to others.[26] It is as persons that the succeeding moments of time are held together in unity, and for this reason Christians are bound to think of God as a person, even though this notion seems to contradict God's infinity:

> It is our duty then to think of God as personal; and it is our duty to believe that He is infinite. It is true that we cannot reconcile these two representations with each other; as our conception of personality involves attributes apparently contradictory to the notion of infinity. But it is not clear that this contradiction exists anywhere but in our own minds.[27]

These "two representations" do not elide each other; rather, they are held together by some imperceptible unity that cannot be conceived within the limits of human imagination.

For Mansel, consciousness is the foundation of all human knowledge, or rather the lens through anything can be known or perceived, though in no way can the philosopher move behind or beyond his consciousness to examine its origins: "This self-personality, like all other simple and immediate presentations, is indefinable; but it is so, because it is superior to definition. It can be analyzed into no simpler elements, for it is itself the simplest of all: it can be made no clearer by description or comparison, for it is revealed to us in all the clearness of an original intuition, of which description and comparison can furnish only faint and partial resemblances."[28] From a theological point of view it would seem that Mansel's emphasis upon the laws and limits of human consciousness are perhaps unusual, even if theologians have employed similar language with regard to the capacity of human reason. Mansel enjoyed marshalling long lists of theological authorities to support his notion that the human mind cannot directly conceive of God, even if the critical tools of Kant and Hamilton were not available for these figures to ground their claims.[29]

But it is in this light that it is important to regard Mansel's debt to Butler and his arguments against deist objections to Christian revelation:

> Since it is as unreasonable as it is common, to urge objections against revelation, which are of equal weight against natural religion; and those who do this, if they are not confuted themselves, deal unfairly with others, in making it seem that they are arguing only against revelation, or particular doctrines of it, when in reality they are arguing against moral providence.[30]

In Mansel's eyes the deist attacks against Christian orthodoxy derived from moral and providential concerns had migrated, in the nineteenth century, into arguments of consciousness and the limits of knowledge. To this extent, he tried to show that the character of human consciousness and Christian revelation are in fact analogous and that the former cannot be used to adjust, modify, or discard the latter. Perhaps Mansel's orthodox critics did not understand the nature of his strategy. The erstwhile Tractarian J.B. Mozley, for example, cautiously critiqued Mansel's skepticism for being too overdrawn because there was "little recognition in these lectures of the truth, that, however theoretically distinct these modes of philosophy may be, yet in practice they will be always entrenching upon each other's ground."[31] This was a common complaint against Mansel's lectures, but any theological account of how these "distinct modes" overlap in practice was never really pursued in response. For Mansel, theoretical precision in accounting for the character of consciousness allowed greater freedom in the reading and affirming of scriptural claims, in all of their obscurity and diversity. This is a theme that I will return to toward the end of this chapter and into the next.

REGULATIVE TRUTH AND THE LANGUAGE OF SCRIPTURE

Regulative Truth

If Mansel's skepticism was received by churchmen as too stark and formulated, his notion of regulative truth was regarded with similar confusion and hesitance. The constraints of consciousness are bound to conceive of God as personal; this is what Mansel calls regulative truth, and he contrasts it with speculative truth. Speculative truth seeks knowledge of God as he is in himself, and regulative truth accepts God's representation of himself within finite symbols – the scriptures – for the purpose of practical living. This is the Christian's first clue to reading scripture in the modern age:

> How far that knowledge represents God as He is, we know not, and we have no need to know. The testimony of Scripture, like that of our natural faculties, is plain and intelligible, when we are content to accept it as a fact intended for our practical guidance; it becomes incomprehensible, only when we attempt to explain it as a theory capable of speculative analysis.[32]

Scripture becomes unintelligible for the reasons outlined previously: How can human reason conceive of an infinite God who acts in time or who responds to human prayers and engages humanity as persons subject to time? Scripture does not resolve this dilemma but rather sets before the Christian the manner in which he or she is to act and think about God in this life.

It was this notion of regulative truth, even more than Mansel's barring of the infinite that struck his contemporaries as absurd and even dangerous. It seemed he was implying, for Maurice and others, that humanity could not actually know God and that the scriptures, rather than revealing God, in fact concealed him. Gavin Hyman has more recently stated the objection in relation to the "real God" and the "available God" as follows: "the constitutive, transcendent God must give way to the regulative 'working God' of practical religion. With this move, truth becomes subjective and realism gives way to non-realism."[33] Distinctions like Mansel's between speculative and regulative knowledge of God contain an intrinsic slide toward atheism or unbelief.[34] But Mansel's argument clearly avoided this conclusion and he related his notion of regulative truth to the central Christological character of Christian doctrine: "Is it irrational to contemplate God under symbols drawn from the human consciousness? Christ is our pattern: 'for in him dwelleth all the fullness of the Godhead bodily? It was when the fullness of time was come, that God sent forth his Son.'"[35] God's condescension to our limited capacities is at the heart of Christian understandings of salvation and should not be dismissed as somehow beneath God:

> Those who, in their horror of what they call anthropomorphism, or anthropopathy, refuse to represent the Deity under symbols borrowed from the limitations of human consciousness, are bound, in consistency, to deny that God exists; for the conception of existence is as human and as limited as any other.[36]

Here Mansel, in fact, reverses the accusation and suggests that the refusal to see God in that which is limited and human is a refusal to see God at all. Mansel clearly believed that there was an analogy between human regulative conceptions of God and God as he truly is, but this analogy must remain imperfect until the beatific vision on the last day:

> So should it be during this transitory life, in which we see through a glass, darkly, in which God reveals himself in types and shadows, under human images and attributes, to meet graciously and deal tenderly with the human sympathies of his creatures ... we may trust that not wholly alien to such feelings will be our communion with God face to face.[37]

It is fairly clear that what Mansel thought he was doing with the concept of regulative truth was simply defending the integrity of scripture against philosophical attempts to subvert its rationality. Yet the concept's origin is somewhat difficult to discern. In an exchange in the *Journal of Theological Studies* (1971), Don Cupitt maintains, against the criticisms of D.W. Dockrill, that Mansel's idea of regulative truth is in fact a theologically and scripturally derived notion. Cupitt suggests,

> Christian theology has always affirmed the incomprehensibility . of God. Scripture is a practical, not a speculative book, and Christian dogmas have always been authoritative guides to conduct rather than authoritative diagrams of deity ... so the doctrine of regulative truth is, quite simply, orthodoxy.[38]

That Mansel was simply trying to defend orthodoxy is undoubtedly true, but that the notion can be found in scripture might be contested. Mansel, in a letter to Goldwin Smith, attributed the idea to Bishop Copleston and Archbishop Whately in their defence of God's passions.[39] But clearly the term itself comes from Kant, though to Mansel's point, it is used in a manner very different than that of Kant: the ideas of God, freedom, and immortality are derived not from the demands of a moral imperative but from the representation of God in scripture, his relationship to his people as described in the very words of the Bible. Thus there is no mediating feature or principle between God and humanity but the words of the Bible, symbolized in the creed and represented most fully in the person of Christ.[40]

Anthropomorphic Language and the Attributes of God

It was hard for Mansel's critics to understand how someone could actually know God if the manner of revelation was only regulatively true. Mozley, for example, was uneasy about the distinction between regulative and speculative truth but felt as though he could not cast off speculative truth of God:

> Either God represents Himself to us as He is, or as He is not; – and leave our readers to make their choice. But, we believe, more fallacies lie beneath these bipartite divisions than is commonly suspected. Dichotomies are almost always arranged for a foregone conclusion; and we, therefore, prefer stating the case more directly; that it is involved in the very idea of God that He will reveal Himself to His creatures, if at all, in a mode which is speculatively true.[41]

The idea that God is couched in language that does not fully express his character is less the issue than that the language may not in fact describe him in any way. Newman's comments to Charles Meynell express some of the same discomfort: "To assert, with the School of Sir W.H. [Hamilton] and Mansel, that nothing is known because nothing is known luminously and exactly, seems to me saying that we do not see the stars because we cannot tell the number, size, or distance from each other."[42] These types of concerns are no doubt legitimate, and perhaps Mansel could have worked harder to make himself clear on this point, but Newman's analogy, however hastily thought out, shows at least some sense of the confusion. Naturally, Mansel would have responded that vague and incomplete empirical knowledge is of a different sort than knowledge of an entirely differ- ent order, in this case of God. Yet how language that is only regula- tively true is able to reveal God needs to be further sorted out.

In a footnote in his first letter to Goldwin Smith, Mansel makes an important distinction by contrasting his position with that of Spinoza:

> Spinoza's views and mine are the exact reverse of each other. Spinoza asserts that there are no mysteries in Scripture; but that things simple and intelligible by all men are taught in figurative language; the figures being mere accommodations to the temper- ament or capacity of each individual writer, which others are at liberty to accept or reject as they please. I assert, on the con- trary, that Scripture reveals mysteries incomprehensible by man, through the medium of conceptions and terms adapted to human comprehension; the adaptation being such as is needed by the laws of human thought in general, and such as no philosophy can enable us to surmount. Spinoza declares that religion con- sists of nothing but moral duties; that the historical portions of Scripture are not necessary for those who can attain to clear con- ceptions without them; and that no dogma which admits of con- troversy among good men can be part of the Catholic faith. This is exactly the position of later German rationalists.[43]

The distinction is admittedly subtle. For Spinoza the "figurative lan- guage" of scripture is an accommodation to human minds that is entirely for a moral effect; that is, it may not say anything about God at all.[44] Furthermore, the language of scripture even risks obscuring God's nature, as in the case of miracles:

Wherefore if we would conceive that anything could be done in nature by any power whatsoever which would be contrary to the laws of nature, it would also be contrary to our primary ideas, and we should have either to reject it as absurd, or else to cast doubt (as just shown) on our primary ideas, and consequently on the existence of God, and on everything howsoever perceived.[45]

Scripture risks this contradiction between primary ideas and depictions of miracles merely to "excite wonder" and command obedience.[46] Likewise, God does not get angry or change his mind, as the Bible might suggest; in the best case, Spinoza argues, these types of scriptural descriptions are used poetically to "excite wonder," but in the worst case they are delusions "foisted into the sacred writings by irreligious hands" who have no knowledge of the natural laws.[47]

It would seem that Mansel's theological critics read his theory of regulative truth as an idea akin to Spinoza's hermeneutics, however the spirit of the respective authors might have differed.[48] Maurice, for example, was bothered especially by Mansel's suggestion that truth and falsehood pertained not to objects but to human conceptions, a common understanding used in logic.[49] Maurice was not a logician, and he was clearly frustrated that such technical rules should be used to obscure a simple scripture declaration such as "I am the truth."[50] In a sequel to his initial criticism of Mansel, Maurice maintains his original point on this theme: "The very question at issue between me and the writer of those Sermons was about the nature of Speculative and Regulative Truth; whether they can be distinguished, what is the distinction, whether truth itself does not vanish if it is such as he tried to make it."[51] Formulated differently, Maurice's question asks, what exactly holds together the reference and the referent if the reference cannot be taken at face value?[52] Or, as in Spinoza, if scriptural language is an accommodation to our limited capacity, how does this language retain any correspondence with the truth, as Mansel still wanted to maintain?

Naturally Mansel had every desire to affirm Maurice's selected statement of Christ: "I am the truth." But Mansel uses this text to describe what he perceived to be the main difference in their argument:

I believe, with him, that God is revealed in Christ. But I believe also that this Revelation (while designed to answer other and most momentous purposes in the Divine Economy, which we need not speak of now) is, as a manner of teaching us the Nature of God, analogous in some degree, however fuller and higher, to those earlier manifestations in which God revealed Himself under symbols borrowed from the consciousness of man. In other words, I do not regard the manifestation of God in the flesh, as a direct manifestation of the Absolute and Eternal Essence of the Deity; but as the assumption of a nature in which the manifestation is adapted to human faculties and limited to a mode in which man is capable of receiving it. In this belief I think I am supported by the language of that Article of our Church which expressly asserts that the Human Nature of Christ is not coeternal with His Divinity, but was assumed, as a subsequent nature, at a certain period of time.[53]

For Mansel, the revelation of Christ does not alter the ordering of human knowledge or the manner in which people come to know. Christ, of course, is a revelation of God, though one that is in accordance with the tradition of God's revealing. Mansel goes on to characterize Maurice's own view as follows:

Mr Maurice's teaching, on the other hand, so far as I can understand it, appears to be this. He holds that the Incarnation of Christ as a Man was not the assumption, by the Son of God, of a new nature; but an unveiling to man of that which had existed from all eternity. He seems to maintain that God the Son is, in His Eternal and Infinite Essence, very and perfect Man; and that, in His manifestation to the world in the likeness of sinful flesh, He did not "empty Himself, taking the form of a servant," but manifested his Divine Glory in all its infinite perfection.[54]

This characterization of Maurice may be unfair; certainly Maurice did not think that he was contradicting the articles of the Church on this particular point especially.[55] But Mansel's criticism perhaps relates more to a perceived trajectory in Maurice's theology that leads to affirmations that, Mansel would claim, contradict the clear words of scripture.[56]

In particular, the issue at stake for Mansel is how the theologian unites the philosophical attributes of God with the representations of God in scripture. Along these lines, Mansel very much follows Butler's assertion of human ignorance of the scheme of salvation: "the account now given of Christianity most strongly shews and enforces upon us the obligation of searching the scriptures, in order to see what the scheme of revelation really is instead of determining before-hand, from reason, what the scheme of it must be."[57] It is from this standpoint – the standpoint of human ignorance of God's ways – that Mansel takes issue with Maurice's rendering of Christ's atonement and universal salvation.[58] The reason for this will become clearer as I lay out Mansel's views in more detail.

The basic problem of God's attributes for Mansel stems from his position that all human thought takes place within the realm of pos-sible human experience. So, logically speaking,

A form of words, uniting attributes not presentable in an intu-ition, is not the sign of a thought, but of the negation of all thinking. Conception must thus be carefully distinguished, as well from mere imagination, as from a mere understanding of the meaning of words.[59]

As we have already seen, a negation in thinking, or a negative limit to thinking, can still imply the existence of God beyond the limit, though God in this respect cannot be conceived in thought. Thus when speaking about the attributes of God, the problem arises as to how such attributes can be predicated of an invisible God who is unavailable to human intuitions. So in a later essay, called "Free Thinking – Its History and Tendencies," Mansel attempts to draw on Aquinas in delineating the manner in which the attributes of God function in human thought:

When the older theologians declared the essence of God to be mysterious and incomprehensible, they were not thinking of Locke's real essence, of which they knew nothing, but of that logical essence which is comprised in attributes, and can be expressed in a definition, and which Locke calls the Nominal Essence. This is most distinctly stated in the language of Aquinas: "the name of God does not express the Divine essence as it is, as the name of man expresses in its signification the essence of man as it is – that is to say, by signifying the definition which declares the essence." The ground of this distinction was the conviction that finite things cannot indicate the nature of the infinite God otherwise than by imperfect analogies. "The attributes of God"

it was argued "must be represented to our minds, so far as they
can be represented at all, under the similitude of the corresponding attributes of man.".... Hence the divine attributes may
properly be called mysterious; for, though we believe in the co-
existence, we are unable to conceive the manner of their
co-existence.[60]

Mansel does not enter into a detailed discussion of Aquinas at this
point but he merely retrieves a rather simple point from what has
become a highly complicated theological topic concerning divine
predication and analogical language in Thomas: namely, God is represented and mediated through human significations.[61]

However, like Aquinas, Mansel argues that these signifying terms
refer to God on a varying scale of signification. The infinite and the
absolute, as already mentioned, are negative conceptions that cannot
be represented by any reasonable intuition. Mill, for example, suggested that Hamilton, and thus Mansel, employed these terms as
meaningless abstractions devoid of any predicates, and as result they
must simply include every possible predicate and so devolve into
endless contradiction.[62] But on this score, Mill mistook Hamilton's
criticism of these terms for his actual position.[63] Mansel was quick
to point this out:

Now, in the first place, "the Infinite" and "the Absolute," even in
the sense in which they are both predicable of God, are no more
names of God than "the creature" and the "finite" are names
of men. They are the names of certain attributes, which further
inquiry may, perhaps, show to belong to God and to no other
being, but which do not in their signification express this, and
do not constitute our primary idea of God, which is that of
a Person.[64]

The terms "Absolute" and "Infinite" are used by Mansel in a manner
that is not unlike David Burrell's understanding of Aquinas. Burrell
argues that Aquinas investigates the simplicity, compositeness, and
limitedness of God as a linguistic exercise to mark off God's otherness, but the terms themselves provide no positive conception.[65] At
least for Mansel, these terms cannot be related analogically to anything
in human experience.

But this is obviously not true for all the attributes of God, such as his goodness, wisdom, and justice, and it was on this score that Mansel had to prove that his theory of regulative truth of scripture could still reliably speak of God in a manner that was not entirely misleading. Again in a manner that is similar to Aquinas,[66] Mansel argues that we know of God's goodness, love, and wisdom, however imperfectly, through human and finite representations of these virtues:

> We have no immediate intuition of the Divine attributes, even as phenomena; we only infer their existence and nature from certain similar attributes of which we are immediately conscious in ourselves … Our knowledge of God, originally derived from personal consciousness, receives accession from two other sources (Revelation and the World).[67]

While the goodness, love, and wisdom of God are only intelligible to humanity through human analogies, Mansel is at pains to emphasize that these humanly understood virtues do not exhaust the manner in which they exist in God. As with the infinite and the absolute, Mansel's concern is that finite definitions of God will be used to measure God as he appears in scripture:

> The main foundation of skeptical arguments, both in ancient and modern times, against the existence of moral and intellectual attributes in God, has been the assumption, that these attributes, if they exist at all, must be literally the same in God as they are in man, and may be reasoned about in the same manner.[68]

The problem that critics of the scriptures raise relates precisely to this point: how can the humanly depicted God in the Bible – passionate, angry, jealous – be united with the supposedly stable virtues of love, goodness, and justice?

Spinoza's answer to this question was to suggest that the scriptures represent God in this way in order to quicken and excite moral sentiment, though these representations inevitably obscure the truth of God's character. Mansel agrees with Spinoza that such depictions of God have moral and religious benefits, but he is unwilling to sever the connection between these representations and God's actual character:

There is a religious influence to be imparted to us by the thought of God's anger, no less than by that of His punishments; by the thought of His love, no less than by that of His benefits: that both, inadequate and human as they are, yet dimly indicate some corresponding reality in the Divine nature; and that to merge one in the other is not to gain a purer representation of God as He is, but only to mutilate that under which He has been pleased to reveal Himself.[69]

Mansel's denial of a "purer representation" does not mean that God does not somehow supersede his representations but only that humanity cannot seek him beyond these signs:

We do not suppose that he sees with eyes or hears with ears, and we have no direct knowledge of any other mode of seeing or hearing. But that language is regulatively true, as stating the fact, that God has a knowledge of what we do and say; though the manner of that knowledge is unknown to us ... But when we speak of the anger or the pity of God, we do not mean that He is affected in precisely the same manner as we are when we feel those passions, and yet we have no positive conception of any other manner. Here again the statement is regulatively true, as expressing God's relation to us to such an extent and is such a manner as we are capable of understanding.[70]

The regulative truth of these figures is not emptied of all claims to the truth; in fact they speak truthfully of God in the fullest sense in which humans can understand him. And naturally, the language of the Bible admits of varying degrees of analogy:

I do not believe that the anger and pity of God are figures in the same sense in which the hand and the eye are figures; nor do I believe that the power and the wisdom and the goodness of God can be called figures, as his anger and pity might perhaps in a wide sense be called so.[71]

Yet all of these representations are accommodated, in one sense or another, to the capacity of human understanding. Outside of these representations, Mansel argues, nothing at all can be known about God's essence: "The mind is thus unable to frame for itself any speculative representation of the divine essence."[72] Furthermore, the images and words of scripture are fixed in a manner that cannot be further adapted or accommodated to particular times or inclinations:

> It is obvious, indeed, that the theory of an adaptation of divine truths to human faculties entirely changes its significance, as soon as we attempt to give a further adaptation to the adapted symbol itself; – to modify into a still lower truth that which is itself a modification of a higher. The instant we undertake to say that this or that speculative or practical interpretation is the only real meaning of that which Scripture represents to us under a different image, we abandon at once the supposition of an accommodation to the necessary limits of human thought, and virtually admit that the ulterior significance of the representation falls as much within those limits as the representation itself. Thus interpreted, the principle no longer offers the slightest safeguard against Rationalism; – nay, it becomes identified with the fundamental vice of rationalism itself; – that of explaining away what we are unable to comprehend.[73]

Mansel was aware that his theory was separated only by a slim margin from the rationalism that he sought to criticize. The words of scripture hover between these "higher" and "lower" referents, and while the original accommodation makes a divine truth comprehensible in a regulative manner, any further attempt to adjust the image to fit it into a speculative understanding of God unravels the entire purpose of scripture. Scripture for Mansel is paradoxical: it is adapted to human minds and to this degree fluid; yet at the same time, it is rigid in its accommodated signification and remains capable of perplexing the readers to which it is accommodated.[74]

Clearly Mansel's view of the regulative truth of scripture allows for the truthful reference of scripture's language. In fact, he employs the theory precisely to provide a manner in which all of scripture can speak truthfully, even when its images and depictions of God appear to violate certain rational principles. It is true that the coherence between scriptural language and the character of God is dependent upon faith – the Christian hopes and believes that these images correspond to God – even though the manner of this correspondence may escape the capacity of human reason. Mansel might have been more precise on the topic of analogy; at times, he suggests that human language "dimly" represents God or will not be "wholly unlike" God in the end. These are not definite terms, and they admit of categorical confusion when cast in the broader theological discussion of analogy. At most Mansel speaks of God's "intention" to represent himself in such a manner, and it is in this way that the analogy is strongest: in scripture we clearly perceive God's intention, which bears upon his character and being, but they also hover behind the foreground of God's intended mode of communication. His imprecision in this regard might have been deliberate, or perhaps he did not foresee the consequences of a more subtle treatment of the topic.[75] He was happy to recognize his position in both Butler and Aquinas, two figures who approached analogical reasoning in markedly different fashions. It is possible that Mansel's view of analogy has more in common with Barth's *Analogia Fidei* than with Aquinas's *Analogia Entis*. But Mansel was not aware of the supposed stakes of this dispute, and his concerns, I suggest, were not remote from either thinker.[76] So while his theory of regulative truth may have appeared to some as a risk, it is clear that in this theory Mansel was searching for a framework in order to defend the scriptures against moral criticisms of Christian doctrine and the scriptural witness.

Scripture and Morality

J.S. Mill's critique of Mansel, while covering the whole range of his philosophy, seemed to center on this very topic of divine and human morality. It is fair to say that regardless of the outcome of the debate, Mill managed to frame the issue in a memorable fashion that survived among even orthodox readers of Mansel. Rather than review this debate extensively, I briefly argue how Mill's criticism seemed to miss the mark on precisely this issue of analogy.

Writing in 1894, the prominent evangelical theologian R.W. Dale fully endorsed Mill's critique: "I wholly agree with the criticism of Mr John Stuart Mill on the famous Bampton Lecture of Mr. Mansel: 'Language has no meaning for the words Just, Merciful, Benevolent, save that in which we predicate them of our fellow creatures.'"[77] Of course, Dale was hardly sympathetic with Mill's overall philosophy, but on this point he sensed that Mansel was pushing God into an intolerably voluntarist mode. To be sure, Mansel had no difficulty affirming Butler's maxim that God's "moral government must be a scheme quite beyond our comprehension."[78] But like Butler, for

Mansel there were clear indications of this governance written into the character of created life, and these created realities – in this case, human virtues – somehow shadowed forth God's life, though in a way that is imperfect.

Ironically, it would seem that when Mill criticized Mansel, he thought he was criticizing long-held theological views that "God's ways are not our ways." In other words, it was not Mansel's conclusions that made him offensive but his attempt to describe these views in modern philosophical language: "the novelty is in presenting this conclusion as a corollary from the most advanced doctrines of modern philosophy – from the true theory of the powers and limitations of the human mind, on religious and on all other subjects."[79] In this light it is not quite clear what Dale thought he was dissenting from. For Mill, theology and philosophy were incommensurate worlds, and Mansel's lectures represented a particularly bold attempt to extend religious heteronomy into the secular sphere. Mill played on this image of Mansel's authoritarian God, and his famous epithet seemed to sum up the entire debate: "I will call no being good, who is not what I mean when I apply that epithet to my fellow creatures."[80] Of course, as I have already shown, Mansel was not a pure voluntarist, and he made an express point of emphasizing the analogy between divine and human virtues and morality. Yet he could not reduce one to the other, for the obvious reason that scripture provides an account of God that presents clear problems for any such reduction.

Still, he did not discard the analogy in his defence against Mill, and he cautioned Mill that they were discussing this issue from vastly different perspectives.[81] For Mansel, the conditions of human morality are created: "[morality] in its human character, depends upon conditions not coeternal with God, but created along with man."[82] Mansel made this argument in opposition to both Mill and Kant, whom he interpreted as holding to an immutable and universal form of morality, however differently construed,[83] whereas Mansel argues that while human morality has its origin in God, it acquires particular and contingent forms in light of created existence.[84] This is not to say that these forms are relative in some absolute sense but only that all human action is situated in particular circumstances.[85] In a human context, the word "good," for example, has a "community of meanings," whether it is embodied by a mother, daughter, ruler, or employer.[86] The argument that the good must always mean the same thing for each person, in Mansel's eyes, is simply not true of reality.

Mansel then extends this analogy to God:

> So, again, there is a divine mercy and there is a human mercy; but God is merciful in such a manner as is fitting compatibly with the righteous government of the universe; and man is merciful in a certain limited range, the exercise of the attribute being guided by considerations affecting the welfare of society or of individuals.[87]

Mill's criticism that Mansel's God is not describable according to humanly derived notions of goodness is inaccurate, at least on a theoretical level. However, for epistemological reasons, and just as much for scriptural reasons, Mansel is forced to place a distance or imperfection within this analogy, which, as I have argued previously, is a legitimate position within the theological tradition, whether stemming from Aquinas or Butler.

Yet, to the extent that Mansel's modifications of the divine and human analogy permit a level of unintelligibility, Mill was perhaps right that this idea can be used by theologians to defend what Mill would regard as indefensible actions carried out by God:

> The divine power is always interpreted in a completely human signification, but the Divine goodness and justice must be understood to be such only in an unintelligible sense. Is it unfair to surmise that this is because those who speak in the name of God, have need of the human conception of his power, since an idea which can overawe and enforce obedience must address itself to real feelings; but are content that his goodness should be conceived only as something inconceivable, because they are so often required to teach doctrines respecting him which conflict irreconcilably with all goodness that we can conceive?[88]

In this respect, Mansel did not shy away from defending what can only be termed the violence of God in the scriptures, in particular in the Old Testament. It is true, at least in the lectures and his philosophical writings, that Mansel defends these difficult texts – for example, Israel's invasion of Canaan[89] – with little theological explanation as to how they might be understood within a larger scriptural framework. In chapter 4 I make this case more carefully. For now it is important to note that while it may appear that he allows these texts to simply hover as deliberate offences to the form of reasoning that he criticizes, Mansel considers the difficulty of these representations of God as critical to central Christian claims.[90]

For example, when Maurice speaks of the atonement, he derides the notion that God could be angry and in need of some kind of satisfaction, and he suggests that early Christian understandings of the atonement were of a different kind: "They have believed that He rescued them out of the power of an enemy, by yielding to his power, not that He rescued them out of the hand of God by paying a penalty to Him."[91] Along these lines Maurice suggests that "Christ satisfied the Father by presenting the image of His own holiness and love,"[92] not by bearing the penalty of sin, as if God needed satisfying. The sacrifice of the Son is an eternal reality that becomes concrete in the life of Christ, a rendering of the atonement that is made possible by Maurice's Platonic metaphysics.[93]

Mansel, however, argued that Maurice's theology of the atonement was driven by an aversion to the plain texts of scripture that depict, in places, God's anger and, furthermore, the sacrificial character of Christ's death. In his response to Maurice, Mansel parallels Maurice's words with relevant scripture passages:

I believe that if God cannot in any sense "be angry," and there-fore does not "need to be propitiated," then is Christ not "the propitiation for our sins"? I believe that if it is inconsistent with Divine Justice that the innocent should suffer for the sins of the guilty," then did Christ not suffer, "the just for the unjust"? I believe that if "it is more reasonable to believe that God forgives our sins freely," without any satisfaction or redemption, then is it not true that "we have redemption through His blood, even the forgiveness of sins"? I believe that if, "because we cannot conceive how the punishment of one can do away with the guilt of another," we are therefore justified in denying that it is so, then is it not true that "with His stripes we are healed"? And I believe that all these consequents are opposed no less to the lan-guage of Scripture, than to the teaching of that Church to whose Articles Mr. Maurice and I have both subscribed.[94]

This is undoubtedly a severe criticism of Maurice's position, and it is likely that Mansel regarded Maurice's theology as a capitulation to the concerns of people like Mill. It is well known that Maurice was

deeply concerned with drawing the "young men" of England[95] who
had strayed from the faith back into the fold. But Mansel's concern
was that such a method of accommodation would only the place the
Christian within a continuing cycle of insoluble difficulties. While it
may appear at times that his method shows little concern for the
scruples of the inquirer or the doubter, Mansel, as much as Maurice,
directed his work toward those who were troubled by unbelief:

> It is painful, but at the same time instructive, to trace the gradual
> progress by which an unstable disciple often tears off strip by
> strip the wedding garment of his faith, – scarce conscious the
> while of his own increasing nakedness, – and to mark how the
> language of Christian belief may remain almost untouched,
> when the substance and the life have departed from it. While
> Philosophy speaks nothing but the language of Christianity, we
> may be tempted to think that the two are really one; that our
> own speculations are but leading us to Christ by another and a
> more excellent way. Many a young aspirant after a philosophical
> faith, trusts himself to the trackless ocean of rationalism in the
> spirit of the too-confident Apostle: "Lord, bid me to come unto
> thee on the water." And for a while he knows not how deep he
> sinks, till the treacherous surface on which he treads is yielding
> on every side, and the dark abyss of utter unbelief is yawning to
> swallow him up. Well is it indeed with those who, even in that
> last fearful hour, can yet cry, "Lord, save me!" and can feel that
> supporting hand stretched out to grasp them, and hear that
> voice, so warning, yet so comforting, "O thou of little faith,
> wherefore didst thou doubt?"[96]

It is perhaps not quite apparent just how far Mansel had considered
Maurice to have wandered out on this "treacherous surface." In all
likelihood, comments like these were directed more toward Mansel's
contemporaries like Francis Newman and Benjamin Jowett, figures
who appear frequently in his lectures. But to be sure, Mansel perceived
in Maurice a more moderate attempt to modify obvious scriptural
phrasing with a set of overriding moral concerns. In cases such as
these, Mansel writes in his lectures, "Theology gains nothing; but she
is in danger of losing everything."[97] What theology stands to lose,
presumably, is its ability to articulate a view of God that derives its
coherence and contours from its own authorized sources. Naturally

this includes reason and the investigation of the world, but there is a certain ordering to these sources that Mansel tries to arrange so that the scriptures are allowed to speak truthfully and, in his own words, plainly.

CONCLUSION

The difficulty in reading Mansel theologically as I have done is that, while his thought bears directly upon theological thinking, he does not frequently engage traditional theological topics head on. In this way, the vast majority of his work reads more as a theological method than as a constructive theology. Maurice, in *What Is Revelation?*, pleads with Mansel that if he does not like Maurice's theology of the atonement, he should at least provide his own account.[98] Further, Maurice argues that even the scriptures need filling out and application, which must undoubtedly be a function of reason working in concert with revelation.[99] Mansel recognized this as a weakness, but he understood it as his vocation to risk the appearance of being theologically thin in order to clarify how he thought theological knowledge should be ordered:

> In one respect, indeed, I have perhaps departed from the customary language of the pulpit, to a greater extent than was absolutely necessary; – namely, in dealing with the ideas common to Theology and Metaphysics in the terms of the latter, rather than in those of the former. But there is a line of argument, in which the vague generalities of the Absolute and the Infinite may be more reverently and appropriately employed than the sacred names and titles of God. For we almost instinctively shrink back from the recklessness which thrusts forward, on every occasion, the holiest names and things, to be tossed to and fro, and trampled under foot, in the excitement of controversy. We feel that the name of Him whom we worship may not lightly be held up as a riddle for prying curiosity to puzzle over ... We feel that, though God is indeed, in His incomprehensible Essence, absolute and infinite, it is not as the Absolute and Infinite that He appeals to the love and the fear and the reverence of His creatures.[100]

Given Mansel's long appeals to the Church fathers, his reliance on Aquinas and the Anglican divines, it seems implausible that he would have any prejudice against dogmatic theology as such. Rather, it is more the case that his peculiar form of skepticism was intended as a ground-clearing exercise in an intellectual climate where philosophical and theological lines had become exceedingly blurred. One might make the case that this has always been the case in Christian history: Platonism in the early Church and Artistotelianism in the late Middle Ages would seem like obvious examples. But it can also be argued that nineteenth-century England, along with the continent, was in a novel circumstance where the traditional status of Christian claims was not entirely clear. Mansel labelled Hegel as a pantheist and a pagan, but if he was either, he was a pagan who placed the Trinity at the heart of his philosophy along with the Incarnation. Likewise, what was one to make of Matthew Arnold's apostle Paul or Jesus, especially considering his ambiguous place in the Church of England? To speak in the abstract about faith and reason, theology and philosophy in this context is potentially confusing and even misleading. These concepts were shifting rapidly within a complicated matrix that spanned figures like Locke, Hume, Kant, and Hegel and the just as complex tradition of English theology. In *The Secular Age*, Charles Taylor tracks the proliferation of what he calls "middle positions" in Victorian England, which claimed to be more reasonable or purified forms of Christianity. But he remarks, "They look rational within a certain framework, indeed, but this framework attracts us for a host of reasons, including ethical ones ... that of a free, invulnerable, disengaged agent."[101] Taylor's comment is only intended to show that frameworks of rationality carry with them a number of considerations that may have little to do with the "purely rational," whatever this might mean. This was certainly the case in Mansel's England, and the strength of his thought was the insight that indeed rival frameworks were competing, however traditional or Christian they might appear.

It is true then, in Maurice Cowling's sense, that Mansel represented a theological retreat, but this was not, as some claim, because he failed to unite faith and reason. He had a place for reason in theological thinking, and he belaboured this point again and again: reason is capable of describing the limits of the human mind and showing in what ways higher truths, grasped in faith, might be represented in human terms. Of course, this configuration of faith and reason did not and probably will continue to not satisfy those who criticize from the outset his commitment to scripture. Nevertheless, his retreat was not into a fideistic world devoid of any appeal to reason; much more, his retreat represented an effort to articulate a consistently scriptural worldview within emerging and vying frameworks of rationality that were, in many ways, incommensurate with the scriptural "scheme." This scheme, in Butler's sense, has a rationality of its own that may or may not cohere with rival frameworks, but on its own terms it is capable, within certain constraints, of describing the world and God's activity within it. In this regard, scripture was profoundly reasonable for Mansel, in its manner of accommodation to the character of human life in the world. This will be the subject of the fourth chapter.

Finally, it should be noted that Mansel's skepticism should not be confused with a simply pious, humble disposition or an antidogmatic attitude. He derided Tennyson's famous phrase that "honest doubt" has "more faith than half the creeds" as yet another veiling of "a spirit of rudeness and bitterness towards the clergy in general,"[102] a spirit that Mansel sensed was not only dubious of but also hostile toward traditional creedal and scriptural claims. But for Mansel, if skepticism led to humility of mind, such humility allowed the ordinary Christian to embrace in faith those aspects of revelation that, in one way or another, confounded many of the instincts of the age. In this sense, Mansel's skepticism carries a strong affinity for what Williams describes as typical of classical Anglicanism. Writers such as Hooker, Andrews, and Herbert – I would add Browne, Berkeley, and Butler – were not indifferent toward doctrine, but rather, the "great doctrinal themes are a steady backdrop, sensed and believed but not to be pulled center-stage for debate and explanation."[103] It is almost the case for Mansel that it is irreverent and in poor taste to "toss to and fro" the mysteries of God. But it was not the case for Mansel, as it was not the case for early Anglican writers, that these doctrinal themes were to be doubted; rather, they were to be wholly affirmed and passively received.

What separates Mansel's skepticism from many of the older Anglican divines such as Hooker and Andrews is that his passive reception of Christian doctrine no longer depended upon the assumption of a society ordered upon Christian principles. Instead, he grounded his skepticism in an epistemological and theological frame that took for granted the presence of competing truth claims in a pluralistic setting that have come to characterize the modern world. To this end, Mansel was a descendant of the Tractarian movement, and he represented its oppositional posture toward an increasingly secularized society. But the fact that many Tractarian figures or descendants such as Mozley and Newman were wholly able to recognize their position in Mansel's lectures would also seem to indicate that Mansel's position did not necessarily symbolize the spirit of the movement.[104] Williams notes that the Tractarian movement unwittingly contained a liberal trajectory: "Once they had claimed the right to redefine Anglican identity from within, they opened the flood gate to an attitude of mind that assumed it was acceptable to debate the nature of this identity with practically no boundaries set in advance, and to opt for a version that you found suitable."[105] While the Tractarians remained doctrinally serious, Williams suggests that this latent attitude generated a skepticism that was more akin to his first, enlightenment, variety, "a skepticism that focused on how I am liable to be deceived by history and community. This was an attitude of mind more liable to collude with a reluctance to believe anything that does not make sense in primarily individual and experiential terms."[106] In this context, Anglican moralism and ritualism developed in a "growing haziness about the integral theological vision within which the Church as a whole, never mind Anglicanism in particular, operated."[107]

It is not clear how Mansel's skepticism fits into Williams's account. Self-consciously he cast himself in the mould of classical Anglican theology represented by figures like Hooker, Copleston, and Butler. But historically he was a product of the Tractarian movement, however he might have differed from its various expressions. While Cowling views Mansel's skepticism as a precursor to the Anglican theological "anarchy" of the twentieth century – perhaps in the way that Williams traces this development through the Tractarian movement – what Mansel desired to offer was the possibility of a scriptural worldview in a society that had begun to see the world otherwise. Unlike Williams's characterization of Tractarian insularity, Mansel struggled to situate his traditional Christian convictions within the emerging philosophical context of the nineteenth century. In other words, despite retreating in a certain way, Mansel was still deeply committed to the public exchange of ideas without altering the shape of Christian orthodoxy. Mansel's skepticism was not a particular cast of mind or an attitude toward doctrinal theology but a structural attempt to make space for the scriptures, rooted in the life of the Church, to form and describe God's created world and his relationship to his people. In this sense, Mansel was very much a traditional Anglican, but what he offered was also a new possibility for understanding reality within the collapse of traditional metaphysics and the rapid rise of unbelief.

4

Mansel and the Theology of Scripture

Despite initial acclaim for the 1858 "Bampton Lectures," Mansel quickly fell into disrepute within Victorian theological publications, in large measure because of the ill association between his skepticism or agnosticism and the materialism of Herbert Spencer.[1] This is the image of Mansel's ideas that would endure well into the twentieth century and, to the degree that they are still engaged, until the present.[2] However, there is something slightly misleading about this description, and in chapter 5 I detail Mansel's surprisingly enduring but hidden influence on the British idealism that would take hold of Oxford for a generation. Despite the continual accumulation of negative reviews, Mansel's lectures seemed to exercise an influence that is not easily captured in the publications of the time.[3] There is a real sense that Mansel's early critics, like the later idealists, were inclined toward a more holistic, integrated vision of the world, and Mansel's ideas became a caricatured symbol for the "project of dividing," or marking off, human knowledge of God.[4]

Decades after the publication of the lectures, R.H. Hutton, for example, was still defending Maurice against Mansel's caricatured ambition

> to prove that God does not and cannot so unveil Himself to men as Maurice believed, but can only give us "regulative" hints, carefully adapted rules of action – working hypotheses concerning Himself – on the assumption of which He directs us for all practical purposes to proceed.[5]

Charles Meynell complained that Mansel's ideas "impugned the light of reason"[6] and commissioned the "end of philosophy" so that we may "burn our books."[7] Mansel had shrunk the world and reduced the powers of human reason, a price that was too high or not necessary to pay for the preservation of Christian orthodoxy.

Mansel's epistemological skepticism and theory of regulative truth were tools intended to protect the Christian scriptures from the pressures of "unbelief," pressures that he regarded as perennial forces that historically have always accompanied the Christian gospel.[8] But more recently, a number of works have appeared that argue that apologetic efforts of theologians to defend the scriptures have in fact contributed to the decline of a scriptural or Christian worldview. William Abraham's *Canon and Criterion in Christian Theology* is one striking example of a genealogical account of scripture's demise that, it might seem, would include Mansel as one of its suspects.[9] Abraham argues that over the scope of Church history, epistemological concerns regarding scripture gained ascension over the early Church's broader, more organic canonical criteria. He defines the contrast as follows: "An ecclesial canon is essentially a means of grace: that is, materials, persons, and practices intended to initiate one into the divine life. By contrast, an epistemic norm is essentially a criterion of rationality, justification, and knowledge."[10] Historically, this transition from ecclesial canon to epistemic norm had to do with the very pressures that concerned Mansel but predated him: concerns about the validity of Christian truth claims and the defense of these claims against rival Christian confessions or rationalist objections.[11] In short, the scriptures came to be the sole locus of canonical authority, divorced from the creedal, liturgical and traditional aspects of Church life.[12]

But the scriptures, Abraham argues, were not intended to bear this kind of epistemological load, and this shift transformed the manner in which they were traditionally used as they came "to misrepresent anew the canonical heritage of the Church by treating it as an inert datum to be captured at will rather than as a subtle gift of the Holy Spirit which should be appropriated with skill, humility, and divine guidance."[13] The troubling consequences of these epistemological developments is that they

> helped precipitate a massive epistemological crisis for Christian intellectuals, which naturally led into Enlightenment theories of knowledge and justification. Equally important, this quest has led to a series of dead ends in modern Christianity, leaving large tracts of it intellectually exhausted and spiritually suffocated.[14]

The loss represented here by Abraham's thesis is the fullness and comprehensiveness of Christian experience, more fully captured in his canonical understanding.

Abraham's thesis turns on different themes than Mansel's contemporary critics, but a common feature is the ensuing spiritual impoverishment that can accompany epistemological accounts of scripture and Christian knowledge. This chapter assesses Mansel's theological views – primarily his anthropology, Christology, and account of revelation – in the context of the criticisms previously described, in an effort to show that Mansel's theology is not necessarily bound to the spiritual "suffocation" that Abraham and others have suggested is characteristic of his approach. While Mansel's ideas have survived predominantly as a link in the genealogy of Western unbelief, I argue that his theory of regulative truth provided him with a method to describe God's providential presence as an all-embracing reality, detailed in the scriptures. It is true that Mansel stands in intellectual proximity to figures like Spencer and Huxley, but his concern to place human history within a scriptural frame challenges our theological narration of ideas to consider the providential context in which they are framed.

The sermons and other works by Mansel referred to in this chapter were all written in the period following the lectures, in which he was forced to clarify the features of his theological thinking.[15] These works, read in conjunction with his better known philosophical writings, I argue, do not describe a world where God is isolated within the nonrealist language of revelation; rather, they confirm the notion that Mansel's theory of regulative truth sought to place the world within the scriptural account of God's personal and providential engagement with creation.

GENEALOGIES OF UNBELIEF

Mansel, like many current writers, had his own genealogical account of the history of unbelief in England and Christian Europe. In his essay on freethinking he documents the passage of Locke's ideas into the hands of eighteenth-century deists, who in turn exercised a profound influence on continental philosophy, especially in Germany.[16] Perhaps mindful of his own fate, Mansel was concerned to commend "the personal piety and sincere Christian belief of Locke."[17] Locke's ideas were vulnerable to distortion, but Mansel argues that the deist's extension of Locke required a certain "hostility" of spirit.[18] In light of this, Mansel's views on the escalating popularity of German philosophy in England were unambiguous: "a good deal of what is paraded as a demonstration of modern German erudition is in substance a *rechauffe* of the forgotten criticisms of one of our old English deists."[19] As in the eighteenth century, Mansel worried that the Church was once again in a position of temptation:

> To such a state we may expect to see the Church of England again reduced, if she consent to listen again to the voice of the charmer, to be allured again by the promise of peace and unity, and to abandon the reaction, which the present century has happily witnessed, towards the Catholic teaching of her earlier and better days.[20]

In this respect Mansel reflected the views of many high churchmen in England – Tractarian or otherwise – who looked to the seventeenth century as the golden age of English theology.[21]

"The voice of the charmer" indicates the theological component of Mansel's understanding of unbelief. While "unbelieving" philosophy has a distinct theoretical or philosophical lineage, Mansel thought that unbelief had a permanent and recurring character:

> When we look at the words of the Apostle himself, so framed as to indicate, not the transient form, but the permanent spirit, of the error against which he is contending, we can hardly avoid the conviction that in this, as in so many other of the prophetic passages of Scripture, the witness of the Holy Spirit is designedly extended far beyond the circumstances immediately present to the human vision of the writer, and conveys its direct lesson and warning to all ages of the Church that were yet to come.[22]

In a sermon on the Church, Mansel writes that, "we are unable to tolerate the thought of a supernatural presence of God in the world, manifesting itself at times in glimpses and partial aspects of a purpose beyond or above that which is carried on by the ordinary manifestations of His natural presence."[23] The history of unbelief has oscillated between materialist philosophies, the "eternal separation" between God and his creation, and the opposite tendency to elevate the created world to the status of divinity.[24]

In this case the "permanent spirit" of error is the enduring desire of human beings to free themselves of their humanity and transcend the humanly accommodated character of revelation. A dissatisfaction with the character of revelation has led to human attempts to build more completed and coherent accounts of reality. In his lectures on the Gnostic heresies, Mansel writes,

> The knowledge professed by the Gnostic teachers, on the other hand, was a knowledge designed to subordinate the revelation of Christ to the speculations of human philosophy, a curious inquiry, searching after an apprehension of God, not in what He has revealed of Himself, but in that which He has not revealed; an inquiry which, under the pretence of giving a deeper and more spiritual meaning to the Christian revelation, in fact uprooted its very foundations by making it subservient to theories incompatible with its first principles, theories of human invention, originating in heathen philosophies, and making those philosophies the criterion and end of revelation, instead of regarding revelation as the discovery by God of those truths which human wisdom had desired to see and had not seen.[25]

This desire to surpass human limits has a moral character for Mansel that is rooted in humanity's fall, which represents the drive to overcome our humanity altogether. The perennial nature of this temptation led Mansel to believe that the current crisis of unbelief in his own time would pass, as it always had, more or less, before. Speaking about the "great anti-Christian movements, the deism of England, the infidelity of France, the rationalism of Germany," Mansel argues that,

> when each of these in its turn had played its little part on the stage of history, giving itself out as some great one, the nation whom it bewitched for a while has turned in very weariness and disgust from its empty boasting and unfulfilled promises, and come back with its baffled hopes and unsatisfied longings to the feet of its forsaken master, taught by its own bitter experience to repeat again and again the words of the Apostle, "Lord to whom shall we go?"[26]

In this case, Mansel's understanding of the theological and historical character of unbelief is not unlike Barth's criticism and understanding of religion. Barth, in his writing on religion, frames atheism or unbelief within the "magic circle of religion,"[27] the constantly fluctuating but ultimately stable forms of "belief in man"[28] that characterize humanity's resistance to God.

Mansel had at least a dim notion and an increasing unease that the unbelief of his own era was unprecedented in its scope. In a sermon on Revelation, he describes the Victorian Church within the figure of the Philadelphian church in chapter 3:

> No one can look at the events passing around us, without being aware that there is fermenting, at the base of society, a leaven of lawlessness, a spirit of violence and intimidation, a spirit so far directly anti-Christian that it acts in open defiance of the Apostolic precept of subjection to the higher powers.[29]

The prospect of such lawlessness, Mansel writes, should act as a warning to his own age, and to those who are "tempted to seek the 'open door' of Christian fellowship elsewhere than in dutiful submission to the revealed word, and full acknowledgment of all that belongs to Christ's name."[30] His belief in the endurance of the Church seemed to remain strong, but like many people today, he began to look abroad for signs of hope:

> It is in this season of trouble and doubt at home, that she is encouraged to lengthen her cords and strengthen her stakes, to consecrate to her service the firstfruits of another race ... knowing that the intervening ages are the time allotted to her to do her Master's work upon earth.[31]

To account for such a development Mansel placed his own generation within the parable of the Labourers:

> To the five classes of labourers mentioned in the parable there might have been added a sixth – those who were offered employment and refused it, and such are all they who, born in a Christian land, living in the midst of Christian institutions, within sight of Christian places of worship, within hearing of Christian preachers, within reach of the prayers and the sacraments of a Christian Church, yet live as men who care for none of these things. In all these things, Christ who hath hired you,

nay, who hath bought you with a price, even the price of His own precious blood, is calling you daily and hourly to fulfil that service which is due to him.[32]

Clearly, Mansel's understanding of unbelief has an intensely scriptural aspect, both in its characterization of unbelief – the various attempts to surpass or deepen the scriptural account – and in the manner in which he located the unbelief of his era within the scriptural narrative.

Mansel's particular theological view of unbelief may not appear strikingly creative or even interesting. It has much in common with that of Barth and countless other preachers and theologians over the centuries who adhere, more or less, to an Augustinian notion of original sin and human pride. But it is important to notice here that Mansel was searching for a way to locate history, and his own moment in time, within the narrative of scripture and God's providential presence in the world. This, I argue in the following pages, is really the heart of Mansel's theology and theory of regulative truth. However, it is important to note that such an attempt to describe modern unbelief within an approximate scriptural frame is not an abundantly obvious move to make. It is, of course, ironic that Mansel's attempt to do this very thing has formed the grounds upon which he has been repeatedly dismissed by subsequent writers admittedly trying to establish a similar vision.

In this way Abraham's argument is typical of numerous recent efforts to locate the loss of a Christian or scriptural worldview – unbelief, in Mansel's terms – within emerging attitudes toward the scriptures themselves. Abraham's point is that a broad-based canonical view of Christianity was streamlined into a strictly epistemological view of the Bible, and in the process Christian understanding of the world became more narrow and impoverished. Peter Harrison's book *The Bible, Protestantism, and the Rise of Natural Science* is another example of a genealogical account of unbelief or secularism, as it were, that is related directly to scriptural interpretation. Harrison argues that the Protestant reformers' attempt to ground religious authority in the Bible forced them to embrace a literalist interpretation of the Bible:

The demise of allegory, in turn, was due largely to the efforts of Protestant reformers, who in their search for an unambiguous

religious authority, insisted that the book of scripture be interpreted only in its literal, historical sense. This insistence on the
primacy of the literal sense had the unforeseen consequence of
cutting short a potentially endless chain of reference, in which
word refers to object, and object refers to other objects.[33]

Allegory, for Harrison, was the device that held the scriptures open
to the world or allowed the scriptures to refer to creation in a broad
and spiritual manner. The loss of allegory, in short, evacuated "nature
of its symbolic significance" and opened the door to naturalistic scientific and philosophical accounts of the world.[34]

In one way, Abraham and Harrison argue persuasively for the
gradual impoverishment of scriptural interpretation and degenerative
effects of these interpretive schemes on Christian belief. But the question that lurks behind accounts like these relates precisely to the goals
that they are both respectively pursuing: namely, in a world that is
created and animated by God's presence – a world both authors seem
to want – what exactly drives the descent toward such a narrowing
of theological vision? Harrison's explanation is straightforward:

> While the Protestants' insistence that passages of scripture be
> given a determinate meaning proceeded from the purest of reli-
> gious motives, they were inadvertently setting in train a process
> which would ultimately result in the undermining of that biblical
> authority which they so adamantly promoted.[35]

On one hand, this might be plausible, at least as an account of what
drove the interpretations of Reformation theologians and the methods
that they actually pursued, though it is not clear that Protestant theologians entirely abandoned allegorical or typological interpretations.
On the other hand, the providential implications are almost stunning:
from the "purest of religious motives," Christian Europe was set adrift
into naturalistic and secular renderings of the world.

Such arguments seem to imply an overwhelming yet unnamed tragic
context that repeatedly turns the efforts of Christian writers and
apologists against their own intentions.[36] One thinks of Reventlow's
conclusion that in Butler's *Analogy* "the Christian substance has
already been largely evacuated so as to become a general worldview"
in which faith becomes an "exclusively intellectual process, based on
the evaluation of grounds for and against the reliability of external

witnesses to facts."[37] This, despite Butler's insistence that Christianity is essentially practical or "existential" in Reventlow's terms.[38] Whether the engine is modernity, secularism, the rise of science, or something altogether unacknowledged, the impression left by these authors is that either Christian writers were helpless to resist the course of history or their resistance contributed to the inevitable change, whether that change is regarded as gain or dissolution.[39]

Yet there is a way in which these accounts are theologically unsatisfying in their inability to relate historical developments to the scriptures and the God of the Bible or to view these developments within a narrative scriptural lens. In the case of Abraham, he reaches for a more comprehensive theological vision with his appeal to the broad canonical context and the Church's life, yet to some degree his own accounting of Christian history relays the same narrow impoverishment that he has set out to expand and enliven.

Of course, commentators on Mansel have not grown weary in highlighting the irony of his orthodoxy and the heritage of his ideas, most notably extended by Herbert Spencer and the Victorian agnostics. Lightman has made this argument most recently, but he, at least, expressed some reserve about the inevitability of this trajectory for Mansel's thought: Spencer, he suggests, had his own reasons of "convenience" for using an orthodox writer to advance his unorthodox ideas.[40] Other writers, as already noted, have not been so cautious. In some sense I wish to reverse this irony by suggesting that Mansel's own theological vision provides a framework for understanding God's presence and activity in the world that cannot permit historical accounts of the Church to be entirely reduced to the succession of ideas, the repetition of epistemological or philosophical crises inclined toward an already known end. In other words, his own theology has the capacity to ease or upend the negative verdict that has clung to his reputation since the controversy that surrounded his lectures. I show how this might be so in the following pages.[41]

THE HUMANITY OF REASON

Mansel's theological and philosophical ideas were intricately bound up with his desire to preserve what he considered to be the basic aspects of the Christian life: prayer, worship, and a personal and corporate relationship with Jesus Christ. In this respect, the entire mode of his thought is determinedly personal, and he viewed everything through this lens, whether philosophy, theology, or science. In a letter written to Pusey he argues against the deterministic conclusions of scientific study and concludes that such engagement need not exclude personal agency, whether human or divine: "If not, may science continue indefinitely without in any way interfering with the duty of prayer? And has not the progress of the majority of science been of this kind?"[42] Whether convincing or not, he regarded prayer as an activity entirely in accordance with human nature and, in fact, what humans were created for. This is what led him into his studies of what was then called "psychology," the study of human nature.[43] If unbelief was a transcending of human limitations, then the Christian faith was the confirmation and fulfilment of what it meant to be human.

To this end, Mansel actually believed that his account of consciousness was an account of what people are really like, not how they ought to be. This attention to particularities and facts was essential for any description of humanity and the world:

> Every existence which we can perceive is definite and particular, limited and related; and every existence of which we can think is definite and particular, limited and related likewise. It must therefore needs be that a science which starts from the assumption of Being in the abstract (which is not a conception, but an equivocal term, capable of relation to many distinct conceptions), and attempts, by pure deduction and division, to reason down to the concrete existences which alone are objects of positive thought, must end by delivering, not differences of things, but distinctions of words.[44]

The notion of an "abstract self" or "abstract world" carried a whole host of dangers that constantly threatened the particular character of created life and, as a result, threatened the very character of God.[45] But unlike Butler in this case, Mansel's conception of the world and God was radically self-referential. So while he was critical of cosmological ontologies, he stated that, "The consciousness of Personality is thus an Ontology in the highest sense of the term, and cannot be regarded as the representation of any ulterior reality."[46] For example, people are only aware of causality in the world so far as they are conscious of their own freedom to act and exert influence; likewise, they are conscious of substance in their own resistance to force:

"Resistance to the locomotive energy is the only mode of consciousness which directly tells us of the existence of an external world."[47]

John Milbank has criticized both Butler and Mansel as extending
Kant's ban on ontology and exhausting the "supposed 'bounds' of
our finitude" that constrain God's activity in the world to these overly
defined finite categories.[48] To some degree Milbank is right, at least
concerning Mansel. While Mansel claims that he is simply defining
humanity by the facts and not abstractions, it could easily be pointed
out that even these facts can become abstractions that place constraints
on experience and, for that matter, God. Yet curiously his understanding of God's activity in the world is not quite what Milbank fears. In
part this is because Mansel's account of the human person, despite
the risk of over-definition and even arbitrariness, is still largely a negative account that holds the individual open to a wide range of theological and experiential possibilities. This is in essence the purpose of
Mansel's psychology.

Mansel's ontological understanding of personality is exhaustive in
the sense that Milbank implies because it reaches into the realms of
human thought, morality, and religion, but there is a sense in which
this is misleading. As an ontological account, Mansel's point is that
personality and relation are the inescapable foundations of human life;
he pushes this as far as to say that an individual's occupation of space,
the resistance to force, observed in consciousness is a basic presentation that cannot be analyzed further.[49] In this regard Mansel is almost
Cartesian.[50] The self is a presented fact, but as a fact it is in no way fully
understood. By virtue of its self-presentation it is a mystery of creation
that cannot be completely grasped. And far from building upon this
foundation a certain mode of reasoning, Mansel places human reasoning within the wide-ranging context within which a person lives in the
world and encounters others. Reasoning, then, is not purely a function
of thought but includes the influence of the affections, the will and the
instinctive needs and desires of individual people.[51]

Philosophies or theologies that reach for a "higher" view of God, not
encumbered by notions of personality, Mansel argues, actually destroy
these aspects of humanity that Mansel desired to retain as central:

Fools, to dream that man can escape from himself, that human
reason can draw aught but a human portrait of God! They do
but substitute a marred and mutilated humanity for one exalted
and entire: they add nothing to their conception of God as He is,

but only take away a part of their conception of man. Sympathy, and love, and fatherly kindness, and forgiving mercy, have evaporated in the crucible of their philosophy; and what is the *caput mortuum* that remains, but only the sterner features of humanity exhibited in repulsive nakedness? The God who listens to prayer, we are told, appears in the likeness of human mutability. Be it so. What is the God who does not listen, but the likeness of human obstinacy? ... Man is still the residue that is left; deprived indeed of all that is amiable in humanity, but, in the darker features which remain, but still man. Man in his purposes; man in his inflexibility.[52]

Mansel's point is that human conceptions of God are bound to anthropomorphism of some kind, but descriptions that seek to rise above this inevitably leave out those aspects of human life that are essential to his whole portrait of humanity.

For this reason it is puzzling how some critics have read Mansel as a conservative who was predictably and uncreatively bent on proving the existence of God. R.V. Sampson's comments in this manner:

[Mansel] is content to list baldly and without argument some fifteen reasons why the claims to authenticity of the Christian revelation are utterly convincing and to conclude that the entire content of Revelation, whatever the intellectual difficulties attaching to any particular element thereof, must be accepted uncritically as the Word.[53]

Gordon Lewis Phillips has argued that Mansel's initial popularity was probably due to the fact that he was read in just this way.[54] But a theory that was "utterly convincing" was not at all what Mansel had in mind; rather, he very much followed Butler by exploring the probabilities of faith within a complex and largely unknown world.

Belief, for Mansel, cannot be based solely upon thought and comprehension:

Belief in a God, once given, becomes the nucleus round which subsequent experiences cluster and accumulate; and evidences which would be obscure or ambiguous, if addressed to the reason only, become clear and convincing, when interpreted by the light of the religious consciousness.[55]

In some sense, by "religious consciousness" Mansel is referring to the whole human person: "If man is not a creature composed solely of intellect, or solely of feeling, or solely of will, why should any one element of his nature be excluded from participating in the pervading consciousness of Him in whom we live, and move, and have our being?"[56] So Mansel argues that religious reflection, or, simply speaking, theology, is not the primary manner in which we encounter God. Rather, such reflection requires experience. Speaking somewhat abstractly, he suggests that an innate sense of dependence and moral obligation are the basic elements of religious experience, which receive their particular character in Christianity.[57] But on their own, divorced from any context, Mansel suggests, these two aspects of religious consciousness are prior to thought, and yet like all natural theology, they are essentially negative in their rendering; that is, these basic desires might resolve themselves into any system of religion that seeks to meet these needs. A sense of dependence, he argues in an adjustment of Schleiermacher,[58] tells us little about God, but it does create an opening that will be filled, in one manner or another.[59]

Granted, it is hard to follow Mansel here unless one thinks of a person in one context or another; given Mansel's commitment to particularity and phenomenal accounts of knowledge, at times he speaks with little sense of context or concrete reality. What person exactly has this consciousness? Might it be different according the traditions in which someone is raised? Notwithstanding this tendency, Mansel's overall point is still reaching for a broader account of religious knowledge that incorporates a wider scope of human experience within a personalist ontology.

It is true that Mansel leaves the question about appearance and reality relatively open. He basically asserts that consciousness of ourselves is that only assurance of reality, the only real thing that is verifiable. Yet consciousness implies an infinite set of relations between things and persons in the world. On one hand, Mansel is uncomfortable with Kant's *Ding an sich* because it implies an invitation to press beyond what is seen. On the other hand, Mansel affirms the notion that appearances do not show forth reality in any kind of conclusive or exhaustive manner. To this extent he is content to live in the world as it seems, and he quotes Butler's comments on freedom and necessity as a way of affirming Butler's more basic commitment: "In religion, in morals, in our daily business, in the care of our lives, in the exercise of our senses, the rules which guide our practice cannot be reduced to principles which satisfy our reason."[60] It is the whole conscious person who must be satisfied with the reasons for belief, because it is with God – "in whom we live and move and have our being" – that Christian belief is concerned. Again, it is much in the spirit of Butler that Mansel makes his appeal to the evidences of religion:

> That if no one faculty of the human mind is competent to convey a direct knowledge of the Absolute and the Infinite, no one faculty is entitled to claim pre-eminence over the rest, as furnishing especially the criterion of the truth or falsehood of a supposed Revelation. There are presumptions to be drawn from the internal character of the doctrines which the revelation contains: there are presumptions to be drawn from the facts connected with its first promulgation: there are presumptions to be drawn from its subsequent history and the effects which it has produced among mankind. But the true evidence for or against the religion, is not to be found in any one of these taken singly and exclusively; but in the resultant of all, fairly examined and compared together; the apparently conflicting evidences being balanced against each other, and the apparently concurring evidences estimated by their united efficacy.[61]

Maybe in the end Mansel is quite close to Abraham's canonical criteria, if it can be granted that an epistemic norm need not be as narrowly conceived as Abraham indicates. In any case, Mansel's argument, which has been overlooked by so many critics, is that Christianity appeals to the whole person, and human reason must in some sense account for this. In contrast to the notion that Mansel "enfeebles" reason, it could easily be argued that he rounds it out or extends it beyond the confines of pure argument and demonstration, which is not to say that he was irrational but that rationality must take account of these considerations. Mansel writes, "It is to the whole man that Christianity appeals: it is as a whole and in relation to the whole man that it must be judged."[62]

Mansel's view is not unlike Michael Polyani's notion of a tacit cognition that forms and drives our explicit knowledge, which underlines the "unavoidable act of personal participation in our explicit knowledge of things: an act of which we can be aware merely in an unreflecting manner."[63] Mansel is operating with different terms, but at least in this case, the personal character of knowledge for both figures is inevitable, though not necessarily restrictive. For Polyani the circularity of personal knowledge is held open if "pursued with unwavering universal intent."[64] Mansel is less concerned on this score, though the theological or created status of personality contains the promise that the human being is fitted for life in the world and relationship with God.

The personal aspect of knowledge for Mansel, and perhaps for Polyani, implies a degree of skepticism or at least a limitation of human knowing. The limited scope of one point of view, the uncertainties of relationships with other free, personal beings and ultimately with God, the creator of that personality, implies that human ignorance is unavoidable. In this respect, Mansel followed Butler to the letter:

> It is reasonable to believe that, in matters of belief as well as of practice, God has not thought fit to annihilate the will of man; but has permitted speculative difficulties to exist as the trial and the discipline of sharp and subtle intellects, as He has permitted moral temptations to form the trial and the discipline of strong and eager passions. Our passions are not annihilated when we resist the temptation to sin: why should we expect that our doubts must be annihilated if we are to resist the temptation to unbelief?[65]

I have argued that Mansel's understanding of human reason and unbelief were connected, and despite claims otherwise, Mansel believed that the speculative and humanistic philosophies of his day were ultimately destructive of human personality. It is worth noting that roughly a century later, Henri De Lubac would say almost exactly the same thing, albeit from a different philosophical perspective:

> What has actually become of the lofty ambitions of this humanism, not only in fact that in the very way of thought of its initiates? What has become of man as conceived by this atheist humanism? A being that can still hardly be called a being – a thing which has no content, a cell completely merged in a mass which is in process of becoming: social and historical man of whom all that remains is pure abstraction, apart from the social relations and the position in time by which he is defined ...

in reality there is no longer any man because there is no longer anything greater than man.[66]

Whether or not this remains the destiny of humanism in our society is debatable, but De Lubac and Mansel are in strong agreement. It is true that the "human" and perhaps "spiritual" aspect of Mansel's thought remains hidden beneath the surface. In part this is because he spent his energy elaborating the context in which Christian knowledge and experience takes place without in fact detailing exactly how this must look. As a result, his view of reasoning in theology calls to mind the observation of Stephen Sykes in the *Identity of Christianity* that theologians in the West have been led "into an uncritical adoption of the role of vanguard in the Christian Community. This self-portrayal implies that it is the intellectual realm which leads the way; the bias of the image is inherently towards discovery and novelty."[67] Sykes argues that the "Christian community at worship" is such a place where the theologian is not the sole bearer of theological truth but one voice among the worshipping community.[68]

In certain respects Sykes's image is an appropriate representation of Mansel's theology. By eschewing progress in theology – "The lapse of time, as all history bears witness, is at least as fruitful in corruption as in enlightenment"[69] – Mansel was not denigrating reason or even progress in knowledge as such.[70] Growth or development in theology relates to our practical duties and the application and interpretation of scripture in this respect. The task of theology then is to describe the context in which this can take place and, of course, to defend this context against threatening alterations. Words like "practical" and "regulative" can easily be misunderstood, as if theology is constrained in Mansel's terms to a strictly pedestrian field. This is how Mansel was read by figures like Maurice and Mozley: Speculative knowledge is spiritual or higher knowledge, while practical knowledge relates merely to duties and actions. In strictly epistemological terms this is true, at least in the manner by which Mansel sets up the dichotomy; even the Incarnation does not overcome the distinction between practical or regulative and speculative knowledge. But in no way is the regulative sphere empty of God's presence or the presence of the Spirit; the regulative function of scripture is not once removed from the spiritual reality of God, but instead it is inhabited with God's presence. So both practical and regulative, as I argue concerning Mansel's understanding of reason, refer to the whole scope of human life, action, and experience; more particularly they refer to the range of Christian experience expressed through prayer, worship, and mission or the life of the Church in the Spirit. All of this is apparent in Mansel's writings, even though his emphasis on the authority of scripture has been taken as arbitrary and severe, imposed on an "enfeebled" human reason, now buckled at the knees. Scripture was authoritative for Mansel in a way that was uncompromising, but it functioned for him as a map of the full range of human experience. In Mansel's eyes, the scriptures exhibited a far broader and more human context to live within in their entire witness to God's presence in creation, that is, broader in relation to the philosophies and theologies of "unbelief" that sought to pry Christian orthodoxy apart in order to encompass a changing world.

THE INCARNATION AND THE PRESENCE OF GOD

Mansel's accounts of human reason, the scriptures and knowledge of God all implicitly refer to the Incarnation, even though the term itself appears in his writings infrequently. W.R. Matthews raises this absence and notes that, "in accordance with his own principles, the doctrine of the Incarnation must be a regulative idea and not the absolute truth ... The fact and the Person of Christ cannot, one would suppose, be regulative ideas."[71] Matthews's point is well taken: there is something slightly awkward if not misleading about describing the revelation of Christ as regulatively true. As to the theological bearings of the regulative truth, F.W. Dockrill makes a similar critique:

> Scripture certainly contains passages which say that our knowledge of God is imperfect and, perhaps, symbolic, but unlike Mansel's theory of regulative truth it does not provide information about the nature of this imperfection nor explain how we should understand the adequacy of religious symbols which conceivably might be true only for man.[72]

Mansel was well aware that his lengthy appeals to scripture and the Fathers were based upon a kinship in spirit, as it were, not in technical detail. Nevertheless, he saw in his theory of regulative truth not a new discovery but a modern and revised method for retaining a traditional orthodoxy. Still, if Mansel is going to be defended in light of this theory, it has to be shown that his ideas can be coherently integrated on the very point that Matthews raises: the Incarnation of Christ.

In one sense, the distinction between speculative and regulative truth is misleading. For Mansel, all knowledge is regulated by the individual consciousness, so in effect the highest knowledge attainable in any sphere is regulative. Even basic observations concerning causality stem from the internal consciousness of freedom and action. All observable facts – the facts of revelation as well – are governed by these laws:

> As mere facts, they are so far from being inconceivable, that they embody the very laws of conception itself, and are experienced as true: but though we are able, nay, compelled, to conceive them as *facts*, we find it impossible to conceive them as *ultimate facts*. They are made known to us as *relations* ... The conception of any such relation as a fact thus involves a further inquiry concerning its existence as a consequence; and to this inquiry no satisfactory answer can be given.[73]

Facts cannot be isolated and explained exhaustively, but they exist in a seemingly endless set of relations that help to define and individuate particular facts without revealing their essence.

Mansel's central point then is quite simple: The Son of God came into the world – a world created through him – and took on the form and limitations of a human being, a form that indicated his divine nature but did not disclose it to human eyes. Like all facts, Jesus was observed in a particular context of relations, but as a "revelational fact," to use Matthews's term, the reference of Jesus's factual life, his divinity, was disclosed in human or finite terms, though grasped, humanly, by faith and not sight. What one sees in Jesus, to use Mansel's terms, is not necessarily a radical disjunction within the order of reality or an opening toward a new manner of spiritual knowledge but instead the fulfillment and summation of God's dealings with his people, the fullest statement of God's presence, disposition and desire for his creatures. The primitive conception of God as a person is fulfilled, gradually in the history of scripture, in the person of Christ.

It is possible that Mansel could give a coherent reply to Matthews's insightful question about the place of the Incarnation in his theology, though it is not clear that this reply is satisfactory to some. Again

Milbank criticizes Mansel, along with Butler, with regard to the actual content of revelation in Christ:

> Given the positivity, and at the same time the derivational vagueness, of the principles of natural law in this tradition, it becomes easy to understand revelation as a supplementary legal system of essential practical injunctions regarding both morality and worship ... The new facts and ordinances belonging to revelation give us no more knowledge than does natural law about the content of the infinite. Mansel was consequently anti-mystical and clearly stressed that the positive critical determination of the "limits of religion" and positive finite knowledge of revelation was opposed to any *via negativa*.[74]

In a certain sense Milbank's comment is accurate, though a phrase like the "content of the Infinite" obscures the matter somewhat. For example, when Mansel uses terms like "accommodation" or "condescension," he could just as easily be speaking of grace or divine action; the "content of the Infinite" could be taken to be God's will or disposition, in which case Milbank's criticism misses the mark. Though it could also mean something more, God's very being, for instance, or God's self-knowledge, this is something Mansel would clearly have opposed. He would have opposed this as an augmentation of the limits of human thought but not as the gift of salvation: the gift of God's own being to humanity belonged to the practical sphere, the whole of human life – forgiveness, redemption and salvation. Once more this distinction is easily lost if "practical" is taken to simply imply a dry, barren, statutory observance of a moral code. Much more, "practical" refers to the field of created existence that God enters, inhabits, and works within; it in no way excludes the spiritual activity of God, but it assumes it.

To make this point more fully, it is helpful to look at Mansel's understanding of scriptural history. In his "Essay on Miracles" Mansel accounts for God's activity in the world in a manner that is analogous to human action. The world was created to be receptive to the actions of free and personal agents:

> We have evidence, also, of an *elasticity*, so to speak, in the constitution of nature, which permits the influence of human power on

the phenomena of the world to be exercised or suspended at will without effecting the stability of the whole. We have thus a precedent of a higher will on a grander scale, provided for by a similar elasticity of the matter subject to its influence.[75]

God's activity in the world does not contradict or interrupt his creation, but rather, the created world was made with this form of agency in mind. God's action as a personal agent is regulatively true – it is not clear, after all, how God's infinite and absolute nature can be reconciled with his activity as a person, but his activity is not the less truthful because of this difficulty.[76]

So for Mansel, the Incarnation – the life and work of Jesus – was the fullest statement of God's relationship to his people and, at the same time, the greatest obstacle for belief:

> The doctrine of a personal Christ, very God and very man, has indeed been the great stumbling block in the way of those so called philosophical theologians who, in their contempt for the historical and temporal, would throw aside the vivid revelation of a living and acting God, to take refuge in the empty abstraction of an impersonal idea.[77]

The assumption of flesh, the living of a human life, was the goal of God's providential presence in the world from the beginning, a God who constantly accommodates and adjusts himself to the human situation to carry out his purposes. The coming of Christ was the goal of all human history embodied in the scriptural account:

> The purpose of God, pre-ordained before the foundation of the world, foretold with the earliest entrance of sin and shame in the announcement of the promised seed, taken up from time to time during four thousand years by a long succession of prophets announcing him that should come, that great central theme of the world's history to which all past generations had looked forward, to which the coming generations should look back, was now completed. The Scriptures were fulfilled that thus it must be.[78]

The entire account of scripture leading up to Christ bears witness to this accommodating, gracious character of Christ's incarnate life because of God's providential plan and because it is consistent with God's character, his desire to reach out and engage his people. It is the character of God's revealing, Mansel writes, to reveal in terms that are close and comprehensible to human beings in any place and any age:

> We behold, as it were, the successive kindling of light after light as the beacon fires speed on their message of good tidings along the generations of mankind from the first to the second Adam, we behold their rays flashing out in various forms, with various degrees of brightness and frequency, changing with the changing features of the regions Which they traverse. At one time, we mark the light glowing as it were in a faint but prolonged line, as it passes over the wide extent of some barren and level plain; at another we see it flashing quickly and frequently from peak to peak of a mountain range; at another it is glancing over the surface of the sea, reflected back in broken and fitful gleams from the shifting waters; and again it is hurrying over some thickly peopled district, taking form after form as it transmits its message horn one spot to another among the habitations of men. That one prediction of the promised seed which should bruise the head of the serpent, gleams faintly as the sole ray of promise over two thousand barren years of early history. Then follow in quick succession the blessings announced and renewed.[79]

Mansel loved this image of revelation as a light that shines over diverse and varied surfaces, and it is an image that Butler employed in his defence against deist objections to the universality of Christian revelation.[80] In this same sermon, Mansel traces the passage of this light through the Old Testament: "the canon of Old Testament scripture closes with a series of inspired announcements of the future deliverer, varying in shape, in clearness, in colour, and feeling, but adding one to another in accumulating light as the day of redemption draweth nigh."[81] These "accumulating" images build a picture of Christ, not just as a means of prediction but as a shaping or forming of Christ's activity in the world. The coming of Christ is a new thing, but it is also the revelation of what has always been true of God's character as it is revealed in Israel's history.

For this reason Mansel is able to say,

In reading the history of the Lord's sufferings and death, we read the history not of one person only but of the whole human race whom He represents, whose nature, whose penalty He took upon himself, and suffered once for all, "the just for the unjust," – we read the history of man's death to sin, of his redemption to righteousness and God's favour, and it is up to that momentous turning point in man's history that the whole series of the earlier scriptures is designed to lead us by the hand. The promise of man's redemption was coeval with his fall, and the whole intervening history as it is told in Scripture is a narrative of the steps by which the world was prepared for the fulfillment of that promise.[82]

It is not clear how all of human history could be represented in one person, at least metaphysically speaking; Mansel offers no account here of a spiritual or imperceptible union between Christ and the Church. What is represented in Christ is the accumulation of historic moments in which God has acted, moved and worked in the world, a vast and endless array of experiences that are ordered and symbolized in the scriptures. Mansel says exactly what Milbank suggests he does:

It [the gospel] not only publishes with authority the duties of natural religion, but it republishes them with moral sanctions and motives of a new kind. It not only enjoins distinct precepts in the consequence of the truth which it makes known to us, but it places the old precepts, which natural reason has dictated to mankind, in a direct relation to those newly revealed truths, which are grafted into them, and which derive fresh life and force from them.[83]

In this case natural religion, along with, though distinct from, the history of Israel, is fulfilled in Christ; in Christ, the continuity of God's providential ordering of the world is most fully visible, and this providential history or precedent is deepened, expanded and set within a new set of relations, to use Butler's phrase.

Mansel insisted that the history of redemption in scripture was a series of facts that culminated in the fact of Christ's life; however, as facts these were still open to strictly naturalistic interpretations:

Whether it was by natural or by supernatural means, it cannot
be denied that he to whom the natural and supernatural are alike
subject has permitted the course of events in the world to bear
a witness to Christ, such as have never been borne to any other
person who has appeared upon earth in the likeness of man. It
cannot be denied that the prophetic writings contain descriptions
which, account for the correspondence as we may, do, as a fact,
agree with the person and history of Jesus of Nazareth, as they
agree with no other man, or body of men; that the rites and ceremonies of the Jewish religion have a meaning as typical of Him,
which no other interpretation can give to them; that the temple
and its services were brought to an end after His appearance on
earth, as if expressly to exclude the claims of any future messiah;
that his dominion has been spread over the civilized world to
such an extent, that by such means, as no other ruler, temporal
or spiritual, can claim; that superstitions have given way before
his name which no other adversary had been able to shake; that
doctrines have been established by his teaching which in the
hands of other teachers were but plausible and transitory conjec-
tures. However, these things may be accounted for, they are sufficient at least to mark him as the central figure of the world's
history, looked forward to by all preceding generations, looked
backward to by all following.[84]

Of course, such facts could and have been debated or denied, but the
point Mansel wishes to make is that the world is arranged and ordered
providentially in a manner that witnesses to the life of Jesus and refers
to him in some ultimate manner. Even when Christ is resisted, he is
historically indicated by the "unwilling testimony of those who have
striven against him."[85]

Historically speaking, "God has so ordered the course of the world's
history, that it bears a witness to Jesus Christ such as it bears to no
other person who has ever appeared on earth,"[86] and yet it is only
through faith that this ordering can be understood as God's; that is,
the ordered history of the world and the testimony about this ordering
are visible indicators that exist within the regulative sphere of knowledge. The Spirit of God is hidden within visible realities, within the
actions of people and events, and most powerfully in Jesus. But such
hiddenness does not imply a barrier, as some have understood the

speculative and regulative distinction – most notably Maurice; regulative truth belongs primarily to the realm of perception. Mansel never suggested otherwise and on the contrary held a vision of the world that was animated and suffused with the spiritual presence of God

> wherein God Himself doth immediately and directly, though invisibly, act upon His creatures; a kingdom through which, so long as the world lasts, the unseen influence of God the Holy Spirit dwells in and interpenetrates the visible world, moulding and leavening it for the second coming of the Lord of Heaven.[87]

The history of the world has been shaped to witness to Christ; even in the midst of unbelief or loss of faith, the visible world is being moulded for the coming of Christ. This aspect of the Incarnation Mansel referred to as a "deep mystery ... when Almighty power condescends to cooperate with the free will of Man" because God's purposes become "liable to be hindered and thwarted by the unworthiness of the human instruments."[88] The deliberations of theologians, the "succession of ideas," are aspects of the Spirit's providential ordering of the world that both frustrate and further God's purposes. The condescension of Christ to humanity, for Mansel, requires this form of contingency that exhibits the frailty of human nature. But it is precisely within the full scope of created life that the world is being moulded to witness to Christ, that is, within the range of humanity's resistance, incapacity and yet enduring desire to perceive God in the world.

MANSEL'S THEOLOGY OF SCRIPTURE

The main focus of the second chapter was to show how Mansel's skeptical epistemology was intended to clear a space where the whole range of scriptural claims could be considered truthful in some sense. Many of his contemporaries considered this appeal to the authority of scripture to be fideistic in the highest degree. Henry Sidgwick, though charitable in his reply to Mansel's lectures, nevertheless remarked that "he talks of Revelation as if the Bible had dropped from the skies ready translated into English, he ignores all historical criticism utterly."[89] These were severe words directed at a man who was proficient in Greek, Hebrew, and Latin and whose commentary on the Gospel of Matthew, written at the end of his life, is notable for its thorough and intense textual and historical engagement, if little else.[90] In a certain way, Mansel's dry and plodding commentary on Matthew was a fitting project to complete his career; he died before completing the final two chapters. As in his "Bampton Lectures," in the commentary Mansel inhabited a language and style that seemed foreign to the vital and personally engaging gospel that he was so concerned to preserve. Yet the painstaking collation of texts, the attention to words and prophecies, the patient consideration of contradictions and seeming errors, was not undertaken to guarantee the historic truth of every reference but to patch together and mend the narrative coherence of scripture that was being pulled apart by biblical critics.

To this end, I would argue that Mansel's understanding of the character and inspiration of scripture fits coherently with the theological account previously provided concerning God's presence in the world through Christ, which is to say that scripture itself resembles the providential pattern of God's activity in creation even as it discloses this pattern. What this means exactly will require some explanation.

On one hand, Mansel is clear that the humanly accommodated language of scripture is an assemblage of facts that cannot be accommodated further. They are immoveable and permanent in their witness to Christ. The permanence of the words and symbols of scripture are guaranteed through the original intention of the Spirit speaking in one historical context or another. This, of course, admits a wide degree of variance in the character of scripture and its witness, but, contrary to the trends of his own age, Mansel did not believe that the historical context needed to be sifted for its permanent meaning. On the contrary, every particular instance in the Bible becomes part of a vast network of referents to God's activity and engagement with the world. These referents cannot be dissolved by an "ulterior significance" but stand solidly as irreducible moments in the providential history of the world.

In this manner, regulative truths refer to descriptions of divine activity that have been accommodated to human conceptions; they are represented in concrete intuitions that are capable of conception in human consciousness, but as representations they do not disclose the full measure of their significance. They reveal the actions, intentions or disposition of God in a particular moment, and they relate these moments to others throughout the narrative of scripture. However, these regulative referents, stable and permanent as they are, carry implications that are not always immediately perceivable.

For instance, Mansel speaks about the expansive character of scriptural words: "In the general tenor of the narrative, and to some extent even in its minuter details as well, a breadth, an expansiveness, a capacity of meeting new facts as they arise, which merely human imaginations and traditions wholly fail to exhibit."[91] Obvious examples of this are Old Testament practices and events such as the Sabbath, the Day of Atonement, and the Passover and their faint though increasingly clear figuration of Christ.[92] In a sermon on the Holy Spirit, Mansel traces numerous examples that are less obvious, though still striking: quoting Hosea, he writes, "'When Israel was a child, then I loved him, and called my son out of Egypt,' is yet, by the use of the significant words 'a child' and 'my son' made to bear a further meaning in reference to an event corresponding by way of antitype in the life of the infant saviour."[93]

Mansel applies this textual expansiveness, perhaps more precariously, to the natural world as well. He admits that scriptural language is couched in contemporary language that dates most notably with regard to the sciences. Yet he writes that in the

> fact of an expansiveness in the text of Scripture, whereby it is enabled in natural things to adapt itself to new discoveries of science, as we have seen that in spiritual things it adapts itself to new revelations of religious truth ... there are parts of the language of Scripture which, when interpreted only by contemporaneous knowledge, seem dark and unintelligible, or even altogether erroneous, but which acquire meaning and consistency, and even scientific accuracy, when viewed by the light of a later advancement in knowledge.[94]

Historically, Mansel claims, this is the case: "Older sciences have had their day of supposed antagonism to Scripture, and Scripture to them, which now move quietly along with it side by side, neither harming nor fearing the other."[95] Writing in the immediate years following the publication of and controversy around Darwin's *On the Origin of Species*, Mansel concludes, "The time may come, may even now be not far off, when the difficulties of our own day may meet with a similar fate, and, like all such difficulties when once fairly overcome, may but add to the strength of the fortress they were designed to overthrow."[96]

It is interesting to note that in the same year Mansel wrote his sermon on Holy Spirit, where he first uses "expansion" as a hermeneutical term, John Hannah's 1863 "Bampton Lectures" engaged a nearly identical theme, and in some cases he used the same word.[97] Hannah is one of few instances of a fellow High Churchman who built upon Mansel's theory of regulative truth.[98] In his "Bampton Lectures" Hannah extends Mansel's arguments about the accommodation of scripture to human capacities into a fuller statement about the antinomies of scriptural language and its double or typological sense. For example, Hannah writes concerning the seeming contradictions of the Bible,

> the method of Scripture rests upon the principle that the most direct way of grappling with such difficulties is to state each alternative, in its own proper place and connection, unreservedly, simply, and emphatically; leaving the task of reconciliation, which surpasses the powers of human intellect, to be either attempted by the higher faculties of the enlightened spirit, or postponed in all the confidence of faith.[99]

For Hannah, as for Mansel, God can only be indicated and described in human language, which inevitably presents speculative difficulties. Much like Mansel, but with a little more clarity, Hannah argues that God is most accurately and capably revealed in antinomous language that presents sides and angles of the truth that cannot be reduced or smoothed over.[100] And yet Hannah insists that scripture represents a unity that can be articulated through the double sense, or expansive sense – the literal and spiritual or prophetic – of scriptural language that is given and drawn out through the Spirit:

> If revelation be a condescension from the higher to the lower, if it be the transfusion of knowledge from a wider to a narrower sphere, the truths thus entrusted to the expressive power of an inferior language must embody a life and expansiveness which only need the fit occasion to burst forth.[101]

Hannah, perhaps, provides a more robust pneumatological account of the scriptures' role and functioning in the Church, but his reasoning clearly extends from Mansel's basic epistemological position toward revelatory language.[102] The scriptures, for Mansel as with Hannah, like the elasticity and receptivity of the created order, are open and receptive to the continued lively and dynamic presence of God and the successive moments of his creatures. Or, put in another way, to use George Lindbeck's phrase, the scriptures are able "to absorb the universe"[103]; the world can be placed within the narrative of scripture that witnesses in various manners to Christ, who "represents" every human life. The scriptures, then, depict a catalogue of God's activities that, gathered together, render a portrait of Christ. Mansel was well aware that not every page of the Bible could be consistently integrated into this picture, but this difficulty was a result of our ignorance, not the incoherence of God: "Necessary alike during this our state of trial, it may be that both conceptions alike are but shadows of some higher truth, in which their apparent oppositions are merged in one harmonious whole."[104] This broad portrait of Christ, Mansel argued, was more encompassing of human experience than any streamlined philosophy of religion could possibly create:

> That mysterious, yet unquestionable presence of Will ... that perpetual struggle of good with evil: – those warnings and prompting of a Spirit, striving with our spirit, commanding, yet not compelling; acting upon us, yet leaving us free to act for ourselves: – that twofold consciousness of infirmity and strength in the hour of temptation ... that overwhelming conviction of sin in the sight of one higher and holier than we: – that irresistible impulse to Prayer, which bids us pour out our sorrows and make our wants known to One who hears and will answer us: – that indefinable yet inextinguishable consciousness of a direct intercourse and communion of man with God, of God's influence upon man, yea, and (with reverence be it spoken) of man's influence upon God: – these are facts of experience, to the full as real and as certain as the laws of planetary motions and chemical affinities; – facts which philosophy is bound to take into account, or to stand convicted as shallow and one sided.[105]

These seemingly scattered notions and experiences, Mansel believed, are represented in scripture and oriented into a framework that is capable of incorporating the full range of human experience. The framework itself is derived from the narrative of the Bible, from the literal accounts of the Old and New Testaments, but the double or typological sense of scriptural words and referents creates a unity across the narrative that does not discard the literal elements but focuses them around the person of Jesus Christ. In the same way, the double or typological sense of scripture presses the history of the world into the images and language of scripture, or, as Hannah puts it, the signs and events of scripture "appear and reappear, though less conspicuously, in the leading incidents of every age."[106]

It would be difficult, I believe, to argue that Mansel's philosophy begets a narrow or constricted worldview, though the phrase itself will be determined by one's own presuppositions. Mansel believed that scripture speaks of the heavenly realms so to speak, but it does so from below, from within the mediated forms of scriptural language. And furthermore, any attempt to begin from above, from the infinite or the absolute nature of God, will only constrain God within frameworks that cannot possibly describe or contain him. Revelation speaks "in partial fragments and by broken lights, to be made known more completely hereafter in a new dispensation."[107] Yet these "broken lights" or divine means adapted to human capacities are sufficient to indicate the shapes of the spiritual referents, though they can in no way exhaust them. For example, in his sermon "It Is Finished" Mansel writes,

> His love, His humility, His patience under suffering, His resignation to the will of God, His prayer for His enemies ... these are features of Christ's human nature, in which we may strive humbly to imitate by God's grace the example which He has given us. But there remains also that in which his death and suffering are unlike all that has ever been suffered by man, that He was lifted up that "whosoever believeth in him should not perish"; He gave as a ransom for many that life which He had power to lay down, and power to take again; He was "made sin for us, who knew no sin"; He redeemed us from the curse of the law, "being made a curse for us "; He "bore our sins ill by his own body on the tree," and " by his own blood he entered into the holy place, having obtained eternal redemption for us."[108]

Christ's life in this sense reveals in his human nature a pattern of living or holiness, but it also refers to a larger spiritual context, which is described in scriptures but impossible to fully comprehend. The historic and visible life of Christ indicates this larger reality, as does all of scripture, but in a manner that struggles at the boundaries of language and human conception.

On this score, Mansel was critical of Butler for understating the theological or spiritual character of evil. In a Lenten sermon in 1866, Mansel writes,

> Our thoughts may be sometimes tempted to dwell on the history of the transgression of our first parents from this human point of view exclusively. We picture to ourselves the apparent light-ness of the one positive precept which they were bidden to keep, the apparent weakness of the temptation by which they were induced to transgress. Simple indeed, and plain, and unadorned, and unaided by one word of philosophic theory or explanation, is that unpretending narrative of facts in which is recounted the temptation under which the first Adam fell as simple, as plain, as unpretending, as that other narrative of that other temptation over which the second Adam triumphed. Yet both alike have one feature in common: the simple tale may be enhanced to what height the imagination may reach, by the thought of the presence of that subtle malignant spirit, bringing every power of evil to bear secretly and invisibly in aid of those suggestions and prof-fers whose outward expression alone we see.[109]

In this case the simplicity of the words are true in their "outward expression," and that expression is not diminished or cast off, even as the words refer to the unknown nature of that "malignant spirit." The words themselves frame human conceptions of these incompre-hensible realities, but the full extent of the reality extends beyond these words without escaping the circumference of the expression's plain meaning. Or in other words, the plain, "unpretending" narrative describes God's engagement – and that of all spiritual beings – with the visible world, and while this narrative is not an exhaustive account of God in himself, it provides indications and outlines that the Christian, in faith, believes will prove to be consistent with God's own being.

For Mansel, a comprehensive theological vision of God and reality is framed from below, though this framework is given by the Spirit. What this means is that the narrative arc of scripture – a fragmentary, accommodated, though sufficient, witness to God's character – refers at every step beyond itself to a greater reality that encompasses the world. In human terms, this greater reality – the Triune God and all manner of spiritual creatures – cannot be encompassed in any kind of broader arc, because it would require the mind to reach into the character of the infinite or the absolute. But the limited and human expressions of scripture provide an authorized, inspired account of God's relation to his creation that does not fully disclose his nature but certainly reveals the pattern of his actions and, for that reason, his character.

Milbank is probably right that Mansel would have been antimystical in some sense; at least, he was leery of certain forms of language that attended the mystical tradition.[110] But there is a mystical aspect to Mansel's theology that comes out in his view of scripture. Mansel, speaking of the revelatory nature of scripture, writes,

> The luminary by whose influence the ebb and flow of man's moral being is regulated, moves around and along with man's little world, in a regular and bounded orbit: one side, and one side only, looks downwards upon its earthly centre; the other, which we see not, is ever turned upwards to the all surrounding infinite.[111]

This image describes well the place of scriptural language in Mansel's theology: The scriptures are humanly composed, and they speak within the capacities and limitations of human thinking, and yet they maintain an independence from their various authors and their intentions. They exist almost as an independent field of language, inspired and held open by the Spirit, active and capable of adaptation without losing their given shape. As in the image of the luminary, they track along with the world and with human history, expanding to make room for the unfolding of time within the strictures of a time-bound narrative. The depth of scriptural language does not depart from its literal or historical reference but extends the reference to shape and illumine evolving circumstances. In this manner, it is clear for Mansel that scripture has a formative power that is derived from the Spirit, who gathers the world and moves it toward the person of Christ.

However one might describe the mystical aspect of scripture for Mansel, it is at least true that it is not a mysticism of ascent. While scripture refers to a spiritual world beyond the visible, the emphasis of Mansel's theology is that the visible is penetrated and infused with the Spirit of God, embodied most fully in the person of Christ. In some sense then, the language of scripture represents a surface that cannot be broken or penetrated; on the contrary, it is a surface that is being moulded and formed from within. It is in this manner that Maurice's confused objections were perhaps not that far off the mark, and likewise, it is here that Mansel can be contrasted most sharply with Coleridge. In the second chapter I argued that Coleridge's maxim "The Bible contains the religion revealed by God" placed the center of Christian living within an interior experience of spiritual communion, which, to some extent, forced the scriptures to answer to a criterion of interior resonance with a higher spiritual realm.[112] The aspects of scripture that fail to strike any chord of resonance with the central experience of spiritual communion can be safely left in the shadows. This logic is more clearly perceived in the well-known distinction of Coleridge's disciple Benjamin Jowett: "Scripture has an inner life or soul; it has also an outward body or form. That form is language, which imperfectly expresses our common notions, much more those higher which religion teaches us."[113] The truth of scripture is buried beneath historical, theological and ecclesial accretions that obscure and conceal the inner character of revelation; language and grammar are shells of meaning that need to be peeled back to get at the kernel.[114]

Whereas for Mansel, the outward form of words, the particular structure of the narratives, are immoveable references that speak accurately about God's action in the world. They refer to a broader spiritual reality, but they do not invite the reader to discard the husk for the kernel: Scripture, in this sense, is all husk; it is the reality in which God works and the medium in which humanity encounters God and comes to know Him.[115] All scripture is oriented toward Christ – the patriarchs, the history of Israel, the blessings and curses, violence, and exile – and these distinct and diverse materials work together through the Holy Spirit to orient human beings and the world they live in toward Christ. To be sure, the scriptures depict God in a manner that is at times difficult to comprehend, and, even more, the character of God's actions can disorient human notions of reason and morality. Though this is not always the case, such difficulties are part of the Church's moral probation, and even more to the point, these difficulties are the chosen means by which the Spirit reveals God in the world.

The preceding statements represent the strength of Mansel's understanding of scripture, but the weakness of this view is that he seemed to stop short of providing an account of the Spirit's work in illuminating the reader of scripture. Of course one can find comments that indicate otherwise. In his sermon on the Spirit Mansel straightforwardly states, "In the revelation of God the Holy Ghost we learn to know His blessed work in supplying the helplessness and strengthening the weakness of our fallen nature."[116] Likewise, his views on the typological and expansive character of scripture seem to invite some kind of spiritual or illuminating approach to exegesis, only he remains relatively silent in this regard. J.B. Mozley perceived this and questioned Mansel on this point: "We should like to know how it is that the innocent and the Saintly have such deep intuitive insight into abstract theological dogmas, such keen perception of false doctrine, in cases where philosophic minds of inferior degrees of holiness are utterly at fault."[117] One might guess that Mansel would have likened holiness in Mozley's sense to humble submission to the created limitations of humanity and God's revelation within these limitations. Such a disposition, Mansel would undoubtedly suggest, is created and nurtured by the Spirit working within the individual; in other words, illumination is a moral or practical reality, not a speculative vista that only a few can approach. Nevertheless, as with scripture in general, any knowledge imparted through the Spirit's illumination would be expressed in human terms and capable of conception within the constraints of human consciousness.

In some sense, then, I argue that Mansel's thought is open to this aspect of the Spirit's vocation, even if it does not present itself in any clear or forceful manner. Mansel's reactions to German idealism and its English followers surely inclined him to diminish any account of an exceptional or additional faculty that allowed for deeper insight into the spiritual realm that surpassed the written structure and form of the words, whether this be Coleridge's version of practical reason or Schelling's "intuition." Scripture was often deliberately "obscure" or "indefinite," but this allowed the text to expand around and embrace a changing world; it showed the depth and character of God's activity in the world, without giving new information about the nature of God's essence.[118] Again, it seems that John Hannah is helpful in clarifying Mansel's theological reticence: for Hannah the Spirit moves in the "ripened judgment" of "those who can look most deeply into the mind of Christ, and can trace most clearly the relations existing between one truth and another, and the respective proportions of the different principles of faith."[119] Proportion and relation are highly apt terms to describe Mansel's approach to a method of interpretation that moves laterally within a range of revealed language that discloses the actions and purposes of God in language accommodated to human capacities.

CONCLUSION

If Mansel's approach to scripture has certain affinities with more contemporary postliberal themes, Lindbeck's criteria of theological legacies might give occasion to pause: "The ultimate test in this as in other areas is performance. If a postliberal approach in its actual employment proves to be conceptually powerful and practically useful to the relevant communities, it will in time become standard. It was thus that the theological outlooks of Augustine, Aquinas, Luther, and Schleiermacher established themselves."[120]

While a quote like this may feel like yet one more dismissal of Mansel's brief flash of a theological career, it derives, in part, from a similar assumption. "Antifoundationalism," Lindbeck writes, "is not to be equated with irrationalism. The issue is not whether there are universal norms of reasonableness, but whether these can be formulated in some neutral, framework-independent language."[121] Lindbeck's concern, to this end, is much like Mansel's: "Reasonableness in religion and theology, as in other domains, has something of that aesthetic character, that quality of unformalizeable skill, which we usually associate with the artist or the linguistically competent."[122] Now, Mansel would not have spoken in such terms – antifoundationalism, for example – but the idea that the full theological picture could not be formulated in rationally binding concepts was one that he endorsed, even if his psychological account of the human person still feels like a nineteenth-century totalizing theory.

The remarkable thing about Lindbeck's comments on performance is that, even in 1982, he did not think that the Western Church was in a position to fully embrace a form of his own position: "The intratextual intelligibility that postliberalism emphasizes may not fit the needs of religions such as Christianity when they are in the awkwardly intermediate stage of having once been culturally established but are not yet clearly disestablished."[123] Clearly Mansel's England was already sliding somewhere along this track, which is part of the reason that his ideas failed to gain any considerable traction. He himself could not have known where the ideas he was contending against were about to lead, but he had a vivid sense that an orthodox, scripturally governed Christianity was being increasingly shadowed by rival and distinct frameworks. In the lectures he writes, "This semi-rationalism, which admits the authority of Revelation up to a certain point and no further, rests on a far less reasonable basis than the firm belief which accepts the whole, or the complete unbelief which accepts nothing."[124] His point here is that the Christian faith has an internal logic that cannot, without damage, be easily merged into or accommodated to other frameworks. While this was taken to be a severe and narrow interpretation of the Christian faith, what many of his critics failed to see was how the scriptural world was open to incredibly diverse experiences of the faith, in different places, times and people.

To say that Mansel was ahead of his time would perhaps be too final a judgment or needlessly congratulatory. It is the argument here that Mansel's theological vision had a firm grasp on the intellectual and spiritual climate of the era but in a manner that was obscure or threatening to many of his contemporaries. Philosophers and theologians alike were not pleased to see themselves or the Church at large in the position that he advocated, and yet if Lindbeck's and others' arguments have any merit, it is a position that has become increasingly relevant to Christian theological discourse. It is less clear, however, that the particular theory of regulative truth holds promise for contemporary theological writing. In part this is due to simple historical discontinuities. Lindbeck himself suggests that Augustine, Aquinas, Calvin, and Luther had diverse methods and manners of making similar claims: all of reality was to be conceived and integrated into the scriptural account of revelation.[125] In this respect, Mansel's aims were scarcely distinguishable from these great figures in the history of Christian thought, and the theory of regulative truth was what allowed him to pursue this course. It was the most effective way, in his mind, of situating the claims of scripture within the intellectual climate of his time, without surrendering the power of the Bible, in its full measure, to shape and form the lives and thoughts of Christians. It is possible that Mansel's apologetic impulse endangered his ideas to some extent, as he sought to make the faith intelligible in an unsettling and confusing context. Maybe the irony still holds, that in an effort to allow the scriptures to identify and describe God he actually rendered God more obscure.

It is difficult to deny that the theory of regulative truth cannot quite shake the specter that what the Bible says about God is only true in some sort of qualified, if not diminished, sense. For example, when Mansel speaks about God as a person, there is a lingering uncertainty as to what this means. On one hand, God reveals himself as a person in a regulative mode in accordance with the strictures of human consciousness. On the other hand, God's personality is not quite what it seems in light of his infinite and absolute nature, as incomprehensible as these terms may be. In light of this, it is interesting to contrast the personalism of Mansel with that of Vladimir Lossky, a more contemporary figure. Lossky, like Mansel, places personality at the center of his theology but it is rooted firmly in the Eastern theological tradition. Lossky's theological notion of the human person is derived from the personal and Trinitarian nature of God. Personhood in God, Lossky writes, "is irreducible to the *ousia*, is no longer a conceptual expression but a sign which is introduced into the domain of the non-generalized, pointing out the radically personal character of the God of Christian revelation."[126] Lossky extends this irreducibility to human personhood as well, claiming that the human person cannot be reduced or isolated within his or her nature:

> Under these conditions, it will be impossible for us to form a concept of the human person, and we will have to content ourselves with saying: "person" signifies the irreducibility of man to his nature – "irreducibility" and not "something irreducible" or "something which makes man irreducible to his nature" precisely because it cannot be a question here of "something" distinct from "another nature" but of someone who is distinct from his own nature, of someone who goes beyond his nature while still containing it, who makes it exist as human nature by this overstepping and yet does not exist in himself beyond the nature which he "enhypostasizes" and which he constantly exceeds.[127]

Unlike Mansel, personhood for Lossky is a non-conceptual reality expressed, ultimately, in terms of relation; within God, the persons of the Trinity must surpass conceptual boundaries of their personality, which is only defined as an encounter with the other persons. So there is a profoundly apophatic aspect to his notion of the personality of God:

> He is a personal absolute who enters into relationships with human persons ... This God reveals himself as transcendent to

every image which could make known his nature, but he does not refuse personal relationship, living intercourse with men, with a people: He speaks to them and they reply, in a series of concrete situations which unfold as sacred history.[128]

This last image is striking for its similarity with Mansel's vision, especially his emphasis on the personal engagement of God. Likewise, Lossky's agnosticism or apophaticism notably resembles Mansel's view: God's nature is unknowable, but he is represented "in a series of concrete situations" known through the scriptures or, in this case, experience. The clear difference, however, is the theological origin of personality. For Lossky, it is encountered in God's nature, though it defies conceptual grasp. Mansel, on the contrary, begins with an account of the human person that Lossky might very well regard as a prisoner to substantival accounts of humanity, though, as I argued, Mansel's account of human personality is largely negative. In this respect it is not experientially constraining, though Lossky might still find this definition of personality to be overly reductive. On this score, Mansel's anthropology might have been enriched by a version of Lossky's theological account of personality. Mansel, in the end, was open to something like Lossky's argument, though he remained understated about it. Part of the discussion on analogy in chapter 3 highlighted the manner of resemblance between the regulative images of scripture and God's own nature. Yet for Mansel, human conceptions of God begin with these images and Christians, in faith, and hope that they will be confirmed in the end.

This is perhaps the point of difference between Lossky and Mansel, despite obvious similarities. Rowan Williams's comments on Lossky help draw the distinction out:

Lossky's "personalism" requires an appreciation of the fundamental importance for him of apophasis, regarded as the expression of the foundation of all theology in the "self-revelation of God in silence," the meeting of human and divine persons in a direct confrontation that does not require the mediation of any image or concept.[129]

On the other hand, Mansel's personalism is an account of the human person, which is designed to make space for the multitude of scriptural images that describe this confrontation. Or put another way, no description of this confrontation is possible without the myriad images displayed in scripture. This is probably true to some extent for Lossky, but the controlling image for Lossky is the inner dynamics of the Trinity; how this image shapes or controls scriptural interpretation would be a good indicator of its performative value. Of course, it is strange to speak this way because Trinitarian concepts are themselves scripturally rooted. Williams's point is perhaps that Lossky's account of personality represents an inner circle around his concept of God, which stands closer to the center than the conventional images employed in scripture.

In part, this contrast is instructive in showing the character of Mansel's apophaticism, if it can be called that. Despite the weaknesses of the theory of regulative truth, I argue that it holds more promise for articulating a scriptural worldview than, in this instance, Lossky's view.

For Mansel, scripture speaks at times in conflicting statements and antinomous images that cannot be conceptually resolved, but it is the character of human knowledge of God that it must be conveyed through "broken lights" and partial statements because a full-orbed or speculative understanding of God is simply impossible. As a necessary result of this conviction, Christians cannot afford to discard the images of scripture – scripture cannot be streamlined so as to leave aside even the most jagged and difficult portions – because there is no fuller account of God's activity in the world than scripture itself that could justify such a selection.

In the next chapter I pursue this conceptual contrast more fully in the particular context of English idealism. Indeed, the theme of theological and philosophical comprehensiveness would become the great concern of late nineteenth-century England: how could emerging and diverse forms of knowledge be united in a single comprehensible scheme? What Mansel offered was a scripturally comprehensive vision of reality, though such a vision fit uncomfortably within clear theoretical boundaries. Even more, it rendered a picture of Victorian England that cut across the grain of the era's more prevailing sense of its moment in history, which is not to say that Mansel's understanding of his own times was the only option available for those who wished to see their world through a scriptural lens. Mansel's understanding of the rise of unbelief drew on the assumption that the Bible is capable of expanding around and describing the world in which we live, but the nature of the Bible is such that the character of these descriptions may not be obvious. The main argument here is that Mansel's theory of regulative truth provides a context in which these descriptions might take place and flourish. However, this is not how Mansel's ideas would come to be known amongst Victorian theologians and philosophers. The subject of the next chapter will explore the way in which Mansel was misread and the theological reasons which made this misreading possible.

Mansel among the Idealists

From the time of Mansel's "Bampton Lectures" up until his sudden death in 1871, his academic life was engulfed in controversy and debate. The majority of his publications during this time involved defending his claims in his lectures against many prominent and unexpected critics. This undoubtedly took a toll on his health, and those close to him certainly wondered if the suspected brain aneurism that took his life was the product of this academic and public strain. It was during this period that he had to contend with the constant reminder that Herbert Spencer had found his ideas amendable in the construction of his own agnostic philosophy. But had Mansel lived longer, he would have witnessed a far more powerful repudiation and refusal of his modest and traditional intentions to depict the world in scriptural terms. The philosophical idealism that would take hold at Oxford and throughout England would have a powerful influence on Anglican theologians in the later Victorian years. This particular brand of idealism was something that Mansel both feared and predicted, and it was this very movement that would seal his reputation as outdated thinker who refused to acknowledge the time in which he lived.

After his death, Mansel continued to have supporters, but his influence trailed off quickly. By 1877, for example, the British historian Montagu Burrows wrote "it will be granted that his fame is under an eclipse, and that his works are not received – at Oxford for example, where men once hung on his words – with the same trusting confidence as of old. Even friendly voices murmur that his day is passed ... The judgment is passed from mouth to mouth that he has failed."[1] Burrows himself admired Mansel deeply and regarded him still as a nineteenth-century Butler:

> We only claim that he has been unfairly attacked, and only
> slightly defended; that his lifelong labours, the labours of one
> of the most conscientious of men ... can hardly be allowed to
> go for nothing at a moment when every aid from every quarter
> is so urgently needed in the battle of Faith and Unbelief.[2]

Though Burrows thought Mansel had been effective in clarifying and challenging certain forms of Christian rationalism, this view was not accepted by many.[3] Instead of being revived to address new forms of Christian rationalism, Mansel became, in the hands of idealist philosophers, the standard of all that must be left behind.

Bernard Lightman's *The Origins of Agnosticism* has already provided a thoroughly descriptive account of Mansel's influence on Spencer and English agnosticism, so it is the intention of this chapter to focus on the manner in which Mansel's ideas impinged upon the philosophical idealism that would soon exert great influence in England. In some sense the irony of Mansel's relation to English idealism is more theologically complex and suggestive than the case of the English agnostics. While Spencer's developmental philosophy had the effect of eroding traditional theological beliefs, it did not contain an ostensible theological aspect that might have made it attractive to Anglican writers.[4]

Both T.H. Green and F.H. Bradley, two of England's leading philosophers of idealism, would use Mansel's epistemology as a foil for their progressive metaphysics of knowledge and history, and yet the Anglican theologians who made their home in this context would eventually draw on certain elements of Mansel's thought to resist the generalizing pressures of idealism that threatened to erode the distinctiveness of Christian belief. In other words, I argue in this chapter that aspects of Mansel's epistemological skepticism remained operative in Anglican theology throughout the remainder of the nineteenth century and into the twentieth century, even if the fuller implications of his theology were not fully understood or acknowledged. It was not until the period following the First World War, when Mansel had long been forgotten in theological publications, that Anglican theologians began to wrestle seriously with the incongruity between the scriptural account of God and the various claims of idealistic metaphysics.

While Green starting writing in the 1850s, it was not until the 1870s, following Mansel's death in 1871, that idealism as such became a widely heralded movement at Oxford and beyond. Though it certainly represented something new in character and form, it stood within the nineteenth-century romantic tradition of Anglican theology represented by Coleridge, the Cambridge apostles, and Benjamin Jowett.[5] Coleridge's resistance to traditional atonement theology and Jowett's dislike for "schemes of salvation" were part of a larger spiritual concern to render Christian beliefs within a philosophical system that coordinated the infinite and the finite in a manner that overcame the materialist and empiricist tendency in the Anglican tradition.[6] But while the thinkers in this tradition were united by a consistent concern, it would be difficult to suggest that the writings of Coleridge, Carlyle, or Thomas Arnold represented a specific school of thought identified by a certain style of philosophical rigor. Yet it was just this appearance that gave the English idealists a certain prestige in 1880s and 90s. In the words of W.J. Mander, English idealism shared a similar goal as its predecessors but promised to deliver something more:

> It was from this culture that Idealism rose, and directly to it that it spoke, for it was a crisis that exposed utterly the impotence of existing philosophies of religion ... the common-sense tradition of Hamilton and Mansel proved itself epistemically too weak to offer up anything more than the emptiness of Herbert Spencer's "unknowable" or of Matthew Arnold's "eternal not ourselves that makes for righteousness." By contrast, Idealism offered a path by which unassailable philosophical enquiry might contribute to the secure rebuilding of what had been lost. Not always explicit or orthodox ... Idealism thus answered a pressing need of the age, seeming to many to offer a rational re-interpretation of religion which, at the same time as shedding itself of blind faith, was able to avoid agnosticism or atheism, and thereby hold on to the things of deeper value and significance in traditional belief.[7]

Of course, the phrase "shedding itself of blind faith" is theologically loaded, much like the "deeper value" of traditional belief. This chapter will be concerned with exploring the manner in which philosophers like Green and Bradley were taken up by more orthodox theologians for the purpose of addressing the demands of the age. It is unquestionably true that the *Lux Mundi* writers were deeply influenced by Green especially, but as Michael Ramsay has insisted, this influence can be overstated.[8] Given the nature of Green's and Bradley's own religious beliefs, this had to be the case. In Timothy Gouldstone's words, this struggle of situating orthodox faith within an idealistic framework was what united figures as diverse as Coleridge, Green, and Scott Holland:

> Coleridge's mind reflected the tension between Christianity and pantheism, between philosophical inferences and orthodox Christian theism, and in this it bears a strong resemblance to later idealist philosophers who felt acutely the tension between their idealistic and holistic vision of the cosmos and the particularities that are a necessary part of orthodox Christian revelation.[9]

My purpose in this chapter is to illustrate and analyze the manner in which orthodox theologians drew on ideas and distinctions that Mansel had already put in place, just before idealism formalized into a forceful movement in Anglicanism.

MANSEL ON HEGEL

In his *A Second Letter to Goldwin Smith,* Mansel defends his philosophical or theological reserve by quoting the famous words of Ridley: "I am so fearful that I dare not speak farther, yea, almost none otherwise than the text doth lead me by the hand."[10] In support of his own position he offers Smith this rather simple reply: "I confess I can give no better than that it appears to me most agreeable to the language of Scripture ... I give this reason only as the one which is most satisfactory to myself: I can hardly expect it to be satisfactory to you."[11] Of course, to Mansel's critics this might have seemed like pious pleading, but the statement expresses his basic belief that human beings approach God by the light of scripture in a world that otherwise conceals him. Though Mansel may not have agreed with the full implications of Hume's maxim that "nature is always too strong for principle,"[12] something like this notion formed the basis of Mansel's criticism of Hegel, except for Mansel it might be rephrased that the human mind is not strong enough for such a principle that unites all things under a theological or logical conception; because all human conceptions are limited or relative to human understanding, no comprehensive vision of God's relation to the world is possible aside from what has been given from God. Furthermore, any attempt to widen the scope of God's providence or relation to creation beyond scriptural language inevitably distorts the manner in which people were created to interact with the Triune God.

I argued in chapter 3 that Mansel inherited his criticism of German idealism from William Hamilton and his *Philosophy of the Conditioned*. No other author is cited more frequently in Mansel's "Bampton Lectures" than Hegel, and Schelling is a close second. While Mansel regarded Hegelian idealism as only one prong of modern unbelief, it was one that increasingly overwhelmed his writing. To Goldwin Smith he writes, "Against the Pantheists, I have insisted strongly on the personality of God: against the Socinians and their disciples, I have maintained that personality, as we conceive it, is but a faint and imperfect reflection of the reality."[13] The lectures would become memorable or notorious for the latter emphasis, but in the last decade of Mansel's life it was really the former that emerged as the greater concern. Historically this is understandable, given the relatively sudden escalation of interest in Hegel that began, in earnest, in the middle of the 1860s.

Mansel's emphasis on the personality of God became a way of holding on to the biblical depiction of God's relation to his people, and even more, personality was a limiting term for the particular character of God in the scriptures. To this end he would have affirmed Charles Taylor's assessment of Hegel's particular theological beliefs:

> The central tenets of this philosophy, that the only locus of God's life as spirit is man, and that this spiritual life is nothing but the unfolding of conceptual necessity, together rule out the kind of radical God to which faith relates. In Hegel's system, God cannot give to man – neither in creation, nor in revelation, nor is salvation through sending his Son.[14]

Taylor's point, perhaps, is that the ability of God to relate and give of himself in the world is taken over, in Hegel's terms, by a "conceptual necessity" or process. Strangely, it is the relatability or porousness of the self that made Hegel's ideas attractive to idealists like Bradley and, to some degree, to contemporary theologians like Rowan

Williams. For instance, Williams regards Hegel's account of consciousness to be in fact highly conducive to the Divine and human encounter: "No perceived reality is stable and self contained for thinking ... Thinking passes through this process as action that realizes itself in 'emptying' itself: and its continuity is secured in and by its challenging or denying of itself."[15] So Williams, not unlike Lossky, invests Hegel's account of the "dialectical process which consciousness executes on itself"[16] with a moral quality that describes the basic character of Christian living. The process of the object becoming internal to the subject and vice versa represents for Williams an "ecstatic" or "kenotic" epistemology that is fundamental for Christian theology: thinking in this sense becomes an act of love, "the self's being-in-the-other,"[17] which is rooted in the Trinitarian God.

It is probably the case that Mansel could not have imagined the application of Hegel in these theological terms. While Williams claims that Hegel remains rooted, in some sense, within the scriptural narrative,[18] Mansel could only see in Hegel's philosophy a form of logic that would eventually dissolve particular scriptural and doctrinal claims. And Mansel's fear stemmed from the very aspect of Hegel that has made him attractive to theologians like Williams and philosophers like Green and Bradley. Mansel writes in his essay on metaphysics,

> In consciousness, two identical thoughts are undistinguishable from each other; and as consciousness is only possible as a cognition of differences, it follows that a system of identical determinations of consciousness is tantamount to the annihilation of all consciousness. The possibility of consciousness, therefore, implies the coexistence of opposites; but, for the very reason that there is coexistence, there is not identity. Any special modification of consciousness is discerned to be that which it is by being distinguished from that which it is not; and in this manner consciousness is only possible on the condition of a relation, not merely between subject and object, but between a plurality of objects opposed to each other.[19]

For Mansel the stability of the conscious self and the reality that it engages with was a central aspect of human personality. The subject/object dualism was a created reality that must be accounted for but not overcome.[20] Thus Mansel writes of Hegel's basic epistemology,

But, in order that these opposite objects should be regarded as identical, or rather as constituent elements of one and the same reality, it is necessary that the notion or thing in itself should be represented, not as a single object of consciousness, but as an unperceived substratum, which underlies the relation between the two opposed objects, and out of which they mutually spring as distinct sides of one and the same reality. Being is thus no longer identical with thought.[21]

For Mansel the essence of reality is personal, and he feared that in Hegel's philosophy personality was simply a phenomenal representation that was superseded in the process of thought:

Thought in the system of Hegel is represented as an impersonal, absolute, indeterminate, universal, unconscious substance, determining itself in opposed and yet identical modifications, becoming all things, constituting the essence of all things, and attaining to consciousness only in man. Consciousness is thus the accident, not the essence, of thought.[22]

The idea that a reality remained accessible outside of the constraints of human consciousness marked the deepest theological concern for Mansel. In relation to God, he argued that Hegel's "Objective Absolutism regards personality itself as a phenomenal manifestation of some higher reality, which alone is truly existent, and to which it gives the name, but not the nature, of God."[23] In more contemporary terms, Mansel worried that in Hegel's thought there was a "God behind the God of theism," to use Tillich's phrase.

Yet Mansel did not seem concerned with the manner in which his criticism of Hegel mirrored his own distinction between what can be known of God and God's actual nature. His comment to Goldwin Smith at least highlights the fact that he was conscious of the degree in which his theological emphases shifted with respect to the ideas he was engaging. But if he was in fact speaking out of both sides of his mouth, his basic position remained undisturbed. The personality of God is on one hand presented to humanity in scripture under the only terms that the human mind can permit; on the other hand, God's presented personality is not a phase in human comprehension but the final and truthful image, even if only partially grasped in faith. This basic understanding of personality was Mansel's primary method in resisting what he considered Hegel's attempt to "rethink the great thought of creation."[24] Mansel may have been wrong that Hegel's logic must always lead to atheism or pantheism[25] – at least it was not at all clear to him how Christian theologians could situate orthodox theology within aspects of Hegel's philosophy. But the remainder of this chapter will explore the extent to which Mansel's skeptical, personalist epistemology would resurface among Anglican theologians who were trying to build their ideas upon the renewed hope for a unified, comprehensive theological vision that English idealism seemed to promise.

BRITISH IDEALISM: GREEN AND BRADLEY

Timothy Gouldstone writes that "Mansel had clearly seen the challenge confronting Christian apologetics in the 1850s," and yet his lectures were not able "to stem the tide of renewed interest in philosophical developments from the continent."[26] But it was not simply continental philosophy that concerned Mansel but the particular form of philosophy that threatened the particular character of Christian doctrine. In his well-known poem *The Phrontisterion* Mansel sarcastically writes,

> The Voice of Yore,
> Which the breezed bore
> Wailing aloud from Paxo's shore,
> Is changed to a gladder and livelier strain,
> For great God Pan is alive again,
> He lives and he reigns once more.
> With deep intuitions and mystic rite
> We worship the Absolute–Infinite
> The Universe–Ego, the Plenary void,
> The Subject–Object identified,
> The great Nothing–Something, the Being–Thought,
> That mouldeth the mass of chaotic Nought,
> Whose beginnings unended and end unbegun,
> Is the One that is All and the All that is One.[27]

But if many of the peculiarities of Hegel's philosophy were lost on English minds, figures like Green and Bradley were able to adapt continental philosophy in order to meet a growing need in England.

In Gouldstone's words, English idealism became "a broad term for a philosophical movement that defines ultimate reality as mental or 'spiritual' rather than physical; the mind and spiritual values are more fundamental than material ones."[28] Under the pressures of scientific materialism, and reacting to the party-driven theological controversies of the era, Green and Bradley attempted to construct a system of religious thought that was capable of unifying the rapidly fragmenting character of English intellectual life by expanding and reordering the traditional Christian concept of God. In order to do this they relied upon a structure of religious faith and the limits of knowledge that resembled Mansel's theory but in essence replaced the scriptures with the eternal consciousness of God or, in Bradley's case, the Absolute.[29]

T.H. Green

Much like Coleridge and other early English readers of German idealism, Green was perhaps primarily a Kantian, though a Kantian who read an opening into Kant's epistemology that allowed for a degree of knowledge about the absolute.[30] The problem with Kant, Green writes, is that "We have asserted the unity of the world of our experience only to transfer that world to a larger chaos."[31] The chaos refers to the unknown world of things-in-themselves that lies outside the cognitive field of rational apperception, in Kant's terms. It was along these lines that Green, in his 1874–75 lectures on logic, criticized Mansel as a formal logician whose rigid epistemic limits upon human understanding prohibited any process in the act of knowing.

Yet, Green argues, Mansel goes beyond Kant in denying that there can be any conception without an intuition, a sensible reference:

Mansel holds (what is quite different from Kant's view) that there can be no conception without intuition; that, attributes being represented by verbal signs, we may and do reason by means of these signs, without at each step referring the attribute signified to an object of intuition, but that in so doing we reason without distinctly conceiving what we are reasoning about, and that if at any stage in the process, for fear of being misled by mere words, we ask ourselves what it is that we mean, we can only answer by an act of conception which involves reference of attributes to an object of intuition.[32]

Mansel argued this point in order to show that there can be no proper human conception of the infinite or the absolute – the conceptions cannot possibly refer to any known intuition. But Green insists that this represents a contradiction in terms: intuitions only acquire attributes through the process of conception, "yet all the while the content of the conception is supposed to be attributes found in, and abstracted from, objects of intuition."[33] Furthermore, Green argues that not all objects of conception are situated within visible reality, and, for this reason, Mansel's theory is ill equipped to deal with moral and spiritual realities:

> When the conceived relations do not purport to be relations between separate things in the physical world, e.g. the relation between man and man, between subject and object, between motives and will, between man and God, or God and the world, there is a tendency to intuitionalize the conception arising from the fact (a) that it is hard ... to think without expressing thought in language, and (b) that our language is primarily appropriate to the physical world ... and that only by a constantly shifting process of metaphor is it made to do other duty. This tendency (which is the ultimate source of dogma) leads us into paradoxes and contradictions, out of which we are apt to find an escape in mysticism. The true way of escape is to recognize the tendency itself as altogether misleading. Is not the true notion of faith, that it is the apprehension of objects which we conceive but cannot present in intuition, an apprehension of which the proper expression is not language but moral action?[34]

Green clearly recognized the theological intent in Mansel's logic, and his appeal to morality – not unlike Kant's – was an effort to suggest that there can be conceptions without concrete references. The moral imperative, in this case, is such a conception.

But even more for Green, the problem with Mansel's epistemology was that it rendered knowledge as a fixed quantity and as a process with a determined end. This concern echoes the more theological criticisms of Mozley and others discussed in chapter 3: namely, that is was difficult to imagine what role the illumination of the Holy Spirit played in theological apprehension. The language of scripture was fixed and immoveable, and Christian truths were presented as accommodated realities impenetrable to human insight. Except Green extends this concern to knowledge as whole:

> The great mistake lies in regarding a conception as a fixed quantity, a bundle of attributes. In truth a conception, as the thought of an object under relations, is from its very nature in constant expansion. Hence the impossibility of really defining a conceived object, unless the relations which determine it from their primariness admit of being isolated. The ordinary definition of an object is available only for rhetorical purposes, as expressing what for the time certain disputants, or those to whom a man is speaking, agree to understand by a name.[35]

This characterization of Mansel's mistake provides, in effect, the opening for Green's metaphysics, which essentially underpins the provisional nature of all thought and experience. As Mander expresses it, "Thought leads always beyond itself."[36] Like Mansel, Green argues that all reality is conceived in relations, but related objects are related not simply to a particular consciousness but to all of reality. This reality is constantly moving and morphing into new forms, and while the possible relations cannot be exhausted, they are held together by an eternal consciousness.[37]

While Green does not speak in the definite theological terms that Hegel uses with respect to the phenomenology of Spirit in history, Green still describes individuals as vehicles for a higher process:

> in the growth of our experience, in the process of our learning to know the world, an animal organism, which has its history in time, gradually becomes the vehicle of an eternally complete consciousness. What we call our mental history is not a history of this consciousness, which in itself can have no history, but a history of the process by which the animal organism becomes its vehicle.[38]

But the eternal consciousness remains, in large part, a moral postulate that cannot be verified or entirely conceived. In this way, Green's metaphysics mirrors Mansel's notion of faith and the regulative truth of Scripture, only the object of faith has expanded beyond the traditional bounds of Christian theology. It is founded on the moral intuition that the mere possibility of moral development implies a completed state, and such a state is nearly synonymous with God himself. So Green writes,

> It is the consciousness of possibilities in ourselves, unrealised but constantly in the process of realisation, that alone enables us to read the idea of development into what we observe of natural life, and to conceive that there must be such a thing as a plan of the world ... the appearance of positive inconsistency between much that we observe and any scheme of universal development, can weaken the authority of the idea, which does not rest on the evidence of observation but expresses an inward demand for the recognition of a unity in the world answering to the unity of ourselves a demand involved in that self-consciousness which, as we have seen, alone enables us to observe facts as such.[39]

Just as Mansel regards causation as a deduction from the character of human consciousness, Green is able to describe the pattern of history – both natural and supernatural – according to the secure inward knowledge of consciousness, though in this case it is a moral knowledge that becomes the measure and the basis on this knowledge, and, Green suggests, in essence, it is by faith that human beings are assured that what is personally true is in fact objectively true.

In these terms God becomes an analogical extension of human moral possibilities. To be sure, God is more than any individual person; God represents an outcome that is impossible to comprehend:

> This consideration may suggest the true notion of the spiritual relation in which we stand to God; that He is not merely a Being who has made us, in the sense that we exist as an object of the divine consciousness in the same way in which we must suppose the system of nature to exist, but that He is a Being in whom we exist; with whom we are in principle one; with whom the human spirit is identical, in the sense that He is all which the human spirit is capable of knowing.[40]

But Green insists that any knowledge of this end in God remains impossible, as the end "is not itself a series in time" but a state that must be "comprehended eternally in the eternal mind."[41] Statements like these are certainly cryptic, but the whole of Green's metaphysics contains an obvious advantage over Mansel's in that it provides a

place for continual movement and progress in knowledge and experience without relinquishing a holistic conception of reality. Mansel,
as I argued in chapter 4, tried to present scriptures as this holistic
reality, the context in which God encounters human history, but the
stress of his work remained upon the distinctions and divisions of
knowledge and the inevitable limitations of human thought. Green
attempts to lift these limitations and render all of life as immersion
in the Spirit, so to speak, though without necessarily attending to the
particularities or personality of God in scripture. But what seemed
to Green and his followers like a widening of the philosophical lens
in the end retained a structure not unlike Mansel's. Though all of
reality is related to and exists in the eternal mind, the realization of
this goal remains hidden in human history; it is grasped in faith. In
other words, Green's epistemology remains skeptical to some degree
even amidst its apparent ambitions.

Dogma and Scripture

It could be argued that Green's metaphysics provided a structure for
a style of thinking that was already prevalent in Victorian England.
Aside from offering the possibility of mitigating growing concerns
over science and the shifting intellectual of the nineteenth century,
Green offered a philosophical account of why theological dogmas
need only serve a penultimate role in religion and morality. To some
extent this was the effect of Locke's *The Reasonableness of Christianity*
– a book written in the aftermath of the English Civil War. Clearly
the Latitudinarian tradition had a foot in both camps – idealism and
empiricism – even while the theological stakes in the classic conflict
remained often unclear.[42] Matthew Arnold's comment in *St Paul and
Protestantism*, for example, is particularly telling:

> If they [heretics] separated on points of dogma they were wrong
> also, because while neither they nor the Church had the means of
> determining such points adequately, the true instinct lay in those
> who, instead of separating for such points, conceded them as the
> Church settled them, and found their bond of union, where it in
> truth really was, not in notions about the co-eternity of the Son,
> but in Christ's injunction, Follow me![43]

What exactly Arnold means with this statement is another matter,
but it expresses, at least partially, a sentiment that is common to

both Mansel and Green: God's nature cannot be fixed in human language, and the essence of Christian faith is practical and moral. However, they differed widely on the context in which these claims are made. For Green in particular, the traditional doctrines of the Christian faith that inform the reading of scripture are not capable of delivering the "bond of unity" that Arnold describes. Even more, a comprehensive theological vision of the world that stops short at doctrinal definitions inevitably arrests the progressive movement of the Spirit in humanity.

With that being said, Green's engagement with scripture seems hardly facile or underhanded. This, in large measure, is what made his ideas plausible and even persuasive to a generation of young Anglican clergyman. Gouldstone writes,

Precisely because of this tendency, it could be a more potent dissolvent of the Anglican cosmos than more naturalistic movements; it could appear as a spiritual sheep in philosophical wolf's clothing when it came to a reassessment of the place of Christian dogma and doctrine.[44]

A particularly potent example of this can be found in Green's lectures on Romans and Galatians. Green provides a skilful account of the Pauline themes of law and gospel, death and life. When considering the conversion of Paul, Green writes,

The subjection of the Son of God to the death in which he found himself was his own deliverance from it, as showing that God was not the giver of an external law which could not be obeyed, but a God who communicated himself to man under conditions which had seemed to separate from him. Thus the death wrought by the law, wrought by it, though spiritual in itself, owing to the relation in which it stood to our carnal nature, through the participation of Christ in it becomes death unto the law.[45]

Green's philosophy is not threatened by the traditional language of salvation in Paul's writing; in fact, he is able to enter into it with conviction and without suspicion of authorship or sources. Even on the issue of the atonement he accepts, at first glance, the obvious reading of Paul's statements in Romans: "We being dead under the curse of the law, the Son of God, in order to save us from the consciousness of being apart from God, had in some way to put himself in that condition too; to put himself under the curse of the law and thus die too."[46]

The theology of the atonement in the nineteenth century was the source of continual controversy. Certainly for Mansel the atonement was a cipher for determining the logic that underpinned any particular theological vision, and in particular, atonement theologies, he believed, quickly revealed an author's attitude toward the scriptures and the Old Testament in particular.[47] Green, in this case, does not dispute the sacrificial elements of Paul's understanding of Christ's work on the cross, but he rather places this work within a larger context of the Spirit:

> Thus, though he did think of the death of Christ as a death in which the penalty of sin was paid, his essential thought of it was as of a death unto sin, in which we ideally partake, while at the same time, by the new consciousness of God's mind towards us which it gives, it enables us gradually to actualise this ideal death unto sin as a new spiritual walk; and his thought of the death of Christ as a payment of the penalty passes into the latter thought, which is what really gives his doctrine its great moral value.[48]

It was not so much that Paul was wrong or needed adjustment; Green does not deny that Christ's death meant what it meant to Paul but only that his death would eventually mean something else. Within the contours of a philosophy where meaning is always slipping beyond the attributes of an object, Green is free to at once affirm the language of scripture, attend to its shape and force, and all the while move beyond it.

So in Green's view, Christ becomes the emblematic type of his epistemological system wherein the paradox of life and death are worked out.[49] To cling to a solid identity, to regard something as fixed by its attributes, represents a clinging to life that leads to death; whereas the dissolution of identity leads to life in the Spirit:

> In like manner the Christ of dogma is an object of intuition become abstract, but not ideal. He is presented to the spirit, not as its own true form objectified, but as wholly external to it. The confinement of his earthly reality, though the attributes assigned to him involve its entire negation, still clings to him. He does not yet fill all things with the fullness of the idea.[50]

Green is speaking here of the Chalcedonian definitions of Christ that, in his words, leave Jesus as a wholly external reality, deprived of his universality by the encumbrance of attributes.[51] As a result, the coming of the Spirit and ascension of Christ's earthly represent less the glorification of Christ, his particular life and action, and more the diffusion of Christ's God consciousness into the world:

> That evolution of dogma, which, as we have seen, emptied the intuition of Jesus of its content, constitutes a gradual determination of the idea of God as an object to himself. This idea becomes more concrete as the intuition becomes more abstract. God has died and been buried, and risen again, and realised himself in all the particularities of a moral life.[52]

As the intuition of Jesus expands beyond his historical person it becomes more capable of embracing a widening range of experience that is characterized by the drive toward self-fulfillment realized in God.[53]

In theological terms, Green's skepticism becomes more severe than Mansel's, largely because the language of revelation is not available to him in any enduring manner. Scripture is not the context in which humanity encounters and knows God throughout history, but it is an instance of the evolution of consciousness – a crucially informing instance – that is elevated within the dynamics of the Spirit.

> The only course which does not land us in contradictions is to admit that we have no reason to suppose, or rather that we cannot suppose, though we may talk of doing so, any personality but that with which our individual experience makes us acquainted, and of which the attributes are as incompatible with an absolute being as are those which experience of nature reveals to us. We may amuse ourselves with guesses about a great personal demon, as about a single primitive force; but God, if he is to be God, can neither be such a demon nor such a force. Either there is no God, or God is the unknown.[54]

Green's reason for making this claim is startlingly close to Mansel's own understanding but without any form of analogical reasoning, Green has no way of bridging the contradictions that arise from the correspondence between the personality of God and humanity. God is simply the sum of human aspiration made concrete throughout experience but ultimately not fully realizable. In a developmental metaphysics, a definitive God who can be identified as one across a range of scriptural references becomes untenable. And Green himself acknowledges this by suggesting that the inevitable progress of the God consciousness in history is toward ineffability:

> We may be passing through a period of transition from one mode of expressing them [the reality of God and moral duty] to another, or perhaps to an admission of their final ineffableness ... Faith in God and duty will survive much doubt and difficulty and distress, and perhaps attain to some nobler mode of itself under their influence.[55]

Though much has been made of Mansel's influence on Spencer's agnosticism, it should be noted that Spencer and Green shared this vision of history, wherein human conceptions gradually ascend to an increasingly unknowable, indeterminate understanding of God.[56]

Ultimately Green rejects the authority of creedal statements and the text of scripture to identify God and God's relation to the world.[57] At least in part, this is because Green could not conceive of how the scriptural narrative was still capable of describing the world in which he lived, much less the future that he imagined approaching. Mansel's use of the expansive character of scriptural terms and the typological unity of the Old and New Testaments was an attempt to allow scripture to form the context in which the truth concerning morality, history, and God are understood and encountered. Where Green saw the ossification and idolatry of propositional orthodoxy as a force that kills the Spirit, Mansel argued that the Spirit brings life to the scriptures and is working in the world in such a way that in the end, they will not be surpassed but fulfilled.

The Metaphysics of F.H. Bradley

While it is possible that Green had more influence among Anglican theologians in the final decades of the nineteenth century, Bradley is considered to have stated the idealist case in England in the most clear and extensive terms. Green's scriptural engagement and theological terminology made him more amenable to theological writers, but Bradley's system of metaphysics has the appearance of philosophical independence and originality. And it was in Bradley, according to R.G. Collingwood, that Mansel was more thoroughly and energetically repudiated within the halls of Oxford. Collingwood writes,

> My suggestion is that Bradley's *Appearance* is in the first instance a polemic against Mansel. It is from Mansel that Bradley borrows the antithesis of *Appearance* and *Reality*; it is against the project of dividing the one from the other that his books is directed, and that project is the task assigned by Mansel to metaphysics in his famous *Encyclopaedia Britannica* article, which everyone was reading when Bradley was young.[58]

According to Collingwood, Bradley's positive objections to Mansel are that all of reality must be consistent with itself and that appearances must belong in some way to reality.[59]

In order to argue this, in the early portions of *Appearance and Reality* Bradley moves through various attempts to establish the nature of reality – primary and secondary qualities, space and time, substance, etc. – to show that the related character of reality renders every affirmation many sided. But his criticism of Mansel comes to a point in his understanding of the self: "But we have heard somewhere a rumour that the self was to bring order into chaos ... Self has turned out to mean so many things, to mean them so ambiguously, and to be so wavering in its applications, that we do not feel encouraged."[60] The rumour could be referring as much to Kant as to Mansel, but the point for Bradley is that reality cannot be limited to the self, because the self is simply an appearance among others. Bradley writes of the self:

> In its given content it has relations which do not terminate within that content; and its existence therefore is not exhausted by itself, as we ever can have it. If I may use the metaphor, it has always edges which are ragged in such a way as to imply another existence from which it has been torn, and without which it really does not exist.[61]

As with Green, no one thing can be defined in any determinate manner because it exists within a state of infinite relations that qualify it. So Bradley's task is to then describe the nature of a reality that can encompass the endless variety of relations that characterize the world.

Bradley's term for this all-encompassing reality is "the Absolute," which is not a being of some kind that defies conception, the type that Mansel was bent on criticizing. Rather, the Absolute becomes almost synonymous with reality itself as a concept that unites every aspect of life:

> Everything, which appears, is somehow real in such a way as to be self-consistent. The character of the real is to possess everything phenomenal in a harmonious form ... The bewildering mass of phenomena and diversity must hence somehow be at unity and self-consistent; for it cannot be elsewhere than in realty, and reality excludes discord.[62]

The pressing need for the unity of experience is what drives Bradley to this conclusion: "The Absolute is one system, and its contents are nothing but sentient experience. It will hence be a single and all inclusive experience, which embraces every partial diversity in concord ... and harmonize all the facts."[63] Because every single thing is related to everything else, there must be something that embraces the whole system of relations.

The Absolute for Bradley, in a similar way to Hegel, must include all of reality, even discord, evil, and error, though in a manner that is qualified by the related character of truth. Bradley writes, "Error is truth, it is partial truth, that is false only because partial and left incomplete. The Absolute has without subtraction all those qualities, and it has every arrangement which we seem to confer upon it by our mere mistake."[64] Logically or experientially this inclusion is demanded by the Absolute if reality is not to be considered discordant or inconsistent with itself, but how this is so, Bradley admits, is impossible to perceive: "We cannot understand how in the Absolute a rich harmony embraces every special discord. But ... we may be sure that this result is reached; and we can even gain an imperfect view of the effective principle."[65] This last statement indicates the fideistic aspect of Bradley's philosophy that is demanded by the features of his philosophical vision or what Stephen Carr calls his "religious faith."[66] The unity or inclusion of all things within the Absolute remains a postulate of all experience – intellectual, moral, and emotional – but it recedes beyond human apprehension; it must exist, even though it cannot be grasped.[67]

Bradley and Religious Faith

In philosophical terms Bradley did not go much beyond what Green had already laid out in his *Prolegomena*, but unlike Green he did not feel the need to engage Christian doctrines or the scriptures in any significant manner. He was not necessarily hostile to traditional faith; however, when put in Mansel's terms, Bradley was more inclined to speak his mind clearly. Though it doesn't mention Mansel by name, if Collingwood is right, it is hard to imagine who else might have been the target of this judgment:

> Present your doctrine in a form which will bear criticism, and which will enable me to understand this confused mass of facts which I encounter on all sides. Do this, and I will follow you, and I will worship the source of such a true revelation. But I will not accept nonsense for reality, though it be vouched for by miracle, or proceeds from the mouth of a psychological monster.[68]

While Bradley had a place for certain Christian doctrines,[69] in general the whole thrust of his philosophy is that creedal or scriptural Christianity represents a one-sided view of reality that cannot possibly unite or embrace the fragmentary and expansive character of the experienced world:

> Religion seems to have included and reduced to harmony every aspect of life. It appears to be a whole which has embraced, and which pervades, every detail. But in the end we are forced to admit that contradiction remains. For, if the whole is still good, it is not harmonious; and, if it has gone beyond goodness, it has carried us also beyond religion.[70]

Whereas Mansel argued that the scriptures mirror the difficult and insoluble contradictions of the world, even while referring to God's providential presence in history, Bradley regarded these difficulties as intolerable inconsistencies.

His argument is aimed at the whole scriptural account of God's character in history, which he seems happy to summarize in the phrase of God's personality, though toward the end of his life he expressed some hesitation in this regard:

I shall assume here, rightly or wrongly, that a personal God is not the ultimate truth about the Universe, and that the ultimate truth would be included and superceded by something higher than personality ... The religious consciousness must represent to itself the Good will in its relation with mine. It must express both our difference and our unity. And must not, it will be asked, that representation take the form of a personal God? I answer that to insist here on this must to myself seems untenable, but on the other hand I am fully prepared to accept "may."[71]

But if Bradley expressed some doubt, it was not because he was tempted by more scriptural accounting of reality; it is more likely that he had been influenced by the personalist trajectory within idealism itself.[72] It remained the case that Bradley fundamentally did not believe that Christian orthodoxy was broad enough to account for the diversity of experience or phenomena, though he allowed that, for practical purposes, perhaps certain religious beliefs were unavoidable. As in all of life, people must "select arbitrarily those ideas which seem best to suit the occasion,"[73] however they might distort the whole. But if unavoidable for practical purposes, metaphysically speaking the personality of God, for Bradley, cannot help but distort the truth: "If in short for religion you need a personal God, you must accept also a creed which is not consistent."[74] Because in the end, "The Universe is a living whole which, apart from violence and partial death, refuses to divide itself into well-defined objects and clean cut distinctions."[75]

It seems Bradley could tolerate Christian doctrines and their practical use, but he could not accept the metaphysical grounding, or lack thereof, in which Mansel tried to situate them. Of course, what Bradley really wanted was a new religion: "We need a creed to recognize and justify in due proportion all human interests, and at the same time to supply the intellect with that to which it can hold with confidence."[76] While Bradley tried to move beyond the project of dividing and distinguishing the world for which Mansel was noted, in a certain sense he only replaced one kind of faith with another. According to Collingwood, Bradley's real accomplishment is that he affirmed that the world of appearances is in fact real[77] but that reality is still received in faith in the Absolute, a reality that is at best only partially perceived, though demanded by his metaphysics. The popular perception that traditional Christian notions of God were too constrictive or limiting found a profound expression in Bradley's metaphysics, though, for all his efforts in establishing the Absolute as the foundation of reality, his philosophy is really another form of immanentism that denies the supernatural character of religion. Collingwood makes this very point: "*Appearance and Reality*, instead of the last word of a decaying idealism, is the manifesto of a new Realism."[78] Mansel's epistemology, despite its weaknesses, still preserved two orders of knowing that corresponded to created reality and the supernatural, in some manner. Bradley retains the structure of the known and unknown, but he encloses all of reality within the realm of appearance, even though appearance is somehow real. There is a similarity here perhaps with Berkeley, who blurred distinctions between ideas such as force and theological notions like grace, but Berkeley's idealism rooted terms like "grace" in a theological context that ensured their scriptural or doctrinal meaning. For Bradley, the context of the Absolute does the opposite: it ensures that such theological terms will be dissolved in the perpetual shifting and sliding of meaning within the world of appearance. This had to be true for Bradley because of his fundamental conviction that Christian orthodoxy could no longer offer an adequate account of the world. In particular, the Christian God could no longer satisfy the definitional demands of a deity in the modern world. This was the challenge that the *Lux Mundi* theologians were faced with, and the demands that this pressure placed on their theology will be the subject of the following sections.

LUX MUNDI

The relationship of idealists like Green and Bradley to the *Lux Mundi* theologians is not straightforward: whatever influence idealism had on the Oxford churchmen was marked by ambivalence, at times hesitance, and the necessary constraints of Christian orthodoxy. The *Lux Mundi* writers were deeply concerned with traditional Christian witness and the integrity of the scriptures, so it was not without serious alteration that idealism was able inform their theology. Nevertheless, the concern of Green and Bradley to articulate a holistic or comprehensive vision of reality – whether tethered to the Absolute or the eternal consciousness – deeply informed the incarnational theology of *Lux Mundi*. It is this aspect of incarnational theology that has since been perpetually controversial. In the words of Michael Ramsay,

When the Incarnation becomes the center of theological system and exposition, the result may be a deep and rich orthodoxy standing firmly upon a biblical basis, yet with a tendency for other biblical themes to recede. There is no doubt this happened in the first years of the twentieth century. Again, the art of presenting the orthodox faith in close relation to a civilization dominated by the ideas of moral and social progress can unwittingly cause the Christian teacher to blind his eye to the perspectives of grace, judgment, wrath, mercy which the Bible presents.[79]

If this "tendency" had become clear by the beginning of the twentieth century, it was less obvious what the outcome of the *Lux Mundi* vision would be. In part, I argue, this was because the theologians in this volume, in an effort to resist the full outcomes of idealism, made use of arguments that closely resembled Mansel's concerning the nature of religious knowledge and the character of scripture. However, if the biblical themes of "grace, judgment, wrath [and] mercy" did at times recede behind the generalizing concept of the incarnation, it was because the theologians of the incarnation shared a hostility with Green and Bradley for the so-called "narrow" or dualistic theology of Mansel or the tradition he represented. In other words, the struggle for a comprehensive Christian theology of reality that takes place in the pages of *Lux Mundi* plays on imprecise or inconsistent notions of human knowledge and scriptural language. This imprecision stemmed from a conflict of interest between satisfying the comprehensive needs of idealism and maintaining the internal coherence of the scriptural account of God's relation to the world.

HISTORY AND THE KNOWLEDGE OF GOD

Like Mansel, the theologians of *Lux Mundi* were anxious to illustrate that the world they lived in could still be described and encompassed in the traditional terms of the Christian faith. For Mansel this required a certain form of skepticism, which would appear in various guises within the pages of *Lux Mundi*, even while it was enhanced and altered by the skepticism of Green and Bradley. While these Oxford theologians could speak about the limitations of human thought and the accommodated language of scripture, the metaphysics of progress, adapted into a theology of the incarnation, created difficulties for scriptural interpretation. In part, this was because the moral and historical difficulties of scripture became relativized in the process of historical development. What this means will become clearer in the following section.

This conflict was especially apparent in the writings of Brooke Foss Westcott, not a contributor to *Lux Mundi* but a figure who is referenced frequently within its pages.[80] In the words of S.C. Carpenter, *Lux Mundi* was the book "Westcott and his friends planned to write after *Essays and Reviews*."[81] While Westcott's influences were wide-ranging – continental idealism, Platonism, German biblical criticism, to name a few – it is interesting to note that when speaking about the knowledge of God, Westcott used language that was identical to Mansel's.[82] Yet he made adjustments that altered the implications of Mansel's ideas. For example, in the *Gospel of the Resurrection*, Westcott writes,

We speak of God as Infinite and Personal. The epithets involve a contradiction, and yet they are both necessary. In fact the only approximately adequate conception which we can form of a Divine Being is under the form of a contradiction.[83]

Even Westcott's definition of personality is indistinguishable from Mansel's – the action of the will and the idea of resistance to external realities.[84] Likewise, Westcott insists, much like for Mansel, that conception requires a sensible intuition, and yet the world constantly presses against the negative and suggestive limit of perceptible experience.[85]

However, despite the similarities between the two men, Westcott's appeal to progress in history subtly altered Mansel's understanding of scriptural language as a permanent accommodated witness to God's character.[86] The incarnation in particular was a way for Westcott to maintain Mansel's epistemological distinction between speculative and regulative knowledge of God and yet move beyond it through the immanent presence of Christ in history. In other words, development becomes a bridge between the two realms, though a bridge that never quite reaches the other side:

The Truth itself is infinite, and it is simply because the powers of man are imperfect and finite that any development is necessary. He can only realize step by step, and by successive efforts, what is indeed from the beginning. According to the position in which he finds himself, he takes now this, now that fragment of the whole, because it meets his wants. Every embodiment of the Truth must be wrought out in this way. And the nearest approximation which we can form to the complete truth is by the combination of the partial realizations of it which history records.[87]

This development of knowledge is made possible through Christ's incarnate presence in history, and the incarnation becomes, in this sense, an epistemological category: "By the Incarnation it gives permanent reality to human knowledge; by the Resurrection it gives permanent reality to human life."[88] Truth, in the absolute sense, becomes partially realizable in history because of the affirmation of humanity in general in the incarnation.

Westcott measure these developments in history in two ways. The first is reminiscent of Hegel:

The slow unfolding of life enables us to discern new meaning in His presence. In His humanity is included whatever belongs to the consummation of the individual and of the race, not only in one stage but in all stages of progress, not only in regard to some endowments but in regard to the whole inheritance of our nature enlarged by the most vigorous use while the world lasts.[89]

The "vigour" and "consummation" of human nature represent the best of humanity, elevated and sustained in Christ's assumption of flesh and guaranteed a place in the history of humanity's development toward God. The second criterion is, perhaps, the more obvious: "The providence of God is at every stage interpreted by His Word. The spirit of the Resurrection tries and transfigures each transitory embodiment of Truth."[90] Scripture, then, functions as a criterion for the measurement and assessment of the broader scope of human development.

Westcott's understanding of the incarnation and the knowledge of God comes nearer to the negative consequences that critics worried were the outcome of Mansel's lectures: regulative truths cannot refer to God in any direct manner. While Westcott uses different language, his emphasis upon the constantly expanding implications of the incarnation force him to place qualifications on historical knowledge because any truth claimed in time must be penultimate in the overall scheme of progress. Mansel tried to accommodate historical change within the expansive nature of scriptural language, whereas Westcott makes use of the incarnation, a perhaps more flexible and dexterous category. For example, Westcott writes in *Christus Consummator* that the real unbelief of the Hebrew people was that they failed to attune themselves to the march of history: "The Hebrews were, as we have seen, in danger of apostasy because they failed to go forward. And that we may be shielded from the like peril, the words which were spoken to them are spoken also to us."[91] The failure to move forward is a failure to recognize the character of God's activity in the world.

Furthermore, Westcott regarded the incarnation as a theological equivalent to the Copernican revolution; the incarnation was a pivot from which all knowledge could now be arranged and illuminated.[92] It is in this light that Westcott's ambivalence to traditional Christian claims comes through:

> It may be that in our day of trial we shall fail to apprehend the new messages of widening wisdom; that we shall cling blindly to fixed traditional forms of opinion which do not correspond with the requirements of our spiritual position; that we shall seek to confine within artificial limits, through timorous distrust, that which is a powerful of infinite growth.[93]

The demands of the age and the belief in a "widening wisdom" that they provoke place "traditional forms" within some kind of limbo. Though Westcott was unwilling to deny the permanence of creedal claims or scriptural language, it is primarily the concept of the incarnation that is capable of "infinite growth." Even Spencer's naturalism was collectible in the expanding universe of the incarnation.[94]

It is in this sense that Westcott was torn between two skepticisms: though he affirmed Mansel's version of the limitations of human thinking, he did so, in part, to make room for the continual adjustment of knowledge that history affords. While his writings often wavered between the two forms of skepticism, the overall picture that emerges in Westcott is not unlike the vision of Green or of Bradley, with Christian terms substituted for the more vague and remote terms of English idealism. Westcott's goal was to cast the Christian vision wide enough to include everything – most pertinently, the rapid intellectual and social changes of his own era. However, it could be argued that the incarnation, in Westcott's rendering, stands loosely at times from the subtle and complicated features of the scriptural narrative. This will become clearer in figures like Talbot and Illingworth, who relied on Westcott for their providential scheme of development.

Development and Personality

Much like Westcott, J.R. Illingworth, in his essay on development in *Lux Mundi*, regards the incarnation as a discovery that provides a comprehensive theological vision of all reality in the face of a narrow doctrinal tradition. Illingworth writes,

> the religion of the Incarnation was narrowed into the religion of the Atonement. Men's views of the faith dwindled and became subjective and self-regarding, while the gulf was daily widened between things sacred and things secular; among which latter, art and science, and the whole political and social order, gradually came to be classed.[95]

Illingworth's point is not that science, art, and politics are to be merely included within the incarnate reality but that the incarnation is the sum and goal of these cultural movements:

> The man of science, as such, can discover the uniformities of His action in external nature. The moral philosopher will further see that these actions make for righteousness and that there is a moral law. But it is only to the spiritual yearning of our whole personality that He reveals Himself as a person.[96]

In some way this statement is a typical instance of an idealist philosophy that tries to put science in its places without discarding its methods and discoveries: science is a piece of a larger whole.[97] Illingworth's method for doing this involves the whole complex of language that is at the heart of Mansel's theology – personality, anthropomorphism, analogy – and in the case of science, he seems happy to have these terms carry the meaning that Mansel intended.

However, the turn to personality in English idealism came not through Mansel but through Hermann Lotze, a post-Kantian logician from Germany who was widely read in England.[98] For Lotze, personality becomes a state that is perfected only in God:

When treating of "Omnipresence" allusion was made to the truth, that God, who is the truly Existent in all Things and comprises them all as mere modifications of his Being, stands in need of no mediation through transmitted effects, in order to be acquainted with the individual elements of the world and the states belonging to them.[99]

Because this unmediated state is not true of finite beings, "Perfect personality is compatible only with the conception of an Infinite Being; for finite beings only an approximation to this is attainable."[100] In his book *Personality, Human and Divine,* Illingworth draws on Mansel's argument about the basic and irreducible reality of human personality,[101] but he extends the notion of personality as a necessary description of the being of God:

> Whereas the Christian doctrine, however mysterious, moves in the direction, at least, of conceivability, for the simple reason that it is the very thing towards which our own personality points. Our own personality is triune; but it is a potential, unrealized triunity, which is incomplete in itself, and must go beyond itself for completion, as, for example, in the family.[102]

Human personality has a triune character that has emerged throughout history in concert with development or revelation of God's own personality.

In contrast then to Green and Bradley, Illingworth follows Lotze in affirming the personality of the Absolute: "it is certainly foolish to prefer to assign the Supreme Principle of the world to an unconscious blind substratum, the conception of which is for us, strictly speaking, something completely dark and inscrutable."[103] While for Green the process of the world moves toward the ineffability of God, Illingworth argues that the world is moving toward the perfect expression of personality, affirmed in Christ and drawn into the very life of God.[104]

So while Illingworth, much like Mansel, affirms the personality of God as a corrective to early idealist notions of God's ineffability or impersonal nature, he transfers the idea of personhood into yet another concept that requires history to become gradually concrete.[105] A reviewer for the *Church Quarterly* noted, in Manselian fashion, "The mystery and incompleteness of our personality in the view of our

intellects is the characteristic which fits it to be the channel of our
access to God and of his access to us."[106] Personality for Mansel was
a negative outline of how human beings encounter the world, an
inscrutable mystery that cannot be accounted for but which God
encounters and enters into. Furthermore, this encounter cannot be
conceptualized outside the full range of Scripture. Yet, for Illingworth,
characteristic of so much incarnational theology, history becomes
about one essential thing: the converging realization of divine and
human personality in time. The history of the Jews and the Greeks
alike is about the desire for and partial attainment of these concepts.

Scripture and Development

Both Westcott and Illingworth employed aspects of Mansel's thought
in order to situate their orthodox convictions within an idealistic
framework or, in Westcott's case, a blend of idealism and Platonism.[107]
To this end, both writers were emphatically traditional in their defense
of orthodox scriptural claims. However, there was a tendency with
many writers of the period to blame rigid and outdated doctrines for
the emerging diffidence toward Christianity while attempting to lift
the scriptures into a more tolerable historical scheme. It was not that
the *Lux Mundi* theologians believed that the Old Testament, for
example, contained difficulties that could be brushed aside, but within
a progressive metaphysics it was possible to isolate certain scriptural
realities within the past. But this isolation was carried out only piecemeal and when necessary. In this respect, the *Lux Mundi* writers,
much like Westcott, wavered between two forms of epistemological
skepticism, and as a result, their attitudes toward the Bible present,
at times, a confusing picture.

E.S. Talbot's essay on "Preparation for Christ in History" is a direct
extension of Westcott's providential scheme: the history of the Greeks
and Jews coalesce in preparation for the person of Christ.[108] This
patristic notion became more than just a providential appeal to Christ's
universality, but even more, this two-fold preparation acted as a
conceptual dialectic that is fulfilled in Christ. Again, according to
Talbot, it is historical process that provides a comprehensive vision
of all reality:

It may seem ... that stricter canons of interpretation forbid for
us that unbounded use of the happy expedient of allegory which

could make everything in the Old Testament speak of Christ. But even if this were so ... is there no countervailing gain to reckon? Have we any reason to hope that our time may be suffered to do ... something for the interpretation of the witness of history to Christ which has not been done before, and which is even an advance upon what has been done? Let us consider for a moment ... what it is which specially engrosses the interest and admiration of all of us in the different branches of modern study and enquiry. It is the beauty of process.[109]

Here Talbot at least states what is implicit throughout *Lux Mundi*: if any continuity can be established between the Old Testament and Christ, it is more likely to be found in the process of development than in a textual coherence that is established by typology or allegory. Though, to be sure, Talbot cannot discard these traditional methods entirely, at least in the obvious cases of prophecy.

But the main force of Israel's preparation for Christ lies in its essential idea of personal communion with God.[110] This is much like Mansel, only in Mansel's case, personal communion with God receives its shape and form from the character of scripture, whereas for Talbot once the ideal is reached it is unclear what happens to the history that prepared it. For example, Talbot writes,

even the very instruments which He was using in the present, the Anointed King, the chosen Royal House, the Prophet-Servant of God, the holy hill of Zion, were charged with a meaning of which the significance was only in the future to become clear. Thus, in this free, deep, spiritual – let us say it – inspired manner, the predictions of prophecy emerge and gather shape.[111]

On one hand, Talbot's description of the biblical images recalls Mansel's notion of scriptural expansion, the gathering of meaning under certain types and symbols. But they remain in part "present instruments," and instruments that are bound up with only one of the great preparations for Christ:

The two preparations pursue their course unconscious of one another, almost exclusive of one another. Greek wisdom and Roman power have no dream of coming to receive from the narrow national cult of humbled and subject Israel. And Israel, even taught by the great prophets, could hardly find a place in her vision of the future for any destiny of the nations of the world.[112]

The shortcomings of each preparation are augmented by the other. The features of the "narrow national cult" of Israel lack the universal aspect that Greek and Roman wisdom could supply the incarnate reality of Christ. The Old Testament is almost a stream that feeds into the coming of Christ – a critical stream, but not the primary narrative itself.

The implications of this view perhaps become clearer in Scott Holland. Holland's essay on faith, like Illingworth's and the others, establishes communion with God as the central controlling concept of Christian faith. Faith is about the gradual grasping of humanity's inherent "sonship," which is "germinal" and constantly seeking its fulfillment in God.[113] All of life is an expression of this impulse toward unity with God: "New knowledge, new experience, far from expunging the elements of faith, make ever fresh demands upon it; they constitute perpetual appeals to it to enlarge its trust, to expand its original audacity."[114] Again, the versatile or expansive category in Christian theology is faith itself and its widening range of apprehension. Faith, for Holland, almost has a story of its own:

> For our faith in Christ becomes the measure and standard of our faith in the Bible. We believe in it as the record of our growing intimacy with God. Faith is, still, a spiritual cohesion of person with person, of the living soul with a living God. No details that intervene confuse this primitive relation. Only, that cohesion was not reached at one leap. It is ancient: it has traversed many incidents and trials: it has learned much: it has undergone patient apprenticeship: it has been bonded by the memory of multitudinous vicissitudes.[115]

Though Holland considered himself a Butlerian, this aspect of his thought is far closer to Coleridge.[116] Though it is not untrue that spiritual "cohesion" is at the heart of the scriptural narrative, scripture's ability to identify the character of God's activity with respect to this union becomes washed out in a conceptual generalization.

For this reason, Holland's appeal to Butler is a little curious. In some respect, he transforms Butler into Bradley:

Butler thus reaches his characteristic conclusion, that every possible act of knowledge reveals itself as being but partial and incomplete. He defies you to know even this world that lies within our human experience, without knowing something of the world that lies beyond it. For every atom that exists demands the entire Universe to explain it.[117]

Knowledge is always many sided and requires the whole to explain the part. But in the case of revelation, human ignorance of the whole scheme of salvation, for Butler, is precisely why human reason is unable to sort through the record of scripture and discard the unpleasant or discordant aspects. Yet, this is exactly where Holland cannot follow Butler:

> While ... asserting the supreme authority of Conscience in moral judgements, he manages to withdraw from the range of its verdict all the particular incidents in the Old Testament that offend, by refusing it the right to pronounce until it knows the ultimate and determining issue. And this it cannot know, without knowing the whole of things in Revelation. Such an argument, so pressed, cannot carry conviction.[118]

Yet this aspect of Butler was decisive for Mansel: while reason is fit to judge the contents of revelation, the main function of reason is to establish its own limits. For both Butler and Mansel, it is not that the Old Testament presents immoral facts about God that must be swallowed whole, but rather, these facts cannot be wholly judged upon the limited information that humans hold.

Holland's contention with Butler is an appropriate example of the *Lux Mundi* approach. The theologians of the incarnation were eager to affirm the history of salvation but unsure of how to render details of God's relationship with Israel. Holland can speak of the "multitudinous vicissitudes" of faith's history, but this does not quite capture the structure of God's covenanted relationship with Israel and the complications of blessings and curses, promises, election, judgment and mercy. Though he speaks of "offensive" moments, in the case of the Old Testament, it is not at all clear where these moments begin and end. The theological skepticism of Mansel, and that of Butler, allowed these features to stand out clearly and not become lost in a historical process that always leads beyond itself. But it is not just Mansel's high tolerance for offensive truths that separated him from writers like Holland; these respective attitudes toward the Old Testament obviously played a critical role in determining Anglican Christology.

Christ and the Atonement

The argument that I have pursued thus far is that the *Lux Mundi* theologians, like Westcott before them, laboured to place Christian orthodoxy within an idealistic framework that adhered to a progressive metaphysics of knowledge and history. However, where the pressures of idealism placed the Christian faith in certain difficulties, they resorted to categories used by Mansel: personality, the limitations of thought and the accommodated character of scriptural language. But this appeal to Mansel, or to ideas represented by Mansel, was done in an *ad hoc* fashion that often confused two different forms of epistemological skepticism. To some degree, this confusion might have been harmless; by and large, these theologians were not prepared to compromise orthodox claims in the face of cultural criticisms. If there is a danger in the *Lux Mundi* method though, it comes precisely at the point where they imagined themselves to be the strongest. The theology of the incarnation was intended to be a way of absorbing a changing world into a theologically comprehensive vision, a vision that was becoming increasingly incredible. Whether in the marginalization of the Old Testament as an account of God's character or the incessant attacks upon the language of the atonement, the *Lux Mundi* writers actually made it more difficult to perceive how the God of the Bible was related to the modern world.

Of all the *Lux Mundi* writers, Charles Gore was perhaps the most sensitive to the difficulties of their position. While he endorsed the same historical scheme of providence as did Talbot and Illingworth,[119] he was eager to show that the Old Testament functioned as Christian scripture and not just as a preparatory religion. For example, in his *Lux Mundi* essay he writes that while Christ is the "test and measure" of the Old Testament's inspiration, the strange and difficult portions of the Old Testament have a secure place in the gradual spiritual education of mankind:

Thus to believe ... in the inspiration of the Old Testament
forces us to recognise a real element of the Divine education in
the imprecatory Psalms. They are not the utterances of selfish
spite: they are the claim which righteous Israel makes upon
God that He should vindicate Himself, and let their eyes see
how righteousness turns again unto judgment. The claim is
made in a form which belongs to an early stage of spiritual
education; to a time when this life was regarded as the scene in
which God must finally vindicate Himself, and when the large
powers and possibilities of the Divine compassion were very
imperfectly recognised. But behind these limitations, which
characterize the greater part of the Old Testament, the claim
of these Psalms still remains a necessary part of the claim of
the Christian soul.[120]

The limitations that Gore speaks of are quite simply the datedness of
the Old Testament and its historical position prior to the incarnation.
Though Gore tries to make a place for the imprecatory psalms in this
case, they can only function as revelatory moments in a scheme that
has moved on. In other words, what they say about God is entirely
unclear. Christopher Seitz makes this very point concerning Gore's
writing on scripture:

The problem is that the writers of the New Testament did not
inquire into the religion of the Old Testament, any more than
"our Lord" did. This did not have to do with kenotic accommodation or some other condescension to human categories. It had
to do with the actual character of God as revealed by the scriptures, according to which Jesus' life, death and raising were
calibrated and acknowledged as fulfilled.[121]

Gore, like Mansel, uses the category of accommodation, but in the
case of the Old Testament, Gore regards the accommodation or condescension of God's character to be directed at a people of inferior
moral development. Even more, the claim of the imperfection of the
Old Testament and the finality of the New, though not in itself unusual,
makes it difficult for Gore to understand how the Old Testament
could speak about God and how this knowledge could be clarified
or integrated with the revelation of Christ.[122]

While Gore has become well known for attempting to protect the New Testament from certain forms of criticism,[123] his particular doctrine of kenosis in relation to Christ's self-knowledge represents an exception. Just as the language of the Old Testament was lodged, to some extent, in a particular history, so certain aspects of Christ's language in the Bible become a symptom of the limitations of the age in which He lived:

> He willed so to restrain the beams of Deity as to observe the lim-
> its of the science of His age, and He puts Himself in the same
> relation to its historical knowledge. Thus He does not reveal
> His eternity by statements as to what had happened in the past,
> or was to happen in the future, outside the ken of existing his-
> tory. He made His Godhead gradually manifest by His attitude
> towards men and things about Him, by His moral and spiritual
> claims, by His expressed relation to His Father, not by any
> miraculous exemptions of Himself from the conditions of natu-
> ral knowledge in its own proper province.[124]

Textually speaking, Gore had some warrant perhaps for this claim: "But about that day and hour no one knows, neither the angels of heaven, nor the Son, but only the Father" (Matthew 24:36, NRSV). With respect to certain scientific observations as well, Gore's claim carried a degree of plausibility. But all the same, as a principle it introduces a division within the scriptural portrait of Christ and the Old Testament references and images that are used to describe his ministry. Darwell Stone wrote in response to Gore that "the acceptance of our Lord of the main features in the ordinary Jewish belief about the Old Testament Scriptures seems to be fundamental to his teach-ing."[125] Stone contends that even the "inspired" writings of the proph-ets, for Gore, represented simply an intensification of their human faculties[126] and only a general extent of foreknowledge that was limited by the prophet's place in the development of the world.[127] Yet surely, Stone argues, much like Mansel, "It is possible that a prophet might be led ... to utter words in reference to some event near at hand which, unknown to him, were destined to have a fuller accomplish-ment in the life of Christ."[128]

The effect of Gore's theory of kenotic accommodation was that it weakened the textual coherence of scripture's witness to Christ across both Testaments. Furthermore, it provided a method to discard or diminish certain aspects of Christ's identity that were drawn from the Old Testament, though Gore himself was not eager to pursue this course. In relation to Mansel, Gore's theory of accommodation is striking, not least for the identity of the term used. But Gore, in this case, at least understood that there was a distinction in the manner of use. In his "Bampton Lectures" on the incarnation, Gore made the following statement concerning Mansel:

> Some thirty-three years ago, a great controversy was originated in this pulpit by a Bampton lecturer, who took for his subject, "The limits of religious thought." Dean Mansel held in little esteem the pretensions of the Hegelian school in Germany to criticize by the standard of rationality the contents of divine revelation. Revelation, he held, was a fact ... Unfortunately Mansel did not confine himself to reemphasizing Butler's strong protest, as valuable today as in the last century, against the easy overestimate of the powers of the human mind to judge a priori of what is probable in a divine revelation. He went further, and exposed himself to the charge of denying that we have, or can have, any real and direct knowledge of God Himself at all. "We cannot know what God is," he seemed to say, "but only what He chooses us to believe about Himself." Thus we cannot, for example, argue against a certain doctrine of the atonement on the ground of its injustice or hardness, because we do not know what justice or goodness in God means. Human qualities are not necessarily of the same sort as the divine. This form of Christian apology produced an indignant protest from Frederick Denison Maurice, and drew from John Stuart Mill the passionate exclamation: "I will call no being good who is not what I mean when I apply that epithet to my fellow-creatures, and if such a being can sentence me to hell for not so calling him, to hell I will go." It was an exclamation, not easy to accommodate to the philosophy of the greatest pleasure, but it finds a response without a doubt in the Christian conscience. For if anthropomorphism as applied to God is false, if God does not exist in man's image, yet theomorphism as applied to man is true; man is made in God's image, and his qualities are, not the measure of the divine, but their counterpart and real expression. Man was made in God's image. The significance of this truth from our present point of view is, that in that original constitution of manhood lies, as the

Fathers saw, the prophecy of the divine Incarnation and the grounds of its possibility. God can express Himself in His own image, He can express Himself therefore in manhood, He can show Himself as man. And conversely, in the occurrence of the Incarnation lies the supreme evidence of the real moral likeness of man to God. All along, through the Old Testament, inspired teachers with growing spirituality of conception had been expressing God in terms of manhood taking the human love of the mother for her child, or of the husband for his adulterous wife, to explain the divine love: and in the Incarnation all this finds its justification ... His qualities are human qualities, love and justice, self sacrifice and desire and compassion; yet they are the qualities of none other than the very God. So akin are God and man to one another that God can really exist under conditions of manhood without ceasing to be God ... Here in Christ Jesus, it is man's will, man's love, man's mind, which are the instruments of Godhead and the fullness of the Godhead which is revealing itself only, it seems, to make these qualities more intensely human.[129]

This is a peculiar statement for a number of reasons. First, Gore justifies his theory of accommodation because of the preexisting continuity between humanity and God, which is based upon the image. For this reason human qualities can serve as descriptors of God's character, at least in the realm of moral action. But when it comes to knowledge, whatever fitness or continuity that exists between God and humanity is clearly broken; this is, in the end, the logic of accommodation because there must be a discontinuity between the two to justify the use of the term. In other words, Christ's knowledge about the world and history cannot be fully trusted, but His actions and teaching, however construed, provide a direct indication of God's being.

Second, it seems clear that Gore misread Mansel, especially at the point where he draws Mansel into contrast with Butler. Surprisingly, Gore seems to draw the same conclusion that Mansel observed in Hume: "He thus reduces the controversy to a choice of two alternatives: either the Divine attributes are identical with the human, or they have nothing at all in common."[130] It is not that Mansel did not believe in the image of God, but he believed that the image could not be employed, on its own strength and logic, as a cipher for delimiting Christian and scriptural claims.[131] This is Butler's position as well. It is true, as Gore claims, that Butler said that human reason can function as a judge of revelation, but this conviction does not operate for Butler as Gore might have wished. On the question of the atonement, Butler vigorously upheld the vicariousness and ceremonial or sacrificial elements of Christ's death as both scriptural and, in one sense, reasonable.[132] While in the end, every person will be responsible for his or her own sin, "during the progress, and, for ought we know, even in order to the completion of this moral scheme, vicarious punishment may be fit, and absolutely necessary."[133] The point for Butler is that human ignorance of the entire scheme does not permit human beings to discard elements that are not pleasing to their reason or moral sympathies.

Finally, it is in the issue of the atonement of Christ that Gore's method comes to fruition. If the imprecatory psalms and other difficult portions of the Old Testament belong to an age when God related to a people of inferior moral development, it is not clear how the framework of Old Testament language used in the New Testament to describe Jesus's work on the cross can continue to inform that work. For Mansel the language of scripture was accommodated to the permanent fallen state of humanity, and for this reason, the language retains a permanence across the spectrum of historical change. Scripture, in Mansel's sense, is a God-given language that can adapt and expand through the power of the Spirit, but the givenness cannot be altered. But Gore's skepticism applied to the scriptural language as such, and though he may have tried to protect the New Testament from the pressures of criticisms, his treatment of the Old Testament had already profoundly affected his reading of the Gospel and Epistle records.

It must be admitted that arguments for various readings of the atonement have always been made within a context of scriptural latitude. Scripture, it would seem, contains overlapping images to portray Christ's work on the cross and his resurrection. The irony of the *Lux Mundi* portrayal of the atonement, and in this case Arthur Lyttelton's, was that while the authors maligned certain narrow renderings of atonement theology – substitutionary atonement in particular – they excluded at least one set of scriptural images in order to make their case.

But of course, it was not the intention of the *Lux Mundi* writers to commit to a particular tradition of atonement theology, but rather they wished to widen the doctrine by setting it within a certain set of relations determined by their theology of the incarnation. Lyttelton, then, in his essay on the atonement, sounds much like Illingworth, Talbot, Holland, and Gore:

> What we call particular doctrines are in reality only various applications to various human conditions of one great uniform method of Divine government, which is the expression in human affairs of one Divine will. The theological statement of any part of this method ought to bear on its face the marks of the whole from which it is temporarily separated; for though it may be necessary to make now this, now that doctrine prominent, to isolate it and lay stress on it, this should be done in such a way that in each special truth the whole should, in a manner, be contained. We must be able to trace out in each the lines of the Divine action which is only fully displayed in the whole. Neglect of this not only makes our faith as a whole weak and incoherent, but deprives the doctrines themselves of the illumination and strength which are afforded by the discovery in them of mutual likeness and harmony. They become first unintelligible and then inconceivable, and the revelation of the character of God, which should be perceived in every part of His dealings with men, becomes confused and dim to us. This has been especially the case with the Atonement.[134]

Such a statement really represents the overarching theme of the entire volume, and at the same time it makes any appeal to Butler by the *Lux Mundi* authors somewhat doubtful: for Butler, or for Mansel, there is no whole outside the scriptures upon which individual doctrines can be assessed. Rather, scripture presents a fragmentary outline of a scheme that is only imperfectly comprehended. However, for Lyttelton to lift the doctrine of atonement from its relative isolation requires denying aspects of the only source available for its articulation. This was Darwell Stone's point in *The Church Quarterly Review*: "However impossible it may be to frame an exact theory of the method of the Atonement, we feel it to be necessary to retain the idea of 'substitution' itself, the belief that Christ suffered in our stead."[135] On one hand, Lyttelton would seem to agree with Stone's assessment that the atonement is difficult to conceive in theory and that it must be guided by the scriptural imagery:

> It may well be that here we are confronted by the final mystery, and that the propitiatory virtue of Christ's death, typified by the

slaying of animal victims under the law, foreshadowed by the almost universal belief in the expiation of blood, acknowledged with wondering gratitude by the human heart, depends upon the unsearchable will and hidden purposes of God.[136]

Yet despite this affirmation of a certain theological method, Lyttelton is able to deny that "the work of Christ consisted in His endurance of our punishment in order that we might not endure it."[137] The vicariousness of the atonement lies not in Christ's bearing of humanity's sins or the penalty of these sins, but in His offering of the sacrifice that no human being could offer.[138]

Lyttelton's view may not be outside the boundaries of possible interpretations, but it does resolutely deny any substitutionary role in Christ's death. Whatever is meant in 1 Peter 2:24 (NRSV) – "He himself bore our sins in his body on the cross" – what it cannot mean is clear: Christ cannot bear a judgment on sin on behalf of others. In Lyttelton's mind, his rendering of the atonement lifted the doctrine out of its narrow confines and placed it within a larger incarnational metaphysics. Much like for Bradley or Green, if a doctrine cannot be related to the whole, then it begins to obscure and dismember the truth. In this case it seems that for Lyttelton, integrating the atonement into a larger incarnational worldview required him to obscure the doctrine's relation to the whole of scripture and the textual setting in which Christ's work on the cross is situated within the New Testament.

The slight adjustment of details in atonement theology was a matter of immense importance for someone like Lyttelton, who believed that substitutionary theories of the atonement were responsible for the escalation of unbelief in the nineteenth century.[139] The substitutionary model made God the Father appear wrathful and vengeful, and, according to Lyttelton, this model placed modern Christians in a situation of conflict between their consciences and certain traditional beliefs.[140] Aubrey Moore placed the blame squarely on Calvin's disproportionate emphasis on the power of God: "Calvin writes in an Old Testament atmosphere when he speaks of God."[141] As many others of his generation did, Moore sided emphatically with J.S. Mill's protest against Mansel.[142] Even more, he suggested that Mill "might have been a loyal member of the Church of Christ, if, when he was asking for the bread of Christ, Calvinistic teachers had not given him a stone."[143] Of course, Mansel was not a Calvinist in the least, but his name had become a symbol of a voluntaristic and irrational theology.[144] But in his own eyes, Mansel was not defending a particular idea of God, but he was defending the ability of scripture to refer credibly to God's character, whether in the blessings and curses of Deuteronomy, the settlement of Canaan, or the prophetic warnings and judgments against the nation of Israel.

As in Mansel's conflict with Maurice, the *Lux Mundi* writers focused in upon the atonement as a symbolic instance that represented a whole host of moral objections to the Christian God. These objections, according to Green and Bradley, were related to the character of truth and the particularity of the scriptural narrative: any true account of reality must be open and transparent toward the whole, a whole that is ultimately indescribable. The *Lux Mundi* theologians employed the same method, but they filled the placeholder of the absolute or eternal consciousness with a generalized notion of the incarnation. It was not so much that Lyttelton and others overplayed the incarnation in their essays but rather that the incarnation, as they rendered it, was not in fact flexible enough to account for the whole range of scriptural realities. Ironically, a method that was intended as a broader approach to Christian orthodoxy in the end closed off certain scriptural possibilities. The inability of the writers to make any place for substitutionary language in the theology of the atonement is a particular and pointed example of this consequence.

CONCLUSION: ANGLICAN THEOLOGY AFTER THE FIRST WORLD WAR

The conventional theories about the collapse of English idealism usually revolve around the overstated ambitions of both personal and absolute idealism. These ambitions naturally fed into the radically reduced scope of the philosophical inquiry witnessed in figures like Russell and Moore.[145] Of course, this shift in thinking was followed closely by the trauma of World War I. In the words of Charles Taylor, "The sense of living in a shattered order has remained at some level as a truth of experience."[146] The obviously German roots of idealistic philosophy and the deepening contrast of a progressive morality and metaphysics with the realities of trench warfare made idealism and its theological corollaries an easy target for critics. As Mander has argued, though, the affirmation of one reality was central for both Green and Bradley, among others: "if in one sense idealism rejects material reality it must immediately be added that in another it wholeheartedly embraces it."[147] The idealists were attacked for their imprecision and speculative metaphysics, but in some way idealistic philosophy had already prepared the ground for a materialistic worldview.

If Mander's argument is plausible, idealism's continuity with twentieth-century philosophical developments further complicated the attempt by Anglican theologians to express the Christian faith within an idealistic frame. This is Gouldstone's concluding point:

> Anxious as these Christians were for intellectual and philosophical respectability in the face of materialist and naturalist challenges, they did not always realize that to sell their theological heritage to idealism, was to give up the authority of their historical tradition which rested on the assumption that the world's creation and preservation was the sole action of the Christian God.[148]

It was not just that philosophical trends had changed but that a new sense of the fragmentation of reality had gained traction within the wider intellectual climate:

> The fears of Yeats and the secular prophets of darkness such as H.G. Wells and Joseph Conrad were fulfilled in the carnage of the trenches. Many believed this disaster was in large part a result of the growth of power of nation states influenced by a Hegelian view of history and philosophy.[149]

The irony is that an attempt to portray the Christian faith in a manner that was intelligible in the modern world – to harmonize the facts of experience – quickly lost its intelligibility and descriptive power.

While the extent to which Charles Gore altered his views toward modern biblical criticism and philosophical idealism is debated, it seems clear that few Church leaders felt the effects of the war and the resultant rise of unbelief as acutely and painfully as Gore did.[150] "God has smitten," Gore wrote in 1921 in *Belief in God*, and "There are few things in history more astonishing than the silent acquiescence of the Christian world in the radical betrayal of its ethical foundation."[151] His conclusion was that the war had "weakened the liberal faith in Progress without strengthening the faith in God. In the case of the most serious, it has left them perplexed; in the mass, it has weakened idealism and deepened a cynical materialism."[152] There is no doubt that World War I effected a deep uncertainty in Gore's theology.

In his late work *The Reconstruction of Belief* Gore insists, more than ever, on the personality of God – his distinction from the world along with his personal activity within it. Gore even approves of Mansel's critique of the absolute and his correlative belief in the divine personality.[153] The text is full of chastened statements concerning the nature of religious knowledge. The following is a collection of statements to this effect:

> The doctrine of relativity, of which we hear so much today ... makes us no doubt tolerant of apparent discrepancies between our conclusions in one department of knowledge and experience and our conclusions in another.[154]

> It may be necessary to entertain contradictory theories simultaneously, at least for a time.[155]

> It proclaims Him in unmistakable terms for a practical purpose, not, that is, with a view to the satisfaction of metaphysical enquiries.[156]

> The Bible, then does not concern itself with the metaphysical question.[157]

> The absolute truth we cannot know. But I suggest that all this sort of language of revelation, is the only language which we can use to express the transcendent truth, and the opposite kind of language is fundamentally misleading and false.[158]

In comments like these it is difficult to discern any difference between Mansel and Gore; all the central aspects of Mansel's theology are in place: the practicality of scriptural language, the inaccessibility of the absolute, the existence of contradictory but irreducible theological claims and the accommodation of scriptural language.

Still, Gore remained conflicted about the implications of these statements, and while he felt the need to adjust his views on progress, the overall structure remained in place: "The prophets also teach us to hold with unquenchable faith to the divine purpose of progress, through all the catastrophes and judgments which widespread apostasy from God brings with it."[159] In this case, Gore at least expressed the shape of progress within the biblical context of God's providential judgment and mercy in the face of human iniquity. So it is somewhat strange to then read Gore's reprise of the Mill and Mansel debate: "The Bible, we may say, justifies John Stuart Mill in his famous refusal to call God righteous if his action did not respond to the ultimate demand of the human conscience."[160] Mill at least rightly perceived that the purpose of Mansel's argument was to justify the varying depictions of God's actions in the Bible.[161] Gore, on the other hand, seems a little confused: World War I represented a judgment of God, and yet the Old Testament depictions of God, in Mill's case, cannot meet the moral demands of the human conscience.[162]

Whatever shift occurred with Gore's theology in the years following the war was marked by some level of confusion and ambivalence. His faith in progress was diminished,[163] but he still struggled to grasp how the Old and New Testaments could speak coherently about the Christian God. It must be said that the effects of the war moved him to begin wrestling with the idealistic metaphysics that once came quite easily, and while in theory Gore made few formal adjustments to his ideas, his understanding of God's providential activity in the world seems to have taken on a more intensely scriptural framing.

Michael Ramsay defended the *Lux Mundi* theologians and Gore in particular. But he has also written that about the excitement of hearing Edwyn Hoskyns's first lecture at Cambridge.[164] Hoskyns is perhaps best known for his translation of Barth's commentary on the Romans, but in the postwar years at Cambridge, he became a symbol of a shift toward a more biblically oriented theology.

Hoskyns, unlike Mansel, was a biblical scholar and not a philosopher, though he operated on assumptions that seem interchangeable with Mansel's approach to scripture. For example, in his essay on the Synoptic Gospels in *Essays Catholic and Critical,* Hoskyns writes,

The failure of most modern scholars to formulate the contrasts correctly has led to their failure to recognize the possibility of a synthesis. The contrast is not between the Jesus of history and the Christ of faith, but between the Christ humiliated and the Christ returning in glory.[165]

This attempt to theologically integrate the contrasting images of scripture into the complex aspects of Christ's work represented a fundamental belief that the text of scripture contains a unity that does not require an exterior framework to uphold it. In a sermon at Cambridge he comments,

> we cannot go and have tea with Isaiah or with St Paul and ask them what they meant, and perhaps indeed they could not tell us if we could do so. If we are to understand them, we can do so only by wrestling with the words they once spoke or wrote, and which have in part been preserved for us.[166]

Thus, many of Hoskyns's writings on scripture contain rich and detailed expositions of biblical words, their resonance across the Testaments and their diverse yet coherent field of reference. He wrote sermons purely on certain words and their range of meaning: "The World," "The Neighbour," "Now–Then," "Here–There," "Tribulation–Comfort," "The Weak and the Strong," "Flesh," "Blood," and "Spirit."[167]

Hoskyns had a metaphysic of some kind that underpinned his scriptural approach, though it was one that functioned with little articulation. Hoskyns operated within a postwar sense of the fragmentary and disordered nature of the world: "The church is the enemy of all romanticism, if by 'romanticism' is meant a flight from the rough and tumble of things as they are into some dream world of our imaginings ... The Church always has a dagger at its heart."[168] These types of the statements permeate his work and reflect his view of biblical language: "So the word *cosmos* is crossed, when we use it, by the whole fragmentariness of what we see, so that the glory of God is seen, not at the point where we are strong, but at the point where we know ourselves to be weak and in need of mercy."[169] In another sermon he writes, "Christian language is a disturbed language; the words we use are, when fashioned to declare the glory of God, bent out of the straight, deflected, and sometimes actually reversed."[170] This sense of the disorder and brokenness of the world marks an obvious departure from idealist theology of the previous century. The distinction between the Old and New Testaments is something that suddenly becomes less clear and increasingly complex: "Between the Old Testament and the New, between the world as we see it and the Kingdom of God as the point at which both contrasted worlds meet, they see the figure of Christ crucified and risen."[171] The relation of the Old Testament to the New is not strictly linear or progressive, precisely because it stands in direct relation to the revealing presence of God. As Christ himself, the words of scripture look forward and backward in their application in a manner that makes relegating the Old Testament to a phase in the divine education far more difficult.

Though Hoskyns did not have a clear sense about the limitations of religious knowledge, at least not in the manner Mansel did, his theological method shares a strong continuity with Mansel:

> Theologians have long since discovered that even this most perfect and rounded off system, even their more penetrating analysis of the Scriptures, even their most brilliant exposition of the Gospel, remain a relative human knowledge. Themselves broken upon the Truth of God, theologians are responsible to protect all newer roads of knowledge from the blasphemy for which theology has itself been punished and by which it has been so deeply scarred.[172]

The relativity of knowledge is a theme that appeared in Gore's writings as well, and while it represents a certain shift in broader intellectual and scientific fields, in Hoskyns's sense it operates much like Mansel's epistemological skepticism. Maybe Christopher Herbert is correct in calling Mansel a proto-relativist.[173] But for Hoskyns, as for Mansel, the relativity of human knowledge places the reader within a certain receptive posture toward scripture, and even more, the idea is used to suggest that the Bible reflects the dynamics of the created world and the theological realities of death and resurrection. Scriptural words are "crossed" in Hoskyns's terms, and their plain meaning has the power to both disorient and transform the reader. In addition, the language of scripture has an expansive sense that exhibits the salvific work of Christ on the cross. In this regard, as John Webster has put it, scripture mortifies and vivifies the reader and the Church.[174]

This chapter presents the argument that while Mansel fell into relative dispute in the generation following his "Bampton Lectures," his epistemological skepticism still proved influential in direct and indirect ways. This was especially the case as theologians struggled to describe the Christian faith within the context of British idealism without allowing the philosophy of the day to erode central Christian claims. Following the war, this proved to be even more apparent, and so the shifts in Gore's theology alongside the emergence of a figure like Edwyn Hoskyns are referenced. The overall question concerns the compatibility of a scriptural worldview with particular expressions of philosophical metaphysics or ontology. While many critics complained that Mansel divorced faith from reason or that he isolated theological claims within a skeptical epistemology, there is a real sense in which his views, in various forms, proved increasingly reasonable to Christian writers in the generations that followed him. Hoskyns, and his early popularity, is a striking example of how the *Lux Mundi* incarnational theology was ill-equipped to cope with an event like World War I and all that it implied about the state of the world in the early twentieth century. The fragmented nature of reality and the disorienting and disruptive power of scripture mark a profound shift from the harmonizing and comprehensive aspirations of theological idealism. For Hoskyns and others, the Bible was often in conflict with human reason; it was a confrontational narrative of judgment and mercy, death and resurrection.

Of course, one can imagine that the largely unexpressed metaphysics or ontology of Hoskyns could in its own way distort or obscure certain scriptural realities. Surely the *Lux Mundi* theologians were not entirely mistaken in their search for some kind of harmony between the disparate facts, changes and experiences of God's world. In different generations the world is bound to seem harmonious and fragmented to vastly varying degrees in accordance with the experiences of people. It was Coleridge's argument that it was perfectly natural for Christians in various times and in various places to draw on different portions of the Bible for different purposes. The argument here is that Mansel's theory of regulative truth and his corresponding use of typology provide a set of rules that might permit various readings of scripture without allowing certain portions of the Bible to damage or obscure others. If it is inevitable that some portions or themes in the Bible will strike certain individuals or people or generations as more reasonable or more resonant with their experience, some account of the limits of human reason must be offered to ensure that the less reasonable portions are allowed to speak truthfully of God nonetheless. In the context of this chapter, this is necessary not just for the preservation of Christian orthodoxy but also to ensure that the entire Bible is available for the Church as a descriptive resource across the inevitable shifts and upheavals of history. In part, the progressive metaphysics of *Lux Mundi* was too monochromatic to adjust to a major historical change that challenged its core principle of moral and cultural progress. It is not a surprise that this worldview transitioned to equally simplified though pessimistic cosmologies witnessed in the writings, for example, of a novelist like Thomas Hardy.[175] Mansel's theory of accommodation and the Butlerian tradition that he imbibed represented an attempt to argue that the Bible graciously reflects and describes reality in a manner that is adjusted to the endless difficulties and complexity of the world. Paradoxically, scripture can provide a more comprehensive account of God and the world than any rational philosophical or theological construct precisely because it is able to "absorb the world" more effectively.

It could be argued that Mansel's skepticism was simply an elaborated defense of the principle of repugnancy found in Article XX.[176] Mansel pursued this principle, albeit sparingly, in his sermons through the use of typology and the expansive sense of scripture ordered around the figure of Jesus Christ. The progressive metaphysics of the *Lux Mundi* writers made the application of Article XX very difficult and at times impossible because their method concealed another form of skepticism, which isolated Old Testaments claims especially within a historical scheme that relativized many Old Testament narratives and types to an immature stage in the process of the world. Mansel wrote enough about the metaphysics of knowledge and the ontology of personality to imply that it was not the pursuit of these philosophical disciplines themselves that pose chronic difficulties to the reading of scripture. Rather, metaphysical or ontological claims need to be curtailed in a sufficient manner to make space for the breadth of scripture to speak truthfully and to form the overarching conception of what it means to live a creaturely life in God's world. Indeed, a skeptical stream is required in any philosophical pursuit because the antinomous and sometimes conflicting language of scripture is the only form of human language that is capable of describing a God who cannot be grasped within purely rational constructs.

Mansel in the Twentieth Century

If Mansel's reputation as a defender of Anglican orthodoxy was fatally imperilled by the association of his ideas with those of Herbert Spencer, his twentieth century interpreters, in certain respects, have done little more to clear his name. This is especially true in the case of Don Cupitt, one of Mansel's most thoughtful and attentive readers. Cupitt's religious nonrealism, most famously published in his book *Taking Leave of God* (1980), bears strong Manselian themes that can be traced back clearly to his early articles on Mansel published in the late 1960s. In this respect, Cupitt is one of the few Anglican theologians to appreciate Mansel's thought in a manner roughly akin to the presentation of third and fourth chapters in this book. Though, as is well known, Cupitt's own thinking has developed dramatically since the 1960s, and while certain aspects of Mansel's thought have not entirely disappeared – the practicality of religion, and the anthropomorphic character of scriptural language, for example – Mansel's governing themes and intentions have clearly been forgotten. In 2006, Cupitt remarked that *The Limits of Religious Thought* is "a book that always has a few admirers – including, in the 1960s, me."[1]

Mansel's nineteenth-century critics judged his understanding of human reason to be overly constricting and exclusive of the spiritual character of human knowing. Whether in terms of the absolute, the eternal consciousness, or the incarnation, writers like Green, Bradley, and the *Lux Mundi* theologians were eager to articulate reality as a spiritual whole that could embrace the rapid changes and seeming progress of the modern world. However, in the twentieth century it has been Mansel's supernaturalism and his high view of scripture that have garnered resistance. To this end, his ideas have been engaged

and implemented by theologians who have sought to advance imman-
entist and nonrealist accounts of the Christian faith that relinquish
the capacity of scripture, in particular, to meaningfully refer to the
character and reality of God.

However, in this chapter I argue that the skepticism and nonrealism
of Don Cupitt and much of twentieth-century Anglican theology is
not a direct extension of Mansel's skepticism but the result of a weakening confidence in scripture's capacity to witness to God's character
and describe God's presence in the world. This is a second form of
skepticism that is easily confused with Mansel's, but in fact it has
more in common with the idealist tendency to dissolve scriptural
claims into the immediacy of spiritual experience in the service of a
comprehensive and all-embracing metaphysics of explanation. Yet,
as argued in the preceding chapters, these varying attempts to place
the Christian faith within a metaphysical scheme that could make
sense of modern developments time and again stumbled over the
question of God's character as it is described in scripture. This pertained especially to the Old Testament and to atonement theology:
notions of God's anger, judgment, and even violence became difficult
to place within a progressive metaphysics that demanded a moral
uniformity, which, in Mansel's terms, the Bible could not quite provide.
Mansel's theory of regulative truth was an attempt to embrace the
full range of scriptural references with all of their puzzling complexity
and startling implications, without compromising the unity of scripture, which speaks of one God across the vast array of written witness.
For Mansel, as for Butler, the difficult and perplexing variety of scripture's witness in fact provided a more compelling descriptive account
of God's world. It is precisely this question of God's character that
continued to trouble Mansel's twentieth-century interpreters, even as
they found in him various theological and philosophical resources.
Thus despite the fact that the postwar atmosphere in England seemed
more hospitable to Mansel's theology than his own era, on the whole
his twentieth-century readers have once again taken him in unusual
and unexpected directions.

I begin by examining Mansel's reputation in twentieth-century
surveys of Anglican theology and the extent to which his contribution
to Anglican theology was erased in the schemes of Anglican idealist
histories. I then turn to the various attempts at rehabilitating his writings in the works of Edwyn Bevan, Gordon Lewis Phillips, Kenneth
Freeman, and Don Cupitt. To these writers Mansel's ideas seemed to

anticipate modern concerns about the nature of religious language and symbolism, and yet the context of this new concern was not always more hospitable to Mansel's theology of scripture.

In a certain sense, this somewhat convoluted and obscure genealogy of ideas in the twentieth century, as in the nineteenth century, serves to raise pointed questions about the place of scripture in modern theology and, more specifically, in the formation and identity of Anglican Christianity. This chapter argues that Mansel's skepticism and theory of the regulative truth of scripture still have the capacity to offer a powerful test and critique of the continuous and competing theological visions of contemporary Anglicanism. And even more, his positive notion of a Church formed by the language and narrative of scripture represents a compelling and coherent theological vision that deserves serious attention.

MANSEL AND THE HISTORIANS

In the original preface to Bernard Reardon's well-known book *Religious Thought in the Victorian Age,* he notes that his inspiration for the work comes from "the needs of students of religious thought in nineteenth century Britain."[2] The previous works that Reardon notes are similar surveys by Vernon Storr, Clement Webb, and L.E. Elliot-Binns.[3] While Reardon himself offers a lengthy and appreciative summary of Mansel's place in Victorian theology, it is striking to note that Mansel's reputation as a theological thinker in England and beyond was almost exclusively in the hands a few idealist theologians and historians for the better part of the twentieth century. The prevailing theme in these complementary histories is that the Spirit has moved the Church and the world beyond the old-fashioned and morally dangerous views of Mansel wherein the scriptural narrative of God's dealings with his people is allowed to stand unaltered by modern developments.

Vernon Storr: A Century of English Theology

Vernon Storr's volume on English theology appeared in 1913 and covered the period of 1800–60 in English theology. Storr's book is steeped in the prewar idealism that was prevalent in English Christianity at the time and reads predominantly as a preamble to the theological movement that would come to characterize his own generation. The Oxford Movement, for Storr, characterized a profoundly negative attitude in Anglican theology that embodied a defensive and aggressive posture towards all forms of modern thought. In this respect Coleridge and Maurice were the figures who represented a deeper and more faithful stream in English Christianity: "After the collapse of the Oxford Movement came a period of reaction and negation, an hour of darkness in which Maurice so nobly upheld the torch of Christian idealism, and carried on the Coleridgean tradition of a more spiritual philosophy."[4] In some respects, the crisis of religious belief in Victorian England was centered upon theories of the inspiration of scripture.[5] And yet the strict adherence to traditional understandings of inspiration by many theologians engendered a certain theological impotence just when the Church was losing touch with the world around it. Storr writes,

> The traditional theology found itself powerless, for it had no religious philosophy worthy of the name. The last forty years of the century saw theologians forced out of their attitude of isolation, and driven to hold commerce with the wider thought around them. Thus began that period of rapid progress and enrichment which has ever since characterized theological development.[6]

Though Storr regards the writers of *Essays and Reviews* and more threatening critics like Francis Newman as dangerous, in some sense, with their heterodox implications, it is the case that such developments in Anglican theology spurred the Church toward a more truthful account of its core doctrines: "Here is the travail of the Time-Spirit; here is the living God at work. We see how this revolution in our thought is the result of the convergence of many lines of movement, how inevitable it was, how preparation had been made for it in a long past."[7] Such a statement characterizes Storr's thesis as a whole: the current trends in idealist theology symbolized the culmination of the Spirit's work in history. For this reason he gives little attention to the critics of this trajectory. Yet Storr does make one exception.

Mansel appears in Storr's history as a confused and obstinate contrarian with little grasp of the contemporary currents in theology. As argued in previous chapters, Mill's objection to Mansel's defence of God's character in the Old Testament formed the ultimate verdict on Mansel in the decades following. Storr, too, despite being critical of Mill's empiricism, forms his judgment on Mansel's reading of scripture along these lines: Mansel's literalism, in the case of the Old Testament especially, threatened to alienate an entire generation of spiritual doubters. Thus, Maurice was absolutely justified in the alarm and distaste that Mansel's theology provoked in him: "Maurice saw that Mansel's attitude, if it were generally adopted, could only lead to a fatal divorce between theology and advancing knowledge. Death must quickly overtake English theology if the clergy were to enroll themselves as Mansel's disciples."[8] This was in effect the judgment of S.C. Carpenter's *Church and History* as well: Mansel's views led to the "abandonment of theology,"[9] though many "hasty theologians jumped at it."[10]

Clement Webb

The other seminal work mentioned by Reardon is Clement Webb's *A Study of English Thought in England from 1850*. Unlike Storr, Webb was an accomplished philosopher and theologian, and his book contains a far more delicate treatment of the major movements of the period under review. Webb was undoubtedly an idealist who, like many idealists in the early twentieth century, had moved in a personalist direction from the philosophies of Green and Bradley.[11]

While Green, Bradley, and the *Lux Mundi* writers were concerned with the threat of religious empiricism (Mansel) or moral utilitarianism (Mill), Webb's idealism is set within the changing circumstances of the early twentieth century. Webb contrasts his position with emerging trends in French sociology. For example, figures like Emile Durkheim

> are apt to speak of the object of their religious consciousness
> as though it were a merely subjective fact, the product of man's
> social nature. But it would in my judgment be better to acknowl-
> edge that the very social consciousness wherein consciousness of
> the supreme Unity has from the first been implicit is rooted in the
> spiritual nature of that supreme Unity itself, which in the move-
> ment of man's spiritual and social life has been carrying on that
> perpetual revelation and communication of itself which belongs
> to its own innermost being.[12]

Durkheim's tendency to reduce the aspirations of religious conscious-ness to relative and temporal considerations was countered by Webb with the argument that the realization of the absolute is progressively realized in the various stages of cultural and historical striving after a primordial spiritual unity. Likewise, Webb criticizes William James's chronicling of religious experience as unduly individualistic and, on the whole, oblivious to the corporate, spiritual character of religious experience embodied in successive stages of world history.[13]

In this respect, Webb's history of nineteenth century theology, like Storr and Elliot-Binns, argues that the true lineage of Anglican theology lies in the tradition of Coleridge and Maurice, a lineage in which Mansel appears as a foil. Mansel, then, emerges in Webb's chapter on nonreligious immanentism directly after a discussion of James's pragmatism.[14] Mansel's theology is based upon the older understanding of Christianity that is built upon the evidence of miracles and the supernatural authority of revelation. And yet Mansel's denial of human reason's capacity to judge the contents of revelation by some independent standard grounded his thought on a "complete skepticism" that provoked the justified condemnation of Maurice and the English idealists after him.[15] Thus, in Webb's view, despite him being a "pioneer of the modern study of philosophy in Oxford," Mansel's philosophical skepticism has become a forerunner to pernicious forms of religious immanentism, whether in the writings of Spencer or James.[16]

Webb's volume concludes with an admission that the Great War "dealt a mortal blow to the optimistic religious immanentism."[17] Yet Webb places the blame for this "optimism" on an abstracted and conceptually banal form of idealism that preceded the personalist turn:

> history, is no mere symbol of general truths for which some other and better symbol might be found, but a process in which unique individual persons perform unique individual acts. Blindness to these facts was bound to bring, and indeed has now brought, a reaction in its train.[18]

In many ways, Webb displays a typical postwar theological confusion that I attributed to Charles Gore in chapter 5. While the progress of history had been arrested by the moral catastrophe of the war, Webb saw little connection between idealistic understandings of scripture and the crisis of belief that emerged in the 1920s.[19] In fact, despite the war, one of the great gains of theological idealism, according to Webb, has been an increase in "candour" and a generous, searching spirit that was capable of absorbing and even encouraging the "critical view of the Bible."[20] Still, he laments that

> a generation should be growing up to whom the Bible stories and the Scriptural phraseology, which were to their fathers as much part of the permanent furniture of their minds as the alphabet or the multiplication table, are altogether unfamiliar.[21]

In essence, it was the alienation of the scriptures, and the God they describe, from common Christian life and experience that concerned Mansel most deeply.[22] And yet the nearly unanimous historical portrait of Mansel, drawn up by Webb and Storr, represents Mansel as a thinker badly out of touch with his times.[23] Furthermore, Mansel's theology risked and actually accomplished a separation of Christian faith and the developments of the modern world. Reardon's history of Victorian theology has gone a long way in repairing the reputation of, in his words, "one of the most original religious thinkers of the century."[24] While "Mansel's work still merits serious attention,"[25] it was not the scope of Reardon's book to offer this attention. I will now turn to a series of writers who interpreted Mansel in light of twentieth-century philosophical and theological developments.

MANSEL THE PRAGMATIST

At the same time as Mansel was being dismissed by idealist historians as a severe skeptic, other writers began to see Mansel as a useful antidote to the idealistic trends in English philosophy and theology. Mansel's insistence that God can only be known within the constraints of human language, and the further point that this language is limited in its capacity to refer directly to God's being, made his ideas amenable to certain twentieth-century intellectual trends. In an increasingly skeptical age, Mansel came to be seen as a forerunner of religious pragmatism, as suddenly his skepticism seemed to "fit" with reality. Still, it remains the case that the portrait of God that emerged from Mansel's understanding of scripture continued to baffle and frighten even his most sympathetic readers. Thus untethered from his scriptural affirmations, Mansel's skepticism becomes open to all manner of applications: Don Cupitt represents an extreme outcome of this possibility, as the language of scripture is deprived of any capacity to describe God. As argued in previous chapters, Coleridge, Maurice, and the *Lux Mundi* theologians brought assumptions to the scriptural text that forced them to heavily favour some images over others. With little sense of how these varying and, at times, contrasting images can be held together in a holistic sense, this dilemma was pushed to the point of denying their ability to describe God at all. I begin by discussing Edwyn Bevan and Kenneth Freeman as a preamble to Cupitt, in order to mark the path that Cupitt himself travelled.

Edwyn Bevan: Symbolism and Belief

I begin with Edwyn Bevan (1870–1943) as a more moderate interpreter of Mansel than Cupitt.[26] Bevan's 1933–34 Gifford lectures were published in 1938 as a book entitled *Symbolism and Belief*, which contains a long chapter on Mansel. Bevan basically affirms Mansel's understanding of religious language:

> all human language applied to Him tries by figures and parables
> to state truth about a Reality which infinitely exceeds all man's
> powers of understanding or imagination. It would be a waste
> of time to prove by a series of quotations something which runs
> through all Christian literature.[27]

It is the theologian's task not to look beyond the anthropomorphic character of religious language but "to make the division between right and wrong anthropomorphism."[28]

In order to make this division, Bevan draws on an aspect of Mansel's thought that was generally ignored by his own contemporaries: namely, that truths of Christian doctrine meet the needs of and fit within the demands and exigencies of human nature. In other words, the truths of Christianity – the existence of God – are indemonstrable realities that can only be known to the degree that one experiences and lives by the practices these realities imply. Bevan writes,

> Yet whatever our conceptions may be, we cannot refuse to admit
> that they are only more or less figurative representations of an
> unimaginable Reality, as Mansel insisted, and that we give them
> our allegiance because they meet the exigencies of the human
> spirit and issue in the mode of action and feeling we perceive
> to be the best, and that further, because they do this, we believe
> them to be in their essence true.[29]

Bevan here is referring primarily to Mansel's understanding of personality and the representation in scripture of a personal God who engages humanity in a manner that is fitting with our created capacities and character. For Mansel, the practice of prayer was particularly important in this regard: in prayer, of all places, the personal and relational aspect is most intensely evident.[30]

Figures like Maurice generally missed this aspect of Mansel's thought, which Bevan brings to light. Though somewhat strangely, Bevan's own approach to separating the discussion of religious symbolism and the actual Bible introduces a limit to the extent that Mansel's ideas can be appropriated. Bevan recognizes this: "Mansel's general philosophy does not stand or fall by the rightness of his belief that the Hebrew and Christian scriptures gave a representation of God every element in which had to be accepted without question, as dictated by God."[31] At a moment when Bevan seems most sympathetic to Mansel, he provides a startlingly uncharitable rendering of Mansel's understanding of the Bible. Maybe Mansel did believe in a dictation theory, but there is no real evidence to suggest it. It is true that Mansel thought the Bible could "meet the exigencies of the human spirit," but he also believed that it was an ancient document that was attested by supernatural authority. His appeal to miracles and the external evidences for the Bible's credibility was already unpopular in his own day and even more so in Bevan's. But Mansel's supernatural understanding of scripture does not lend itself easily to a more generalized account of religious symbolism outside of the scriptures themselves.[32]

In the end, Bevan's reading presents a mixed picture: his own views on religious language seem indistinguishable from Mansel's, and yet he cannot quite acknowledge the primacy of scriptural language in a manner that could make complete sense of Mansel's intentions. His pragmatism in this regard works against his scriptural commitments, whether intentionally or not. This is true to the extent that the "exigencies of the human spirit" claim a controlling force in his ultimate theological argument:

> Those who believe the Reality behind phenomena to be Spirit, to be God, hold that we see the character of that Reality in the manifestations of the human spirit, and since we see those manifestations in a scale of worth, some higher than others – a more perfect goodness and loveliness of character, a more ardent loyalty to truth, a richer genius in apprehending beauty and making

beautiful things – it is as they rise in the scale, as they are brighter and purer, that they are for us more perfect manifestations of the character of the Supreme Spirit. For Christians the human spirit reaches its highest possible point in Christ.[33]

Thus, while making use of Mansel's skepticism, Bevan, like the idealists that he too criticizes for their unwarranted metaphysical assertions,[34] provides an external criterion that makes reading the Bible as a unified witness difficult, if not impossible, to perform. And like for so many of the authors discussed in my first four chapters, the great obstacle in reading the Bible as a coherent revelation from God is frequently the moral picture of God that the Bible presents. So Bevan thinks that Christian symbols fit well within the "exigencies" of the human spirit, but the picture of God that the scriptures present does not, in fact, fit within these "exigencies." If the Bible were to be read in the way that Mansel suggested, Bevan says in passing, "we should be delivered over to a welter of contradictory superstitions."[35] But I have argued that it is within this "welter" that Mansel found the most powerful and truthful account of God's character and activity in the world. Furthermore, Mansel, like Butler, argued that the form and content of scripture did in fact "fit" with the character of human life.

Kenneth Freeman and the Death of God

While Bevan understood Mansel within the framework of religious pragmatism, Bevan, and much less Mansel, was not quite willing to relinquish the objectivity and identity of the Christian God. Though Bevan was inclined to speak of religious or Christian symbolism in a manner that was abstracted from the actual contents of scripture. In part, Bevan did this because the scriptural narrative and images interfered in some sense with the pragmatic "fit" that should and does exist between Christian symbols and the "exigencies" of human life. Kenneth Freeman's book *The Role of Reason in Religion: A Study of Henry Mansel* (1969) and an earlier article on the same topic (1967) build on the aspects of pragmatism in Mansel's thought but extend and deconstruct Mansel's ideas in a manner that reflects the concerns of the death of God or radical theology that was popular in the 1960s.

Freeman was a philosopher of religion who taught at Cornell and Harvard in the 1960s, and though he was not an Anglican, his book marks the most sustained and singular reading of Mansel as a radical theologian. Radical theology was introduced in England most memorably by John Robinson's *Honest to God* in 1963, and many of the concerns of Robinson's book were altered and forcibly extended over the next three decades by Don Cupitt. I discuss Cupitt shortly, but in what follows I briefly examine the manner in which Freeman adjusts and interprets Mansel for the purposes of articulating a purely finite conception of God.

Freeman, in a slightly different vein than Lightman, suggests that Mansel initiated an inadvertent

> first step in a development which leads through J.S. Mill, William James, John Dewey, E.S. Brightman and Henry Nelson Wieman and culminates in the theology of the mid 60s which emphasizes the "death of God." For the common denominator of the radical theology is the denial of the radical metaphysical transcendency which Mansel stressed.[36]

In effect, Mansel's insistence on the transcendence of God – both infinite and absolute – paired with his assertion that human knowledge can only operate within the finite realm of distinctions and relations led to an obvious removal of human reason from the realm of religion.[37] For Freeman this result illustrates the impossibility of a transcendent God or at least the usefulness of such an idea. Yet Freeman argues that Mansel's criticisms of rational theology are useful and constructive for a finite conception of God.[38]

Freeman's own position does not make use of the heavy theological language of someone like Altizer, but the structure of his argument is effectually the same. Altizer's famous claim in *The Gospel of Christian Atheism* was that "As the God who is Jesus becomes ever more deeply incarnate in the body of humanity, he loses every semblance of his former visage, until he appears wherever there is energy and life."[39] The death of God in Christ effected the gradual erosion of all religious identity and created a space in which a pragmatic religious relativism could flourish. This is the conclusion that Freeman draws out of Mansel:

> Implicit in any application of religious pragmatism is an affirmation of relativism with respect to religious truth. Such a relativism can easily be absorbed into the position of finitism. Within

a particular culture...one finds a certain religion which emerges as that which most nearly satisfies the wants and needs of that culture.[40]

Freeman points to one of the principal difficulties with Mansel's theology today. Much as with Kant's transcendental categories of human thought, Mansel's appeal to the fittingness or natural correspondence between human nature and Christian revelation has been eroded by pluralistic and local accounts of what it means to be human.[41] In other words, theological or philosophical attempts to provide abstract or generalized accounts of human nature are no longer in vogue.

In spite of this objection, Freeman agrees with Mansel that the question of God's objectivity remains undecidable, and he makes no effort to prove beyond question the veracity of a strictly finite God.[42] Rather, Freeman's point is that God's finitude is in fact more useful or pragmatic in a pluralist world and less dangerous than Mansel's fideism: "Mansel's analysis provides no framework within which one may consistently resist the various superstitions and flights of fancy which crowd in upon modern life."[43] The implication here is that Mansel's strictures upon reason in the realm of theology could lend themselves to any manner of beliefs and practices. Mansel believed that Christian practices and belief should be formed by a continual engagement with Scripture through a process of Christological and typological reading that has been common throughout the history of the Church. But this is not an option that Freeman considers. In fact, Freeman credits the finite understanding of God and all reality – "the single realm theory" – to pioneers in biblical criticism such as Strauss, F.C. Bauer, and the authors of *Essays and Reviews*.[44] Furthermore, Mansel's belief in the supernatural reality of God in the Bible – miracles and all – is, according to Freeman, a view that in light of recent "Biblical scholarship ... has been generally discredited."[45] Freeman goes on to conclude, "Without this presupposition, however, Mansel's approach is largely vitiated."[46] Naturally, this goes without saying; Mansel would never have denied that his whole worldview hung without reserve upon the reality of God and the credibility of the Spirit's witness in scripture.

While Freeman's reading of Mansel is creative and at times complimentary – "Mansel had struck at the vital center of the new wave of religious thought"[47] – more than anything, his book demonstrates the profound weakening of confidence in the capacity of scripture to describe and form Christian practices and beliefs. Freeman may be right that the philosophical apparatus that surrounds Mansel's understanding of scripture contains problems and vulnerabilities. But as argued in chapter 3 of this book, Mansel's work is best understood from within his greatest commitment – that scripture, as a whole, provides a unified witness to the actions and character of God in history. Any philosophical or theological theory that tries to pull this apart must be examined and criticized from the position of faith. So, like Bevan, Freeman assumes that the scriptures in their entirety cannot describe and illuminate the contemporary world. His goal is pragmatic in the sense that he wants to articulate a religious philosophy that can accommodate a limitless pluralism, which he regards as the true characterization of the contemporary world. Freeman's assumption, more baldly stated than Bevan's, is that the contemporary world, its knowledge and achievements, is so unprecedented that the God of the scriptures appears irrelevant and lost, in some way, within the past. It is this simple assumption that informs the whole of Cupitt's work.

DON CUPITT AND RELIGIOUS NONREALISM

At the time of Freeman's book, Don Cupitt was a young priest and theologian with a teaching post at Emmanuel College in Cambridge. In the articles he published in the late 1960s on Mansel, there were slight indications of the direction he would eventually go with books like *Taking Leave of God*. Cupitt has become known for his claim that religious language does not refer to an objective God outside or even within the world. Indeed, there is a clear path of development between the two stages for Cupitt, but my purpose in what follows is not to simply describe this development but to relate it to Mansel's central ideas concerning the limits of knowledge and the character of the scriptures. My argument is that Cupitt's skepticism about the realistic nature of scriptural language has little to do with Mansel. However, there are clear affinities between Cupitt's position and idealists like Green and Bradley, and it is within this tradition of English religious skepticism that Cupitt's nonrealism is more accurately located.

Early Articles on Mansel

Cupitt's article on Mansel's theory of regulative truth (1967) makes the case that Mansel's theory simply represented a traditional theological notion that God's very being is incomprehensible, though God's action in the world and relation to his creation are revealed in scripture. Far from advocating a skepticism that removes God from the world, Cupitt suggests that, "Mansel stands for continuity between things human and things Divine. God mercifully attaches us to himself by engaging our human thoughts and affections."[48] Cupitt goes on:

> To Mansel the power of the Christian revelation to develop human nature to its full capacity is a most important evidence of its truth, and the God who wills to be thought of as Father and Husband not only enriches those natural relations, but is known in them. Revelation is adapted to our powers of thought, moral activity, and affection alike; but still more to human nature as a whole ... Mansel is rather concerned for a wholeness, a "kindness" which he finds in orthodoxy and would not see diminished.[49]

This is, to some extent, the picture that I present of Mansel: despite the dominant image of Mansel as a severe and cold skeptic who defended an image of God that was offensive to so many, the prevailing theme for Mansel is the gracious "kindness" of a God who inhabits and indwells human reality in order to know and save his people. Yet within this picture of God's nearness or proximity to human life, Cupitt writes that for Mansel "theology is continually haunted by the thought of God's transcendence, even though that thought can never be brought to perfect clarity in reflection."[50]

Despite these sympathetic reflections, Cupitt is not uncritical of Mansel. First, he questions whether Mansel should have located the limits of thought strictly within the religious realm and not applied them to all fields of knowledge. Mansel, Cupitt suggests, was possibly "led astray in *The Limits* by the demands of his Butlerian scheme."[51] But it is difficult to see how this could be the case, at least in Mansel's mind. The lectures open with the quote from Hamilton that all problems of theological knowledge are mirrored in philosophy, in respect to knowledge of God and the nature of the infinite or absolute. For better or for worse, it would be hard to contest this notion within Mansel's work. Cupitt, however, may have had his reasons for suggesting this, as will be seen.

Secondly, Cupitt argues that Mansel's understanding of analogy was a relative latecomer to his thought, a notion he went searching for in response to Goldwin Smith.[52] It is true that Mansel introduced the idea of his fairly straightforward view of analogy after he delivered his lectures, but it seems like a natural suggestion on the heels of his theory of regulative truth: the language of revelation is primarily practical – it forms the thoughts and actions of believers – but in faith, if not in conception, the Christian believes that there is an analogical relation between the language and God himself. But Cupitt seems to prefer a version of regulative truth without the possibility of any known correspondence: "If Mansel to some extent abandoned the original strictness of his doctrine of regulative truth, and developed it into a kind of theory of analogy, he made no progress. His original position, bleak though it is, is surer."[53] How this more "bleak" position could cohere with Cupitt's other assessment of Mansel's kind and holistic orthodoxy is not clear, and Cupitt does not explore it. It does suggest, perhaps, an uncertainty in his own mind.

Indeed, several years later, in a series of exchanges on Mansel with F.W. Dockrill, Cupitt seems to adjust his view of Mansel. In one instance he summarizes Mansel's view by suggesting that "Christian dogmas have always been authoritative guides to conduct rather than authoritative diagrams of deity."[54] Suddenly Cupitt sounds more like the reckless critics of Mansel's own day who did not grasp the tension between knowledge and practice that he was attempting to hold together. In a more definitive statement, Cupitt restates his own view of the debate between Mansel and Maurice:

Mansel allows that our knowledge of God is in the form of the consciousness "of the relation of a Person to a Person." But the concept of God as personal is a concept of him that is limited and finite. It cannot be a constitutive concept, that is, a concept which truly represents him as he is in himself ... Maurice believes that the basis of knowledge is a real ontological communion between knower and known. We can have and we can speak of such an experience in the case of God. Our talk of God is not metaphorical but refers directly to a genuine and conscious experience of him. A few years ago it seemed obvious to me that Mansel was nearer the truth. He is clear, Maurice is obscure: yet if Maurice is right, how can Maurice be obscure, and how can Mansel hold the opinions he does? Moreover, Maurice clearly lost the argument. Elsewhere in his writings he talks more like Mansel, and I had the impression that his passionate nature, and the demands of controversy, led him to rhetorical exaggeration. Now however, I feel a little more sympathy for Maurice's opinion, but it would be a long story to say why.[55]

The reference here to his "story" leaves the reader guessing, but Cupitt has subsequently left us with no shortage of material to trace this story. What is curious, however, is that Maurice's notions of "ontological communion" and direct and conscious experience of God should become attractive to Cupitt at a moment when he began moving in his non-realist direction.

Christ and the Hiddenness of God

Cupitt's now well-known book *Taking Leave of God* appeared in 1980 to much controversy and attention. While it was an announcement of Cupitt's nonrealist position, any careful reader of Cupitt could well have seen it coming. By his own account, in a written reply to Rowan Williams's critique of his book, Cupitt makes this comment:

> *Taking Leave of God* is strongly Kantian, and reflects the influence of Mansel's theory that religious truth is regulative, and of Wittgenstein's interpretation of Kierkegaard. In retrospect I now see it as completing a development which began as far back as *Christ and the Hiddenness of God* and even earlier. *The World to Come*, by contrast, reflects the recent joining of hand between American and French philosophy as seen, for example, in what Rorty has lately been writing about Derrida ... Thus ... *Taking Leave of God* rounded off what I had been trying to say for the previous dozen years, and it was followed rather than preceded by the conversion which led me to write the second book.[56]

Unlike the retrospective Cupitt provides in 2006, here he clearly acknowledges Mansel as a formative influence in his progression toward a non-realist position, though it is a version of Mansel that has been severely altered.

Already in *Christ and the Hiddenness of God* (1971) Cupitt provides evidence of this alteration. This book demonstrates an analysis of the person of Christ and his role as an object of human faith and apprehension. Cupitt pursues this study largely within the context of Anglican theology, and he provides a rare exposition of the tradition that figures largely in Mansel's background. Cupitt discusses the work of Mansel, Peter Browne, Archbishop King, Richard Whately, Copleston, and Hume as varying representatives of the negative tradition within English theology. However, in a large measure Cupitt already gives Hume the upper hand against the "Demea" theologians of the Anglican tradition who employed skeptical arguments about human knowledge of God in order to create a space for Christian revelation. Cupitt writes that these theologians

> were prone to argue, mistakenly I believe, that all human repre-
> sentations of God are on the same level. They maintained this
> partly out of a respectable protestant dislike of any double stan-
> dard or hierarchy of degrees or proficiency among the regenerate,
> and partly out of suspicion that if imagery of scripture is admitted
> to vary in authoritativeness or adequacy the pass would be sold
> to the biblical critics. Both these reasons are unsound. Even in the
> very earliest Christian ascesis there was an important distinction
> between "milk" and "meat" stages, and the religious life cannot
> move at all unless the religious symbols guiding it be arranged,
> as they plainly are arranged, in some kind of hierarchy.[57]

Clearly Cupitt takes the central claim of these writers – that God's nature cannot be directly apprehended – and blends it with a mystical or negative component that allows for a progressive overriding of certain scriptural claims. He is right about the concern over biblical criticism, and the claims about milk and meat stages are not entirely unwarranted. The overall trajectory of this argument, however, recalls the idealist tendency to dismiss certain biblical claims and narratives as primitive or immature within the course of history.

Cupitt goes on to appropriate the narrative of idolatry that was prevalent among writers like Green:[58]

> But in so far as the story is told successfully and convincingly it
> has made of God not God but a man. And so in its transcendent
> or prophetic mood theism is iconoclastic, it must negate its own
> symbolism, it must insist upon the inexpressibility and the myste-
> riousness of God ... The image of God as in perpetual movement
> suggests that there can be no fixed positions and no incorrigible
> formulations of doctrine ... For what God is, is not so much
> expressed in our success in speaking about him as rather indi-
> rectly suggested by our failure.[59]

Fixed conceptions of God and "incorrigible formulations of doctrine" are described by Cupitt as antithetical to the character of Christ's own ministry, which was iconoclastic: it broke down the rigid religious

idols and substituted an indeterminate gradient of spiritual exploration with no definite goal. This is an obvious departure from Mansel's
own reading of the scriptures; he did in fact regard all of scripture as
on an equal field of meaning, but the field of reference was organized
and interpreted by a Christocentric logic. Cupitt also employs a
Christocentric hermeneutic, but it is one that sheds referential meaning rather than gathering it. In this way, as early as 1971 he was
expressing views that were consistent with writers like Altizer.

Cupitt was aware that he was only using a portion of Mansel's
ideas, and like Freeman, he rejects his views of scripture. In part this
is because Cupitt, like other radical theologians, holds to a narrative
in which the old ontology that upheld analogical reasoning about the
knowledge of God had collapsed and given way to sheer authority.[60]
But the authoritarian view – Mansel's own, he suggests – hovers list-
lessly in a void that cannot justify the claim:

> The anthropomorphic imagery through which we relate ourselves
> to God is incapable of rational justification. In H.L. Mansel's ter-
> minology, it is not speculatively true: but it may nevertheless be
> regulatively true. The imagery may be used because it is autho-
> rized, it is to be believed and obeyed … We have argued against
> this that no satisfactory justification can be given of the claims to
> authority of the Bible, the church or whatever else is supposed to
> be the authoritative source of action guiding religious imagery.[61]

In severing this connection between the Bible and its divine authoriza-
tion, Cupitt places the whole range of scripture in a highly precarious
position. An example of this is his reading of Christ's death:

> Jesus' own living out of his anthropomorphic faith disclosed that
> its own logic led to its own loss. In obedience to God as he con-
> ceived God, Jesus was obliged to lose the imagery, to experience
> the distance of God, the Messianic Woes and the Cross. The opti-
> mistic imagery which pictured God as fatherly, good and loving,
> if it was lived, led to its own renunciation.[62]

Whereas someone like Austin Farrer, for example, suggested that
Christ "clothed" himself in Old Testament images as he went to the
cross, Cupitt only acknowledges one family of images and suggests
that all biblical imagery is lost and renounced in Christ's death. The

suffering servant of Isaiah or the judgments of God upon the nation of Israel are excluded by Cupitt in favour of the "optimistic imagery" of God's overriding goodness and love. However, in Mansel's terms, God's goodness and love were informed and coloured by scriptural narrative in all of its particularity, an interpretation that Cupitt does not seem willing to consider.

Thus *Christ and the Hiddenness of God* interprets Jesus as ultimately unknowable and yet as a symbol of God's hiddenness that constantly destroys and removes fixed conceptions of God. Such an interpretation implies a developmental reading of history that places Cupitt in close proximity to idealists like Green and Bradley who could not countenance the idea that the Bible might describe God and the world in any kind of definite manner. In addition, Cupitt, in this early stage, reflects the ambivalence of Bevan's reading of Mansel, for whom Mansel's skepticism functions as a theory of religious symbolism that relates only sporadically to the actual biblical record.

Taking Leave of God

Inherent within Cupitt's early views that religious symbolism – scriptural symbolism – required constant supersession was a progressive theory of knowledge that impinged upon his conception of modernity. Like Bevan, Cupitt seems to merge scriptural symbolism into a more generic account of religious symbolism that becomes subject to a process of continual purgation: these symbols have only temporal use in an intellectual process that approaches the truth through a constant supersession of traditional language and symbolism. Nearly all the books that surround *Taking Leave of God* (1980) – *The Leap of Reason* (1977), *The World to Come* (1982), *The Sea of Faith* (1984) – contain genealogies of modernity that document the emergence of a new consciousness that demands the alteration of traditional religious beliefs.[63] Yet Cupitt's desire to retain the usefulness of religious symbolism complicates his own narration of modernity in a manner that illustrates some of the difficulties of his own position.

For example, in *The Leap of Reason,* Cupitt asserts that traditional belief in a realist God has become increasingly difficult, but the role of faith remains integral in human life. He follows a version of Kierkegaard and suggests that faith does not have to be oriented toward an object, but in itself it represents "an ecstasy, standing outside one's habitual ways of thinking."[64] This ecstatic character emerges from the ability to recognize our situation in the world: "So religion aspires after absolute knowledge, while yet it recognizes that our situation is such that absolute knowledge is not attainable ... precisely because we can grasp what relativism is and asserts, we can transcend it."[65] By us standing outside of our moment, or transcending the present, relativism is no longer a threat to the truth but an explanation of the world. Here Cupitt expresses an ontology of his own: "The interpretive plasticity of the world describes the curious way in which the world of our experience is seemingly willing to lend itself to interpretation in terms of a great variety of different programmes."[66] This intense form of subjectivism is, for Cupitt, compatible with the nature of the world, and the act of grasping at once both the possibility and relativity of one's framework is what Cupitt calls the act of faith.[67]

Cupitt would not hold to this definition of faith throughout the rest of his career, but it still helps to underline some of the difficulties with the nonrealist position. For example, at the end of *Taking Leave of God*, Cupitt expresses himself in Feuerbachian terms: "I continue to speak of God and to pray to God. God is the mythical embodiment of all that one is concerned with in the spiritual life."[68] For Cupitt, these concerns of the spiritual life have shifted dramatically in the modern world and, correspondingly, so has the "mythical embodiment" of God. It is clear that the religious language he holds on to – prayer, spirituality – has been abstracted and no longer has a definitive place within a tradition of faith, much like for Bevan before him.[69] In the end the language that does survive, already unrelated to a scriptural context, is powerless to describe the world. The act of description is left to the rarefied feeling of ecstatic faith, which comes to terms with the metaphysical closure of the world and the unreality of God. While Cupitt's genealogy of modernity retains certain loose theological indicators like "death" and "rebirth,"[70] it is clear that history is now under the control of a force that has nothing to do with providence in any biblical sense. In his own words, "The attempt to retain religious meanings fixed must fail, because the process of historical change slowly evacuates them and turns them into superstitions."[71]

If there is a power behind this "evacuation," it is not represented by any variation of Christian doctrine, such as the incarnation and death of Christ is utilized by Altizer. Rather, Cupitt speaks about the real context in which this shift has occurred as an earthly encounter with the void:

Everyone must eventually come to terms with his own transience and the Void that encircles him. Religion is about that; not about consolation, but first and foremost about the truth of life. You must enter what *The Cloud of Unknowing* calls a nothing and a nowhere, full blind and full dark.[72]

The history of modernity for Cupitt is about the unveiling of the void and the immediate encounter that occurs between humanity and reality once religious illusions have become unmasked. Morality is constituted by moral action without the promise of any eternal reward: morality for its own sake, carried out in the void.[73]

But this narrative – the emergence of the disinterested and the autonomous, fearless self – would again shift for Cupitt. As Gavin Hyman has noted, in the 1980s Cupitt, like many intellectuals of the time, began to transition from a Kantian epistemology toward a post-modern understanding of the subject and morality.[74] Steven Shakespeare notes that Cupitt's early nonrealism was simply a form of classical Kantian Liberalism: "Theology is presented in a thoroughly dialectical guise, in which its positive images must always be treated as contingent creations, to be shattered as soon as we are tempted to cling to them and confuse them with the reality of God."[75] The reality of God is unknowable and cannot be spoken of in any stable manner.

But in the 1980s Cupitt would shift his views in this respect toward a more postmodern understanding of language. He had already been reading Wittgenstein, but his encounter with Derrida moved his non-realism to another level. For example, instead of God being a void beyond or hidden within experience, Cupitt writes,

God is not selfsame, but creates precisely by an endless moving on and pointing to something else. He is not a being, but the universal sign of relation, a principle of otherness and difference that divides the Void to form the field of meanings and gradations of value. He creates not by hugging his own divinity but by renouncing it.[76]

The endless moving and pointing of language is no longer part of a narrative of progress or of the emergence of human responsibility but is simply "an immanent process of dialectical development without any inbuilt and overriding purposiveness, and only a flux of differentiations without any substances or sheerly given atomic units to build with."[77] This represents yet another metaphysical conception of the world in which the Christian faith has only a fading purpose, as it is merged into the infinite field of signs and meanings. Cupitt writes,

> The general metaphysics picture that we work towards – it is only a picture, and we work only towards it, because these must not be done too crudely – seems to be a little reminiscent of F.H. Bradley's metaphysics of feeling, and also of Russell's neutral monism in its attempt to achieve a flat two dimensional surface.[78]

To be sure, Cupitt's idea here does sound much like Bradley's absolute, an objectless totality of all experience without any reference to an outside.

The shifts in thinking that characterizes Cupitt's thought represent a relentless press towards an immanent and immediate religious faith. This, perhaps, can account for his growing appreciation of Maurice and his corresponding uncertainty about Mansel stated earlier.[79] Indeed, according to Shakespeare, Cupitt's evolved position represents an even more severe form of immanentism than Derrida's: Derrida spoke of the "secret," the unknowable embedded in the world, which is possessed by no one and which holds the immanent world, and persons within it, open toward the other.[80] But for Cupitt, "The text seems trapped by an overwrought dualism. Either Platonism or 'nothing is hidden.'"[81]

Yet, despite these differences, Cupitt's vision of life in this new world, "solar loving," is typically postmodern. Life is lived through "ecstatic" immanence "immersed in and unreservedly given over to its own utter transience."[82] Solar love is "ardent and heedless,"[83] unbounded in some way, unstructured by traditions but set loose among the infinite variations of reality. Cupitt argues that there is nothing hidden within human beings or outside of them, and this metaphysical doctrine commands "you to live as the Sun does, expending yourself in communicative life giving self-externalization."[84] Atheism, Cupitt suggests, "sides with the Son against the Father," which, in effect, overthrows the established order and calls for a continual clash with fixed and established norms.[85] The contrast of law and gospel is a derivative of the Father-and-Son contrast:

> Gospel ethics tries to live beyond the distinctions, and therefore to live purely affirmatively, without *ressentiment*, without

differences of respect, without dividing, discriminating or exclud-
ing. It is an ethical style for an "open" world that no longer has a
fixed structure.[86]

Certainly these words recall Collingwood's comment that Bradley
was seeking to amend Mansel's "project of dividing" reality into
distinctions and limitations.[87] For Cupitt, as for Bradley, even the
distinction of the natural and the supernatural threatens to tear the
fabric of the world.

Cupitt's vision of the world is not unlike John Caputo's, another
philosopher of religion strongly influenced by Derrida. In *The
Weakness of God*, Caputo writes,

> The name of God is the name of an event transpiring in being's
> restless heart, creating confusion in the house of being, forcing
> being into motion, mutation, transformation, reversal. The name
> of God is the event that being both dreads and longs for, sighing
> and groaning until something new is brought forth from down
> below. The name of God is the name of what can happen to
> being, of what being would become, of what rising up from
> below being pushed being beyond itself, outside itself, as being's
> hope, being's desire.[88]

For Caputo, the indeterminacy of God "calls us beyond ourselves,
down unplotted paths and into unexplored lands, calling us to go
where we cannot go, extending us beyond our reach."[89] While Caputo's
use of the "impossible"[90] as a hidden promise within the immanent
world may have been more than Cupitt might concede, the overall
effect of Caputo's philosophy upon the traditions of Christian theology is largely the same: the particularities of doctrine, the specific
narrative of scripture and spectrum of Christian beliefs that anchor
piety, are dissolved in the cycles and circles of indeterminacy.[91] The
scriptures, for Caputo and Cupitt, have their place within the flux of
reality, but they, like everything else, are set adrift within a more
comprehensive metaphysical scheme.

Despite the fact that Cupitt's religious nonrealism underwent certain
shifts throughout his career, he was clearly drawing on trends that
began in the nineteenth century and even earlier. In this way, the differences that mark his thought between a more explicitly Kantian
phase and his subsequent postmodern adjustments are perhaps

overstated.[92] In either case, Cupitt is advocating for an alternative metaphysics that places traditional theological claims under a master system that is purported to be closer to reality. Rowan Williams draws attention to this aspect of Cupitt's work and suggests that Cupitt appeals "repeatedly to the self-evidence of what he is saying in respect of the contemporary consciousness" as if the character of the world were obvious to all.[93] Williams's own strategy in replying to Cupitt is not to disprove his vision "but rather to ask whether the vision commended is quite as consistent, attractive, and liveable as it is made out to be."[94]

In this respect, the comparison of Mansel and Cupitt is revealing. Clearly, by 2006 Cupitt had largely forgotten about Mansel, but even his earlier suggestions that he appropriated Mansel's theory of regulative truth now seem suspect. Williams's question about the consistency and attractiveness of Cupitt's vision is obviously important, but with respect to Mansel, it is clear that within Cupitt's metaphysics the scriptures, unhinged from any theological reality, cannot even serve a regulative function. In fact, it was Cupitt's doubts about the validity of the Bible, the moral portrait of God that it presents, and the overall narrative that it describes that provoked his nonrealism in the first instance. Despite his attempts to embrace "ordinary" reality and the world as it is, his works are full of sarcasm and cynicism with respect to the "mythological" beliefs of "ordinary folk."[95] He condemns the pastoral theology of *The Book of Common Prayer*, which along with the scriptures has lost so much "explanatory utility."[96] Whereas Mansel's intention was to uphold the faith and piety of common Christians and to place that piety within a scriptural context, the effect of Cupitt's work has been to undermine that piety at every turn, to question the notion of prayer and to deride any providential concept of God that permits the agency of the Holy Spirit within the created world. Like Bevan and Freeman, Cupitt reads Mansel as a kind of pragmatist, and yet it is not clear that Mansel's view of God as represented by the whole of Scripture is pragmatic in any way. In fact, in Cupitt's terms, the "traditional" notion of God is destructive of personal piety and creates contradictions and insoluble difficulties for individual spiritual experience.

Still Cupitt's work is highly important for illuminating the crisis of faith within which we continue to live. The "self-evidence" that Williams alludes to is not without warrant, and Cupitt's assumption that the Bible has lost all explanatory value and moral credibility is a serious consideration for modern theologians. However, Cupitt's attempt to recast certain aspects of the Christian faith within an alternative metaphysical vision clearly fails to do justice to the integrity of the Scriptures. The scriptures look utterly lost in Cupitt's world of "solar living" and eternal flux. In some respect Cupitt is an allegory of Mansel's deepest fears, that the scriptures cannot live long in metaphysical systems that pull apart, reorder and subject the coherence of the Bible to the scrutiny of a higher or lower principle.[97] At the very least, Cupitt has the courage of his convictions, and his work illustrates the incongruence of two, maybe more, vying worldviews. Whether as a pragmatist, idealist or some kind of postmodern theologian, the effects of these varying influences for Cupitt continually disrupt and break down the stability of scripture's witness to God's character and reality in the world. The basic assumption that Cupitt accepts wholesale from a certain strand of Anglican idealism is that the world has moved beyond the point at which the Scriptures in their entirety can refer meaningfully to God.

MANSEL AND THE UNITY OF SCRIPTURE

Mansel's reputation was solidified early in the twentieth century by historians who read him as a foil for the dominant movement of the Spirit in history. Writers like Bevan, Freeman, and Cupitt sensed the Spirit moving in a different direction and found in Mansel an early opponent of certain strands of metaphysical idealism and theological realism. But both of these interpretations of Mansel were agreed that the scriptures in their entirety could no longer speak convincingly, accurately or reliably about God and the world. The scriptures, for Bevan, seemed to inhabit a shadowy region somewhere between religious truth and outdated fiction. This was initially true for Cupitt, but he pushed the confusion toward at least one possible outcome: that the Bible does not actually describe a real, supernatural God at all.

But for Mansel the theory of the regulative truth of scripture was a device to defend the power of the whole Bible to shape and order human life, in the midst of the metaphysical and historical difficulties within scripture itself. Human reason itself has no vantage point from which to adjudicate the contradictions and complexities of scripture's witness to God's presence in the world. Thus, scripture can only be regulatively true if it is free to operate as an indivisible whole. This is Mansel's concluding point in his lectures:

> The life of man is one, and the system of Christian faith is one: each part supplying something that another lacks ... But we may avail ourselves of that which satisfies our own peculiar needs, only by accepting it as part and parcel of the one indivisible whole.[98]

For a rhetorical flourish, he uses the image of a tree:

> The tree is not then most flourishing, when its branches are lopped, and its trunk peeled, and its whole body cut down to one hard unyielding mass; but when one principle of life pervades it throughout; when the trunk and the branches claim brotherhood and fellowship with the leaf that quivers, and the twig that bends to the breeze, and the bark that is delicate and easily wounded and the root that lies lowly and unnoticed in the earth.[99]

This is the kind of appeal to the diversity of religious experience that Freeman and Cupitt were after, perhaps, but Mansel – without warrant, they would say – encloses this experience within the scriptural world of Christian faith, which "so strangely yet so fully adapts itself" to human experience.[100]

This point concerning Mansel's work found expression in Gordon Lewis Phillips's little-known book called *Seeing and Believing* (1957).[101] *Seeing and Believing* is a short and somewhat obscure work that is intended as a criticism of modern Anglicanism and its inclination toward the "historian's" sense of probable faith and mistrust of the Bible. It is in this sense that Phillips turns to Mansel as a long-forgotten figure who argued for a form of Christian faith that embraces the whole of revelation. "There is plenty of room," Phillips writes, "for 'spiritual search.' But not, for a Christian, to find the truth – only to penetrate ever deeper into its reference and meaning."[102]

Mansel's understanding, Phillips writes, of the act of faith as an acceptance, in total, of scriptural revelation is based upon his understanding of human knowledge and God's indwelling of human reality: "This means that the knowledge we have of God in this life is not a knowledge of God in his absolute nature but only as he is reflected in the life of us, his creatures."[103] This reflection within creation marks the essential character of the scriptures, which cannot be separated into divine or human aspects:

> Most valuable of all, his conclusion establishes the essential unity of divine revelation and the utter impossibility of accepting some truths on the basis of their divine authority and rejecting others, when it suits, by appealing to human reason as the ground for their rejection.[104]

Human reason, in the case of the Bible, is inhabited by God's intentional presence, and while God is transcendent, He approaches the world from within the created constraints of human life.[105]

Phillips's own purposes for endorsing Mansel's views is bound up with the notion of the regulative truth of scripture as Mansel explained it. But Phillips uses the more straightforward theological language of holiness and sanctity. Holiness or sanctity, for Phillips, can only be forged in the posture of submissiveness and reception, and this is precisely what Mansel's theology accomplishes.[106] Phillips writes,

> We should be alarmed at the absence in our communion of that specific type of Christian living which we call sanctity and we should be uneasy that clash between modern culture and divine revealed truth, has not produced in our land and in our tradition that vivid sign of supernatural operation, which we see in France.[107]

Phillips goes on: "The methods of historic theology lead only to probable certainties. And probable certainty makes no saints."[108] The frequent polemic in his book against "historic theology" is one that Phillips astonishingly never really develops, but it is a clear reference to the contemporary tendency to relativize theological claims within varying traditions, whether within the biblical world or subsequent ecclesial traditions. Furthermore, the "probable certainty" that he pillories is not the probabilism of Butler, Mansel, and Newman, for whom the weighing of probabilities demands decision and commitment. Rather, he is referring predominantly to the weakening effect of historical studies on the credibility of the Bible and the traditions of the Church.

Despite its unusual argumentation and at times tendentious presentation, Phillips's book is surprisingly prescient. For example, much like Stephen Sykes in *The Integrity of Anglicanism*, he questions the assumption that Anglicans have played a mediating role between rival traditions. But he asks, "have Anglicans so mediated from principle? And if so, what is this principle? Is it the principle ... that absolute truth is not revealed?"[109] Such a claim "seems to make nonsense of the Scriptures ... For we must pay serious attention to the fact that this generalization of what Anglicans have in fact been found to do, is now itself being offered as a canon of theological truth."[110] In other words, Phillips grasps hold of Mansel's concern that a search for a comprehensive theology or metaphysics that can contain a constant questioning of biblical credibility, and that can erase fundamental theological differences, risks pulling apart the comprehensive totality of the scriptural witness. The cost of such a risk, for Phillips and for Mansel as well, is nothing less than the holiness and sanctity of the Church.

Phillips issues another challenge, which might be well received today: "It is surely time that the dogmatic theologians of our communion plucked up their courage ... and stretched out hands in holy alliance to the biblical scholars, their proper allies and who, left to themselves, look so forlorn."[111] This plea stems from his belief that scripture must be received and read as a comprehensive whole that is not intended to be divided and separated along critical or traditional lines. In this respect, Mansel has never had a more sympathetic reader.[112] In Phillips, Mansel's view that the scriptures provide a comprehensive account of reality and God's providential engagement with the world receives a very forceful expression. To be sure, since *Seeing and Believing*, very few of Mansel's readers have taken up this case.

If the goal of idealists like Green and Bradley was to articulate reality as a spiritual whole, they found this holistic framework in a developmental metaphysics that appeared broader and more comprehensive than the biblical account of God's presence in the world. The *Lux Mundi* writers were not willing to do this, but their demand for a spiritually holistic theology struggled to relate portions of scripture to the strictures of their progressive scheme. While twentieth-century writers like Bevan, Freeman, and Cupitt did not employ the same idealistic framework, they nevertheless took over the assumption that a truthful account of reality, whether theological or philosophical, cannot be found within the entire scriptural account. These writers used the limitations of human thought as a device to not limit their own speculations but rather the writings of the scriptural authors themselves. In Phillips's terms, this kind of "historicism" inhibited the power of scripture to form Christian lives. For Mansel, these developments obscured the image in which God is known in the world, and because holiness concerns the whole person, the whole breadth of scripture, and the strange, mysterious, and loving God it describes, must be allowed to address itself to the Church.

CONCLUSION:
SCRIPTURE AND CONTEMPORARY ANGLICANISM

While Cupitt's philosophy of religion represents a radical departure from mainstream Anglican theology, there can be little doubt that it draws on themes that have been present within nineteenth- and twentieth-century Anglicanism. For example, the 1922 report *Doctrine in the Church of England* reveals the clear influence of an idealist metaphysics that was prevalent at the time. The section on scripture talks about the unity of the "whole" Bible but cautions that the "limitations of the human writer and his age distort for us the presentation of this central theme [God's love], as when vindictiveness is attributed to God."[113] Likewise, the brief statement on scripture includes the following qualification of prophecy: "We cannot now regard as a principal purpose or evidence of Inspiration the giving of detailed information about the future."[114] This claim is made in light of "knowledge now at our disposal" and the "progressive self-revelation of God in history" through the Spirit's work within but also without the narrative of Scripture.[115] The history of the Bible describes "higher conceptions of God supervening upon lower ones, through the continual communion and conflict between the spirit of man and the Spirit of God."[116]

These types of claims, typical in many ways of *Lux Mundi* and Anglican idealism, flow from a shared assumption with Cupitt: namely, that the historical isolation and limitations of the biblical authors require the reordering and, in some cases, the modification or disposal of certain portions of scripture. In the case of the report, the Holy Spirit, rather than leading the Church into the truth of scriptures, leads the Church into the truth almost in spite of the many scriptural irregularities. Obviously Cupitt represents an extreme form of this method, but both *Doctrine in the Church of England* and Cupitt are operating within the same assumption that the witness of the whole scriptures has been severely weakened by the critical analysis of the Bible. Perhaps more fundamentally, the historical limitations of scripture provide an escape from the difficult moral and character depiction of God that proved so challenging for Mansel's contemporaries and has continued to be so into the twenty-first century.

In the third chapter I discussed Rowan Williams's suggestion that within Anglicanism there have been two forms of skepticism at work: the first considers the limitations of human thought and dangers of dogmatic closure "because the search for definite boundaries suggests that you might be 'in possession' of the territory." The second form is "generated by Enlightenment suspicion of authority, in which the target of the questioning is the formulae as such and the processes by which they were shaped.[117] Williams's distinction is very useful, and it highlights a feature of Anglicanism that is commonly suggested but less commonly understood. Williams speaks about the place of "sanctioned words" but not always knowing "where the boundaries" are within these words. But in order for these words to be available as "territory" to move within, they must be allowed to function beyond the limitations of historical context. To be sure, it is not totally clear if Williams is referring to the words of scripture or strictly doctrinal formulae. But in either case, there has been a strong tendency in modern Anglicanism to limit the breadth and capacity of certain portions of scripture for fear of letting the claims of one age speak to another.

There is a way then in which the two skepticisms that Williams speaks about become difficult to distinguish, at least with respect to the reading of scripture. Clearly Cupitt, while holding on to certain generalized theological notions, no longer believed that the Bible, in its entirety, was capable of speaking to the unprecedented developments of the modern world. This was not true for the writers of *Doctrine in the Church of England* or the *Lux Mundi* theologians, but clearly the limits of human thought became useful as a strategy, not so much for curtailing human speculations but for limiting the claims of certain biblical writers. The fear of theories like verbal inerrancy is obvious in the report and in the writings of many theologians of that era, and yet the alternatives so often suffer from a piecemeal approach to the Bible.[118] As I have argued through the preceding chapters, certain streamlined theological views – God's love, spiritual communion – were shaped and formed often with little appeal to the complicated and complex narrative of God's covenantal relationship with his people.

Therefore, if a certain kind of skepticism is indeed a virtue within Anglican theology, there appears to be a need for greater clarification of the term's use. Skepticism, of Williams's first variety, is typically paired with a theological and ecclesial vision of comprehensiveness and a reluctance to claim full "possession" of any particular truth. In L. William Countryman's terms, this represents the difficult but profound vocation of Anglicanism, to exist somewhere between the "Pope" and the "Paper Pope."[119] Yet Stephen Sykes has questioned the coherence of this notion: "Comprehensiveness is, therefore, per se, a radically unclear notion, requiring qualification to give it precision; and it is for this reason that when it is used in Anglican apologetic it has to be used in contexts which make clear both what is comprehended and what is still excluded."[120] In Sykes's terms, if it is indeed Anglicanism's vocation to live within a unique ecclesial position without the customary confessional or authoritative boundaries, some kind of theological account of this position must be given.

Stephen Ross White, in his book *Authority in Anglicanism*, attempts to offer such an account, though it suffers from the same ambivalence toward scripture that has characterized Mansel's readers. White acknowledges that writers like Cupitt have clearly touched a nerve with many people, and Cupitt's work raises profound questions for Anglicans: "Indeed, if scripture, creed and doctrines are found to be relativistic through and through, then where can such authority any longer be convincingly located?"[121] White remarks that modern fundamentalism and returns to scriptural inerrancy have been effective in resisting radicalism, though this has never really been an option for Anglicans.[122] To suddenly revert to a strict scripturalism would upset the delicate balance of scripture, reason, and tradition. White accepts Cupitt's view that all knowledge is relative to time and circumstance, and he also agrees that the biblical notion of a God who acts and intervenes in history is now impossible to accept.[123] Thus White's own proposal is a radical return to a simplified belief in the person of Jesus freed from the imprisonment of traditional doctrinal formulations:

> Such a doctrinal method, if followed, allows Christianity to become infinitely flexible in its response to the world without

ever abandoning its basic conviction as to the centrality of Jesus Christ and his place as the locus of God's self revelation to humankind. We are set free from the shackles of rigid doctrinal formulations (which as relativism rightly acknowledges are always cast in the mold and language of a particular age) and allowed to formulate our own more provisional ... estimates of how and what we can rightly be said to believe.[124]

White's comments could be interpreted in a variety of manners. What is clear, however, is that once again the limits of human thought and the relativity of all truth claims seem to have more purchase on the past than on the present. This, according to Timothy Gouldstone, has long been one of the pervading themes of Anglican Liberalism, "a radical transformation of the concept of revelation which sees it as a created reality rather than as a reality given from above."[125] "Given from above" need not imply any specific theory of inspiration, but at the least it must mean that the words and narrative of scripture are not realities that can be isolated within the relativity of the past without implication for contemporary Christian theology and practice.

Sykes does believe that a partial account of Anglican comprehensiveness is possible:

The dispersal of authority in Anglicanism is rooted in the conviction that Christians to whom the Scriptures are read in their own language are able to judge of the essentials of the faith. Because it is a liturgical provision that the Scriptures should be heard, and because the Scriptures are contextualized in worship which seeks at once to evoke the fundamentals and induct the worshipper into the heart of Christian experience.[126]

Sykes here assumes that the scriptures are a living reality within the life of the Church and that within the breadth of scripture the "heart of Christian experience" is found and negotiated. Such a position does not beget an obvious clarity on matters of belief and practice, but it does ensure the context in which Christians will discuss and determine these realities. Furthermore, it states that the scriptures as a whole form this experience.

Sykes's understanding of the comprehensiveness of Anglicanism coheres with Ephraim Radner's in an essay entitled "The Scriptural Community: Authority in Anglicanism." Radner suggest that the conception of a scriptural community allows the Church to remain open to historical realities while remaining under some kind of communal authority.[127] Indeed this was the vision that Thomas Cranmer set in *The Book of Common Prayer*. Radner writes,

> Cranmer is adamantly opposed to viewing Scripture primarily as a source of right doctrine, and therefore as the object of human reasoning and interpretation; rather Scripture is to act as the practical "organizer of life" for the whole people, and its meaning is accessible only to the "virtuous" who submit to the corporate demands of the church's "body."[128]

Cranmer's intentions in this regard represented

> a broad theological argument about the nature of the Christian Church's authoritative witness within a "communion of the scripturally molded" whose contours lay in the practices of a people's common worship and order ... and in the virtues of a person's scripturally-infused social relationships ("duties") rather than in the dogmatic integrity of a person's discourse.[129]

Such a reading of Anglican origins might be contested, but it is my argument that Mansel's theology was intended to uphold a vision of the Anglican Church as a scriptural community that is moulded by and lives within the language and narrative of scripture. To the degree that modern forms of skepticism have made such a vision inconceivable, Mansel's limits of thought and theory of regulative truth were intended to create a space in which the Church could find its life within the scriptures. The fear of Cupitt and others that such a view would sever the connection between Christianity and a changing world only holds if the Bible itself is incapable of describing and encompassing the world as it is currently known. Clearly for Sykes, Radner, and, I argue, Mansel, the scriptures are capable of forming and moulding the contemporary Church. Mansel's notion of the practicality of the Bible and the capacity of its language to "expand" around a changing world favoured a strong understanding of biblical inspiration without committing the Bible to specific theories of inspiration. Indeed, the foil of verbal inerrancy seemed to have obscured this possible understanding of Anglicanism's ecclesial identity for writers like Cupitt, Bevan, and White. Yet it seems that a programmatic skeptical and relativistic approach to the Bible in modern Anglicanism has had an alienating effect between the modern Church and the scriptures in which its life is to be found. One of the most grave consequences is that modern Christianity in general has been given over to historical narratives like that of Cupitt's and its more mainstream variants, wherein the development of the world has begun to outstrip the history in which God has formed and shaped his people.

Conclusion

In the preceding chapters I argued that Mansel's theological skepticism and theory of regulative truth have been rarely understood and summarily dismissed as counterproductive to his actual purposes. I have argued in this book that Mansel deserves to be read today not as a Kantian philosopher or as the father of English Agnosticism or as an early death of God theologian but as an orthodox theologian who engaged the place of scripture and its role in the Church. Mansel's theology should be remembered today not as a halfway house between belief and unbelief but as a robust account of how traditional and scriptural Christian faith can flourish in an increasingly hostile context. The philosophy of Herbert Spencer and the later theology of Don Cupitt stand within a stream of English thought that Mansel resisted at every turn. Though the contemporary image of Mansel has been branded by his association with these two figures, it is time to acknowledge the real context in which Mansel made his arguments and the particular claims that he made concerning the Bible. By way of conclusion I will offer a discussion of Mansel's place among a few contemporary Anglican theologians in order to briefly suggest a manner in which his thought might be applicable today.

The recent surge of interest in typological or figural reading of the Bible has served to once again highlight the question of metaphysics and ontology in relation to theology and the scriptures. If the historical-critical tendency to focus upon the text itself and the historical context from which it emerged has not rendered satisfactory results for many contemporary theologians, what reality within or behind the text enables a typological reading of the Bible? A Catholic theologian, Matthew Levering, has argued persuasively that Christian exegesis "will need a theological–metaphysical (sapiential) stance critically adequate to the theological and metaphysical realities whose active historical presence the Bible depicts."[1] Whatever the details of this stance, Levering suggests that "such typological exegesis cannot stand on its own" but requires the magisterium of the Church to gauge and assess the various performances of these readings.[2] Of course, such appeals to the Church's magisterial authority are not quite so straightforward for Protestant theologians. Though, if the entire scriptures are to continue in their role as a practical organizer of the Anglican Church's common life – or the common life of any Christian Church – the question of what holds the scriptures together and allows them to describe and shape our current existence remains as pressing as ever.[3]

Mansel's theology today may be most relevant in its ability to test and examine theological systems that seek a grounding in scripture but explore that larger philosophical context in which scripture is rooted. I have argued throughout that Mansel's skepticism was a method designed to allow the full range of scriptural "facts," language, and imagery to stand out against the, at times, obscuring effects of philosophical or theological systems. He schematized these effects through the concepts of dogmatism and rationalism, not concepts represented by moods or argumentative tenor but by an actual method of intellectual engagement with theological realities. For example, he writes:

> The one [dogmatism] seeks to build up a complete scheme of theological doctrine out of the unsystematic materials furnished by Scripture, partly by the more complete development of certain leading ideas ... The other [rationalism] aims at the same end by opposite means. It strives to attain to unity and completeness of system, not by filling up supposed deficiencies, but by paring down supposed excrescences.[4]

It was not so much, as some contemporaries feared, that Mansel disliked the actual discipline of theology but rather that all theological reasoning must continually adjust to the contours of scripture, which "supplies him [the theologian] with facts to which his system has to adapt itself."[5] These facts, Mansel argued, reveal one God that is received in faith through the medium of an "incomplete system," the missing portions of which cannot simply be supplied through our reasoning.[6]

Kant's application of certain moral standards to the character of God – a common move, as I have argued, throughout the nineteenth century – provided Mansel with an easy example of rationalism at work in theology.[7] However, dogmatists were perhaps more difficult to locate, in part because the definition Mansel provides admits a certain level of ambivalence: at what point does theological writing begin the process of filling out an incomplete system?[8] This question becomes even more vexed when these so called dogmatists make use of a wide range of scriptural reference to build up their systems. While Mansel defended criticisms of the sacrificial or penal aspects of the atonement, he was nervous about atonement accounts that were rooted in some kind of logical or theological necessity.[9]

Thus, for Mansel there is a danger of saying too little or saying too much about the character of God: "Throughout every page of Scripture, God reveals himself,"[10] and the needs of any theological system need to be assiduous in allowing and illuminating the manner in which scripture does this. Mansel's deeper concern was not just exegetical: if God truly reveals himself and is apprehended on "every page of Scripture" then the frameworks or systems that we bring to the scriptures needs to be flexible and spacious enough to adjust to "the many colored rays into which God's presence is refracted in its passage into the human soul."[11] Inversely, the incomplete character of scripture – its many coloured rays – implied a scheme of salvation that was broad enough to include and expand around the endless peculiarities of created life without surrendering its unity. Scripture's breadth, for Mansel, was a function of its divine inspiration, which relays wisdom, knowledge and events in human terms, but not derivable from any independent human source. Rationalism and dogmatism, while trying to create a wider, more comprehensive system, in fact narrowed the scope of scripture by attempting to dull or smooth over the edges of a language that was chosen as the most appropriate manner in which to speak of God.

It is interesting then, to read the contemporary Anglican theologian John Milbank in light of Mansel's criticism of dogmatism in theology. Milbank's theology is an interesting example not only because of its powerful influence in contemporary theology but also because of its stated ambition to unite all reality within a theological perspective. His critique of modern liberalism and its genealogical roots in the medieval theology of Duns Scotus, while not entirely original to Milbank, has still provoked deep resonances and profound criticisms amongst his readers. Radical orthodoxy in general, the movement Milbank has championed, has been influenced by Cupitt's nonrealism and the challenges it presents for modern theology.[12] Milbank's ontological claims can be read as a response and counter to Cupitt's skeptical and nonrealist theological positions. However, like Cupitt's, one of the most common criticisms of Milbank's theology has been that his ontological arguments have been used as a wide brush to paint sweeping judgments over the historical genesis of modernity and over the scriptures themselves.[13]

But it is not the case that Milbank is unconcerned with scripture. For example, in *Theology and Social Theory* Milbank is sympathetic to the narrative concerns of theologians like Lindbeck and Frei: "George Lindbeck and Hans Frei have been quite right to call us back to narrative as being that alone which can 'identify' God for us."[14] However, Milbank goes on to say, "But more attention must be paid to the structural complexity of narrative, and especially the way it has to assume a never fully representable synchronic setting, which means that it always in a fashion anticipates the speculative task of ontology and theology."[15] While Lindbeck argues that the narrative of scripture is ruled by a Christological focus, Milbank argues that Lindbeck's focus upon the narrative of scripture lifts the actual stories out of their historical setting as they become a speculative norm that is applied to varying historical moments.[16]

This does seem to be an accurate depiction of Lindbeck's view. In *The Nature of Doctrine* he writes, "it is the religion instantiated in Scripture which defines being, truth, goodness and beauty, and the nonscriptural exemplifications of these realities need to be transformed into figures of the scriptural ones."[17] Lindbeck's worry about the ontological status of doctrinal statements is, in part, that they lack the first order versatility of scriptural images: "If ... the doctrine is a proposition with ontological reference, only one type of theory has a chance of being true."[18] Thus, in a similar manner to Mansel, and even Butler, Lindbeck argues that the scriptures form a framework within which people "live their lives and understand reality."[19]

However, it is this precise aspect of Lindbeck's thought that Milbank wants to distance himself from, in some respects, because he does not seem to believe that the scriptures can perform that function. Though Milbank at least agrees with Lindbeck and Frei on the narrative character of theological truth, the narrative he has in mind is perhaps something larger: "The metanarrative is not just the story of Jesus, it is the continuing story of the Church, already realized in a finally exemplary way by Christ, yet still to be realized universally, in harmony with Christ, and yet differently, by all generations of Christians."[20] This statement alone is not alarming, but the implications of this "metanarrative" begin to accumulate some familiar concerns: "It is, in fact, at the point where the metanarrative requires a speculative ontology to support its meta-status, that Christian counter-history is revealed as also a 'Christian sociology.'"[21]

It is within this speculative ontology that Milbank's moral concerns about violence come into view as a controlling idea in his theology. The stories of the Bible serve this larger vision in an aesthetic fashion that makes concrete and persuasive the ontological priority of peace: "We need the stories of Jesus for salvation, rather than just a speculative notion of the Good, because only the attraction exercised by a particular set of words and images causes us to acknowledge the Good and to have an idea of the ultimate telos."[22] Within this "ultimate telos," rooted in an ontology of peace, Milbank states that punishment and judgment have no real theological reality:

> For every time we punish, or utter a judgment against someone held in our power, we deny that person's freedom and spiritual equality: she does not have equal rights to speak about or act against our sins. This stance of judgment and punishment is never occupied by God, because he pronounces no sentences that we do not pronounce against ourselves.[23]

What exactly this statement means with respect to biblical interpretation is not necessarily clear for Milbank. For example, is it scripturally possible to speak of a God who does not pronounce and enact judgment and punishment? Of course, this not quite what Milbank is saying: *Theology and Social Theory* concludes with the affirmation that God has judged, once and for all, the violence of secular reason that has worked destructively inside and outside the Church.[24] But there remains at least some question about the scriptural character of the God who makes this judgment. For example, the Church's "break with Judaism" forms part of its political critique of violence.[25]

Hans Boersma has criticized Milbank's seeming rejection of God's use of redemptive violence but has also pointed to Milbank's more recent adjustments.[26] Certainly in *Being Reconciled* Milbank takes a more complicated stance on the question of violence and pacifism, but it is also in this work that some of his philosophical assumptions come to bear, perhaps awkwardly, on the central theological question of atonement.[27] It is not so much that Milbank's account of forgiveness and Christ's atonement falls outside of some kind of orthodox limits, but more that it receives a rather narrow scriptural profile. For example, Milbank speaks of forgiveness in contrast to the position of Duns Scotus:

> Once more, Scotus's ontic conception of God makes him think of divine initiative and human response as external to each other, in such a way that our merit becomes too much ours, or at any rate something that does not of itself return to God, but rather something which God may or may not graciously receive. One consequence of this loss of a sense of participation is therefore a loss also of a sense of exchange between infinite and finite.[28]

Milbank understands Christ's death on the cross as an instantiation of an infinite divine gift exchange, a circulating process that knows no beginning or end:

> Christ's earthly self-giving death is but a shadow of the true eternal peaceful process in the heavenly tabernacle, and redemption consists in Christ's transition from shadow to reality – which is also, mysteriously, his "return" to cosmic omnipresence and irradiating of the shadows.[29]

At every opportunity Milbank qualifies and downplays the sacrificial language that surrounds the scriptural representation of Christ's death in favour of his all-embracing theological vision:

> Hence the divine answer to the original human refusal of his gift is not to demand sacrifice – of which he has no need – but to go on giving in and through our refusals of the gift, to the point where these refusals are overcome. Christ's abandonment offers no compensation to God, but when we most abandon the divine donation it surpasses itself, and appears more than ever, raising us up into the eternal gift-exchange of the Trinity.[30]

One could argue that Milbank's theology of atonement expands into an almost impersonal process of eternal gift exchange that receives concrete and finite reality in the life of Christ.[31] But I do not think Milbank intends to remove the personal and relational aspect of forgiveness that is so characteristic of Christian piety.

However, in Mansel's terms, it does seem that Milbank's moral and speculative concerns place the scriptural depiction of God's character in a difficult position. Milbank himself admits that an ontology of peace and the ontological participation in that reality is a speculative idea that cannot be demonstrated.[32] Yet despite the contingent nature of the claim, Milbank states that this "Catholic vision of ontological peace now provides the only alternative to a nihilistic outlook."[33] Of course, all Christian claims stand within this paradoxical scenario of being indemonstrable but to those who hold them necessary and morally compelling. However, in Lindbeck's terms, the ontological status of Milbank's claims make it such that "only one type of theory has a chance of being true," and it is for this reason that Milbank's theology has provoked such wide criticism.[34]

Perhaps the greater issue though is that Milbank's all-embracing theory and morally driven concerns – admirable in their own way – render portions of the Bible nearly unavailable for the sort of figural application that Lindbeck describes. Indeed, this was Mansel's precise concern about theological speculative knowledge, or "dogmatism": that unprovable speculative claims would be used to adjust, improve, or criticize the scriptural depiction of God. Mansel criticized Maurice for allowing speculation about the nature of God's eternal life to control his reading of scripture. Such a criticism can be made of Milbank as well, even if these speculative ideas arise in some sense from the scriptures themselves. For Mansel, our theological ideas – speculations, perhaps – required the qualification and adjustment of the whole range of biblical material.[35]

But for Mansel, it was not just correct exegetical methods that were at stake but the actual capacity of his generation to be able to recognize its Lord in the only source that revealed him. This ability, Mansel perceived, had everything to do with the perception of the actual character of the Biblical God and his activity in the world. Milbank's desire to describe the world in all embracing theological terms, from a Christian perspective, is admirable. But there is a way in which Milbank's ontology takes over scriptures' role in doing this. While Milbank's theological ontology offers a strong alternative to Cupitt's assertion that we can no longer believe in the metaphysical reality of God, Milbank does less to counter Cupitt's equally unsettling conviction that the scriptures have lost their capacity to describe the modern world. This was the simple intention of Mansel's theory of regulative truth, but it is possible that his theory brought the language of scripture too close with its, at times, frightening, threatening, and perplexing revelation of God's character. His commentary on Matthew and his sermons made a modest attempt toward providing an internally coherent and consistent portrayal of God's activity in the world, read through the lens of Jesus Christ. But his skepticism, for which he was better known, did at times leave the loose ends and seeming contradictions of the Bible adrift outside the limitations of religious knowledge. To this extent, Mansel saw his own work as preparatory for the greater task of interpreting the Bible from within its own structures, themes and particularities in order to render the scriptures alive, unified, and available to order the Church's life. In many ways, this is a task that remains very much alive and contested today.

The recent book *Divine Evil? The Moral Character of the God of Abraham* contains a series of essays and responses that emerged from a 2009 conference at Notre Dame. Many of these essays bear the now classic objections, so current in Mansel's era, to the moral character of God depicted in portions of the Bible, in particular the invasion of Canaan.[36] Concerning these objections, Christopher Seitz writes in his essay "Canon and Conquest,"

> In the words of Paul, to the degree that God can be grasped in his mystery as God at all, it will be in his severity and mercy equally. As with Paul, this grasping of God, or being grasped by God, takes place inside a struggle to understand the totality of his dealings with humanity – the long story – for which Paul in Romans 11 supplies the conclusion: "behold the mercy and the severity of God" (11: 22). Mercy and severity both, for only as related, inseparable, can they convey the truth of the mystery of God's imperative manifestations with us – what the classical tradition called God's economic life revealed through the totality of scripture.[37]

God's justice, for Seitz, is revealed in his mercy and severity, a claim that emerges from within the heart of the New Testament gospel account and is attested to throughout innumerable scriptural passages. Even more, God is grasped, or we are grasped by God, from within this contrast, which is a mystery, Seitz claims, but a mystery that receives its logic from the entire scriptural canon: "Goodness is understood from within the context of a life lived in relationship, and not by an external grid, when the OT reflects on how goodness might be measured."[38]

In one sense, Seitz is making, in his own words, a "low flying" claim about the simple literary character of the Bible: "By its very form, the canon assists in making sense of how serial statements about God's life in relationship to Israel are to cohere."[39] Gary Anderson's essay "What About the Canaanites?" provides an excellent demonstration of this conviction. He argues from within the text that God was in fact dealing justly with the Canaanites by allowing them 400 years to amend their ways. Furthermore, Abraham himself made every effort to obtain the land fairly and equitably.[40] Therefore, in Anderson's words, the text itself "does not award a land to Israel in a manner that immorally voids all previous claims."[41] Maybe Mansel's appeal to a "moral miracle" is not necessary if the text itself is careful enough to attend to this difficulty. However, the hard fact of Israel's injunction to destroy the whole people of Canaan still remains, and in Mansel's eyes, the truth of such an action remains hidden in the mystery of God's mercy and judgment.

Thus in another sense, the deeper implications of Seitz's argument seem to suggest that God is encountered most truthfully amidst the contrasts of scripture's portrayal. While accounts of human knowledge – its limitations, range, and capacity – will no doubt vary in detail, at some point, if the scripture's canonical unity is allowed to emerge, the image of God that is presented must simply be accepted as a truthful account of his character.[42] For Milbank, it is not so much that the reciprocal and peaceful exchange of the Trinitarian persons is unfaithful to this account, but the risk is that the full range of scriptural imagery that gives rise to this reality is no longer needed to adjust and calibrate the particular moments of the Church's life. The Church, for Milbank, lives within a new narrative that makes a formal break with the history of Israel even as it takes its departure from the Gospel records of Jesus's ministry. This break with Israel is motivated, at least in part, by the Church's renewed vocation to provide a moral counter-ontology to the secular ontology of violence. But the risk of this counter-ontology is that the character of God, revealed in the scriptures, becomes increasingly difficult to grasp throughout the whole range of the biblical canon.

Milbank's genealogy of modernity is one of many similar but varying theological account of the modern world and the problems of
secularism and unbelief. [43] In Mansel's time he was confronting a
different narrative of moral and metaphysical progressivism represented by varying strands idealism. Mansel's concern was that the
all-embracing frameworks of idealism, even in its most theological
variants, placed the world in the hands of a power that no longer
resembled the God of scripture. In fact, as the power of these frameworks expanded the scriptural portrayal of God became increasingly
problematic. Contemporary narratives of modernity tend to be devo-
lutionary – they describe the fragmentation or the downfall of a world
that once seemed more solidly Christian. Milbank's is now perhaps
the best known of these narratives, but in Mansel's terms, it can be
argued that Milbank's participatory ontology of peace functions in
a "dogmatic" sense to the degree that it fills up the missing portions
of an incomplete system of revelation. It is not so much that an ontology of participation inherently misrepresents the Biblical narrative;
rather, the demands of the system and Milbank's account of its gradual
eclipse describe a process that appears almost providentially implausible in scriptural terms. Seitz's argument that God is grasped in his
mercy and severity throughout the range of scriptural material, means
that the degree to which the Church apprehends the presence of God
in history must somehow be found within this contrast.

This book began with an interest toward the nature of unbelief in
Victorian England and in the Church of England in particular. Mansel,
like many others, addressed himself to this concern and attempted to
describe the scriptures as a reality in which the Church continues to
live and find its life and vocation. I have not addressed the origins of
unbelief in this period or provided a genealogy of the pressures on
traditional Christian faith that emerged in England. Instead I offered
an account of Mansel's response, and I explored this response in
contrast to the expressions of these pressures as they reached clarity
in the works of various philosophers and theologians. In addition, I
argued that Mansel's understanding of the knowledge of God in the
Bible represented a fairly basic and traditional position within the
Anglican theological tradition and the wider tradition of Catholic
theology – even Mill acknowledged this to be true. What made
Mansel's position novel, perhaps, was that he tried to situate the
conviction that God is revealed in the scriptures within the philosophical idealistic framework of his own day. To this end, the

particulars of Mansel's skeptical epistemology may not be entirely relevant today – Seitz and Anderson clearly have no need of it to make their claims – but some framework needs to be in place to profile the risk of allowing speculative theological or philosophical programs to control or dull the full range of scriptural testimony concerning the character of the Christian God.

Mansel's more positive vision was that the world lives within the scriptural narrative, as the images of types of the Bible have the power to expand around a changing world without altering their revelatory character. This conviction was rooted in the theological notion that God continues to live and dwell within the created world in a manner that is consistent and graspable in scriptural terms ordered around the person of Christ. The degree to which this idea was misunderstood, ignored or dismissed has had tragic consequences in the Church of England. This may seem like a gross exaggeration, but it is clear that Mansel's lectures were read by nearly everyone we now consider notable in the period's ecclesial life. The explicit rejection of Mansel's theology by so many leading figures in the Church of England, I argued, has provided a lens into the secularizing forces that increasingly overwhelmed England's intellectual life. At the heart of these forces was unease about the character of God revealed in the Bible and providentially present in the Church's life throughout history. Mansel might have done more to alleviate his critics' concerns – his distinction between regulative and speculative knowledge continually provoked distrust – but on the whole it was his insistence that God is and continues to be just like what the whole Bible describes that provoked the most visceral rejections.

Mansel's limitations as a theologian are fairly obvious. But his basic conviction that the Church continues to live within the narrative of the entire Bible is one that can be, and is being, explored in more concretely theological and biblical terms. The brief essays of Anderson and Seitz that I referred to are examples of Mansel's conviction that the Bible represents a unified witness, the coherence of which is at times obvious and at other times needs to established, sought out and built up. In addition, the questions about a Christian metaphysics or ontology will continue to circulate as the Church situates its convictions in a changing world. Mansel's personalism was as close as he came to an ontological worldview, but helpful as this was for his purposes, it will probably not do justice to contemporary ecclesial and societal concerns. In this way, a scriptural ontology or metaphysics might be necessary or helpful in rooting and establishing the coherence and unity of the biblical witness. But whatever form these accounts take, Mansel's rule, that our conceptual schemes must not stifle the difficulties, complexities, and unity of the biblical account, I believe remains in full force.

I agree with Rowan Williams's argument that a certain kind of skepticism has been a virtue in Anglican theology, only I question whether Westcott is a compelling example of this virtue. What Mansel offers the contemporary Church is a way of configuring this skepticism so that it applies equally to the present, the future, and the past. Inasmuch as skepticism has been a feature of Anglican theology, so has the desire for a comprehensive theological vision that can incorporate and explain the historical moment of any given age in which the Church lives. But as I argued, this desire has too often employed skeptical arguments to distance the entire scriptural witness from contemporary reality, instead of rendering this witness as a means to describe the Church's location within a changing world. Mansel was not over-committed on the theological sore spots of his era: penal substitution, predestination, or eternal damnation.[44] But nor was he willing to deny that the scriptures, at times, spoke in these terms. Theological skepticism, properly configured, requires that the Church must make sense of these realities along with the whole range of canonical writings for the simple reason that, somehow, they describe the character and activity of God. Whether this represents an exceedingly narrow vision of the world, as Mansel's critics claimed, or a vision that is broad enough to relate and incorporate the vast array of human experience at any moment, as Mansel claimed, is a question that may indeed be undecidable. I argue that the skeptical and comprehensive trajectories of Anglican theology can indeed coalesce if the scriptures are allowed to form the providential pattern in which the Church encounters a changing but God-created world.

Notes

INTRODUCTION

1 Rowan Strong, "Introduction," 19.

2 Francis Newman, *Phases of Faith*, 69.

3 Ibid., 65.

4 Calderwood, "The Philosophy of the Infinite," 435.

5 Ibid., 437.

6 Michael Wolff highlights the fact that the Henry Mansel/Frederick Denison Maurice debate was reviewed in 1859 by fourteen of the twenty-five most prominent literature periodicals of the era. Charles Darwin's *On the Origin of Species* received twenty-two reviews. Wolff's representative list does not necessarily favour theological reviews. Wolff, "Victorian Reviewers and Cultural Responsibility," 273.

7 R.G. Collingwood, "The Metaphysics of F.H. Bradley," 236.

8 George Lindbeck, *The Nature of Doctrine*, 117. I do not wish to simply cast Mansel as a proto post-Liberal in Lindbeck's manner, however the similarities are obvious, despite largely dissimilar methods of philosophical and theological reasoning. The following statement by Lindbeck, though, could have been pulled from the "Bampton Lectures": "The primary focus is not on God's being in itself, for that is not what the text is about, but on how life is to be lived and reality construed in the light of God's character as an agent as this is depicted in the stories of Israel and of Jesus." Lindbeck, *The Nature of Doctrine*, 121.

9 Mansel, *The Limits of Religious Thought Examined in Eight Lectures*, 74.

10 Ibid., 6.

11 Calderwood, "The Philosophy of the Infinite," 438.

12 J.S. Mill, *An Examination of Sir William Hamilton's Philosophy*, 103.

13 John Burgon, *The Lives of Twelve Good Men*, 173.

14 Ibid., 182.

15 B.A. Know, "Filling the Oxford Chair of Ecclesiastical History," 68. In a letter (3 December 1866) by Lord Carnarvon to Lord Derby concerning the appointment, Carnarvon writes that Mansel had earlier declined an appointment to a living that would have afforded him £1,700 a year, a significant increase. However, Mansel declined "because he considered that his Oxford life and habits had not sufficiently qualified him for the parochial work of a country clergyman," 69.

16 Burgon, *The Lives of Twelve Good Men*, 230.

17 Henry Parry Liddon to E.B. Pusey, 2 August 1871.

18 Peter Knockles distinguishes eighteenth-century and nineteenth-century high churchmen from the Tractarians according to their broader outlook, incorporation of the Reformation heritage in the Church of England, and their more general appeal to the Church fathers. Mansel shared Newman's hostility toward nineteenth-century liberalism in the Church and the nation of England, but he did not share, at least explicitly, Newman's hostility to the Reformation, and certainly Mansel's views of scripture have something in common with that of Luther and Calvin. Knockles, *The Oxford Movement*.

19 Burgon, *The Lives of Twelve Good Men*, 223.

20 Strong, "Introduction," 1.

21 Mansel, "The Phrontisterion," 403.

22 Charles Taylor, *Sources of the Self*, 408.

23 I will discuss the relationship of Kant and English theology more fully in chapter 1. Mansel was very aware that while there was a religious and theological aspect to Kant's philosophy, it also rendered portions of the Bible incomprehensible and even irrational. See Immanuel Kant's, *Religion Within the Limits of Reason Alone*, 178.

24 Bernard Lightman, *The Origins of Agnosticism*.

25 Ibid., 66.

26 Timothy Fitzgerald's article "Mansel's Agnosticism" takes a similar approach by measuring Mansel's philosophy by the standard of Kant. In a slightly different tone, Hamish Swanston's book *Ideas of Order* describes Mansel's philosophy as an inventive but ultimately flawed attempt to renew theology through philosophical synthesis.

27 Christopher Herbert, *Victorian Relativity*, 36.

28 Ibid., 40.

29 Edwyn Bevan's chapter on Mansel in *Symbolism and Belief* takes a parallel approach though with respect to the symbolic and anthropomorphic

character of religious language. While he is more sympathetic to Mansel's scripturalism than Herbert, he too concludes that this aspect of Mansel's thought is no longer plausible or even necessary. Kenneth Freeman takes a more radical approach to Mansel in *The Role of Reason in Religion: a Study of Henry Mansel*, where he argues that Mansel's philosophy can be appropriated into a death of God theology, which argues for the wholly immanent and finite presence of God in history.

30 Mansel, *A Second Letter to Goldwin Smith*, 26.

31 The recent interest in typology and figuration in exegesis has a long history. Henri De Lubac's *Medieval Exegesis: The Four Senses of Scripture* remains a touchstone on the topic of the return to medieval and patristic practices in reading scripture, over and against modern historical critical methods. The following is a list of more recent notable contributions: Matthew Levering, "Participation and Exegesis"; Richard Hays, *Echoes of Scripture in the Letters of Paul*; Telford Work, *Living and Active*; Christopher Seitz, *Figured Out: Typology and Providence in Christian Scripture*; Ephraim Radner, *Time and the Word*. The *Brazos Commentary* series is perhaps the most sustained and collaborative recent effort to approach scripture through the lens of typology and the history of interpretation throughout Church history.

32 Rowan Williams, "General Introductions," xxv. I will discuss Williams' own understanding of theological skepticism in the third chapter.

CHAPTER ONE

1 Thomas Carlyle, "State of German Literature," 41.

2 This chapter will focus on Hamilton as a representative of this school, but insofar as Mansel represents the theological extension of Hamilton's philosophy he will be mentioned, and to some extent taken for granted, in order to clarify the theological implications of Hamilton's philosophical approach and reception of Kant.

3 Richard Popkin, *The History of Scepticism*, 15.

4 Lightman, *The Origins of Agnosticism*, 66.

5 Kant claimed that inferring the existence of God from the patterns and laws of observed nature was an exercise in speculative reason: "If, again, I infer from the form of the universe, from the way in which all things are connected and act and react upon each other, the existence of a cause entirely distinct from the universe – this would again be a judgment of purely speculative reason; because the object in this case – the cause – can never be an object of possible experience. In both these cases the principle

of causality, which is valid only in the field of experience – useless and even meaningless beyond this region, would be diverted from its proper destination." Kant, *Critique of Pure Reason*, 356.

6 John Toland, *Christianity Not Mysterious*.

7 Ibid., 2. Of course, this argument was not original to Toland. Spinoza made very similar arguments concerning the character of scripture and its miraculous content. Benedict De Spinoza, "Theological Political Treatise," in *The Chief Works of Benedict De Spinoza*, vol. 1, 86. See also David Friedrich Strauss, *The Life of Jesus Critically Examined*.

8 John Locke, *Reasonableness of Christianity with A Discourse on Miracles and Part of a Third Letter Concerning Toleration*, 77.

9 In his essay on English freethinking Mansel writes, "The English Deism of the last century, like the English gentlemen of the same period, has made the grand tour of Europe, and come home with the fruits of its travels." Mansel, "Freethinking – Its History and Tendency," in *Letters, Lectures and Reviews*, 334. This is a conclusion that is affirmed by W.R. Ward: "By the end of the Napoleonic wars the cultural relations of theology in England and Germany were the reverse of what they had been three quarters of a century before. Then radical English criticism in the field of the philosophy of religion had given a lead to German theologians, a lead enhanced by an English reputation justified to the extent that deist literature could actually appear in print." Ward, "Faith and Fallacy," 53.

10 Mansel, "Freethinking."

11 Ibid., 313.

12 How exactly Mansel did this I discuss more fully in the second chapter.

13 I discuss Mansel's reading of Hegel in particular in the fifth chapter on British idealism and *Lux Mundi*.

14 "Pure reason, then, contains, not indeed in its speculative, but in its practical, or, more strictly, its moral use, principles of the possibility of experience, of such actions, namely, as, in accordance with ethical precepts, might be met with in the history of man. For since reason commands that such actions should take place, it must be possible for them to take place; and hence a particular kind of systematic unity – the moral – must be possible. We have found, it is true, that the systematic unity of nature could not be established according to speculative principles of reason, because, while reason possesses a causal power in relation to freedom, it has none in relation to the whole sphere of nature; and, while moral principles of reason can produce free actions, they cannot produce natural laws. It is, then, in its practical, but especially in its moral use, that the principles of pure reason possess objective reality." Kant, *Critique of Pure Reason*, 453.

15 Mansel, *Limits of Religious Thought*, 12.

16 Mansel, "The Philosophy of Kant," in *Letters, Lectures and Reviews*, 175.
Mansel's interpretation of Kant in this case was directly derived from
Hamilton: "Kant had annihilated the older metaphysic, but the germ of
a more visionary doctrine of the absolute, than any of those refuted, was
contained in the bosom of his own philosophy. He had slain the body, but
had not exorcised the spectre of the absolute." William Hamilton, "The
Philosophy of the Unconditioned," 25.

17 Mansel, *Limits of Religious Thought*, 32.

18 In the fourth chapter I more fully detail Mansel's views of Hegel in relation to English idealism and figures like T.H. Green and F.H. Bradley.

19 Hamilton, "Philosophy of Perception," 21. Hamilton read Kant through
the eyes of Jacobi, the Christian disciple of Kant, who reached similar
conclusions about the revelatory quality of knowledge. Jacobi was in turn
influenced by Reid and what is known as the position of "natural realism."
Manfred Kuehn, *Scottish Common Sense in Germany, 1768–1800*, 8.

20 Hamilton, "Philosophy of Perception," 90.

21 Mansel, *Limits of Religious Thought*, 12.

22 In the next chapter I will discuss more specifically the English theology
heritage many nineteenth-century Anglican writers were reacting against.
While William Paley became the symbol of the poverty of eighteenth-
century English theology – Mansel too was critical of Paley – there was
another tradition in English theology which stemmed from writers like
Peter Browne, George Berkeley, and Joseph Butler.

23 For example, in 1800 the *Anti Jacobin Review* had made it a priority to
attack the foreign incursions of German philosophy into England's intellectual life as the threat of continental political unrest created fear and
unease in England. Giuseppe Micheli, "The Early Reception of Kant's
Thought in England," 286.

24 Micheli quotes an early interpreter of Kant, Benjamin Snowdon, who
writes that German idealism that resembles "A mass of obscurity and confusion, which instead of assisting the mind in the acquisition of true science, tends to sink it in doubt and skepticism." Micheli, "The Early
Reception of Kant's Thought in England," 216.

25 Kant's critique of "Physico-Theology" was particularly compelling for
English theologians like Coleridge who felt that the design arguments
of natural theology distracted Christian writers from the spiritual and
moral foundations of the Christian faith. Kant writes in the first critique:
"Physico-Theology is therefore incapable of presenting a determinate conception of a supreme cause of the world, and is therefore insufficient as a

principle of theology – a theology which is itself to be the basis of religion." Kant, *Critique of Pure Reason*, 352. Kant famously turned to morality as the foundation of belief in God: "the moral laws not merely presuppose the existence of a Supreme Being, but also, as themselves absolutely necessary in a different relation, demand or postulate it – although only from a practical point of view." Kant, *Critique of Pure Reason*, 355.

26 A.O. Dyson points to the Locke and Leibnitz debate of the late seventeenth century as cementing the varying trajectories in English and German thought. In particular, Locke's refusal of Leibniz's notion of innate ideas in favour of the "tabula rasa," a passive mind that receives sensory data, clarified a separation in styles of thought that would persist until the nineteenth century. While Kant would criticize Leibniz, and innate ideas in particular, the effect of this separation established a tradition in Germany which elevated the powers of reason and granted them a constructive and formative agency in cognition. Dyson argues, as have others, that the great debates between the orthodox and deists, which climaxed between 1720 and 1740, presented a shallow and misleading resolution. Dyson, "Theological Legacies of the Enlightenment," 48.

27 Ibid., 53.

28 Ibid.

29 Ibid., 54.

30 Ibid., 60.

31 Ibid., 55.

32 Micheli, "The Early Reception of Kant's Thought in England 1785–1805," 151.

33 Paul Tillich, *The History of Christian Thought*, 359.

34 Rene Wellek, *Immanuel Kant in England, 1793–1838*, 80, 68.

35 Kant writes in the *Critique of Pure Reason*: "Now I maintain that all attempts of reason to establish a theology by the aid of speculation alone are fruitless, that the principles of reason as applied to nature do not conduct us to any theological truths, and, consequently, that a rational theology can have no existence, unless it is founded upon the laws of morality. For all synthetical principles of the understanding are valid only as immanent in experience; while the cognition of a Supreme Being necessitates their being employed transcendentally, and of this the understanding is quite incapable," 356.

36 S.T. Coleridge, *Aids to Reflection in the Formation of a Manly Character*, 209.

37 Wellek, *Immanuel Kant in England, 1793–1838*, 101.

38 Coleridge, *Biographia Literaria*, 77.

39 Wellek's concluding words are telling: "Finally he gave up any attempts at a solution and came to take for granted the dualism of speculation and life, of the head and heart. The monistic aim demanded precisely the solution of these dualisms ... At length, he seduced the struggling spirit to acquiesce in immediate knowledge and faith, he lured it to enjoy a mere feeling of mystery and to give up the labor of thinking penetration into problems ... he simply did not seem to have the ability to conceive in thinking what he felt he should confess and preach as a person ... He fell back into an ontology which is fundamentally the same as the ontology of the great systems of the seventeenth century and from there he fell into a mere philosophy of faith." Wellek, *Immanuel Kant in England, 1793–1838*, 134, 135.

40 Readings such as Wellek's continued with scholars like Norman Fruman and his book *Coleridge, The Damaged Archangel*. Fruman probes more deeply into the personal problems Coleridge dealt with, and the conclusion is similar: Coleridge simply cannot be taken seriously as a philosopher, despite his immense abilities and intrigue. Norman Fruman, *Coleridge, the Damaged Archangel*.

41 Ward, "Faith and Fallacy," 58.

42 Douglas Hedley, *Coleridge, Philosophy and Religion*, 194.

43 Ibid., 196. Jeffrey Barbeau is another scholar who has argued that Coleridge's philosophy was controlled more by orthodox theological convictions than by Kant's philosophy: "Coleridge creates a polarity between the Divine and self-Will that does not collapse the two, in pantheistic fashion, but instead distinguishes them and demands subordination of the finite to the Absolute. At this point, it is important to recall Schelling's idea of freedom; although Schelling did acknowledge the difference between self-Will and universal Will, he failed, unlike Coleridge, to subordinate the finite to a personal God." Barbeau, "The Development of Coleridge's Notion of Human Freedom."

44 Carlyle, "State of German Literature," 86.

45 Ibid., 85. Carlyle is quoting August Wilhelm Schlegel and does not reference the source.

46 Wellek, *Immanuel Kant in England*, 193.

47 Frank Turner, "Victorian Scientific Naturalism and Thomas Carlyle."

48 Ibid., 146.

49 Carlyle, *On Heroes, Hero-Worship, and the Heroic in History: Six Lectures*, 7.

50 Herbert Spencer writes in *First Principles*, "The abstraction of these conditions and limits is, by the hypothesis, the abstraction of them only;

consequently there must be a residuary consciousness of something which filled up their outlines, and this indefinite something constitutes our consciousness of the Non-relative or Absolute. Impossible though it is to give to this consciousness any qualitative or quantitative expression whatever, it is not the less certain that it remains with us as a positive and indestructible element of thought." Spencer, *First Principles*, 84.

51 Ibid., 94.
52 Turner, "Victorian Scientific Naturalism and Thomas Carlyle," 141.
53 Timothy Gouldstone, *The Rise and Decline of Anglican Idealism in the Nineteenth Century*, 26.
54 "Coleridge's mind reflected the tension between Christianity and pantheism, between philosophical inferences and orthodox Christian theism, and in this it bears a strong resemblance to later idealist philosophers who felt acutely the tension between their idealistic and holistic vision of the cosmos and the particularities that are a necessary part of orthodox Christian revelation." Gouldstone, *The Rise and Decline of Anglican Idealism in the Nineteenth Century*, 32.
55 Even the tough-minded and contrarian leaders of the Oxford Movement for a time saw the promise of philosophical idealism's ferment in England: Pusey's *An Historical Enquiry into the Probable Causes of the Rationalistic Character Lately Predominant in the Theology of Germany* (1828) is a testament to this tentative hope. And yet Pusey's later ambivalence toward this work and Newman's own attempt to distance himself from Coleridge speaks to the confusion and perceived danger of Kant's influence in England. Later in life, Newman would deny that he had ever read Coleridge and, for that matter, Kant. Johannes Artz and others think that this must not be true and have shown in the work of Newman various points at which he references Kant. Yet Newman's desire to say such a thing shows how the implications of German idealism placed Anglican interpreters in an awkward position. Artz, "Newman in Contact with Kant's Thought," in *The Journal of Theological Studies*, 519.
56 Taylor, *Sources of the Self*, 409.
57 Hamish Swanston writes, "It was, perhaps, the recognition, however obscure, by their contemporaries that the theologies of Hampden, Mansel and Maurice, impressive and sensitive beyond the ordinary, were yet insufficiently careful of the human, that prevented any one of them becoming the author of a general revival of confidence in theology." Swanston, *Ideas of Order*, 211.
58 Alan Ryan, "Introduction," xxix.
59 Ibid., xi.

60 Ibid., xxx.

61 "That philosopher [Kant] did recognize a direct object of our perceptions, different from the thing itself, an intermediate between it and the
perceiving mind. And it was open to Kant to do so; because he held what
Sir W. Hamilton calls a representative theory of perception. He maintained that the object of our perception, and of our knowledge, is a representation in our own minds." Mill, *The Collected Works of John Stuart
Mill, Volume 9*, 27.

62 Ibid., 103.

63 Ryan, "Introduction," xiv.

64 Lightman, *The Origins of Agnosticism*.

65 Ibid., 60.

66 Donald Mackinnon, "Kant's Influence on English Theology," 361.

67 Stanley Hauerwas's essay "How 'Christian Ethics' Came to Be" is an
example of a theological critique of Kant's ethics. John Milbank's *The
Word Made Strange: Theology, Language, Culture* contains a sustained
critique of Kant and the destructive effects of epistemology on Christian
understandings of the world and God.

68 Kant, *Religion Within the Limits of Reason Alone*, 47.

69 Ibid., 178.

70 Ibid., 167.

71 Ibid., 126.

72 Mansel, *The Limits of Religious Thought Examined*, 142. Kant's enlightenment understanding of primitive religion's gradual moral purification
and purgation was central for nineteenth-century English intellectuals:
"Hence, also, we find in the history of human reason that, before the
moral conceptions were sufficiently purified and determined, and before
men had attained to a perception of the systematic unity of ends according
to these conceptions and from necessary principles, the knowledge of
nature, and even a considerable amount of intellectual culture in many
other sciences, could produce only rude and vague conceptions of the
Deity, sometimes even admitting of an astonishing indifference with regard
to this question altogether. But the more enlarged treatment of moral
ideas, which was rendered necessary by the extreme pure moral law of our
religion, awakened the interest, and thereby quickened the perceptions of
reason in relation to this object. In this way, and without the help either
of an extended acquaintance with nature, or of a reliable transcendental
insight (for these have been wanting in all ages), a conception of the
Divine Being was arrived at, which we now hold to be the correct one, not
because speculative reason convinces us of its correctness, but because it

accords with the moral principles of reason." Kant, *Critique of Pure Reason*, 458.

73 Taylor, *Sources of the Self*, 404.

74 Newman, *Phases of Faith*, 69.

75 Mansel, *A Letter to Goldwin Smith Concerning the Postscript to His Lectures on the Study of History*, 48. Mansel goes on in this vein, "the one embodying the good, the other the evil principle in the history of mankind; the one generous, the other selfish; the one representing 'the moral instincts of Man person onwards, in obedience to his conscience, toward the further knowledge of Religious Truth'; the other 'the defenders of ecclesiastical interests,' endeavouring 'to save their threatened dominion' by 'civil sword' or by 'intellectual intrigue and the power of sophistry.' This is but a repetition of the old cry of Priestcraft, – a cry common among the demagogues of a former generation, but which I hardly expected to see revived by the philosophers of the present."

76 John Milbank, *The Word Made Strange*, 9. Here Milbank refers to Mansel as a typical Kantian theologian of the nineteenth century.

77 Milbank, *Being Reconciled*, 12.

78 Milbank, *The Word Made Strange*, 44.

79 Ibid., 50.

CHAPTER TWO

1 Thomas Aquinas, *Summa Theologica*, part 1, question 13, article 2.

2 Newman, *Phases of Faith*.

3 See Owen Chadwick, *The Mind of the Oxford Movement*.

4 Samuel Butler, *The Way of All Flesh*; George Eliot, *Adam Bede*; Humphrey Ward, *Robert Elsmere*.

5 For examples, see Chadwick, *The Secularization of the European Mind in the Nineteenth Century: The Gifford Lectures in the University of Edinburgh for 1973–4*; P.T. Marsh, *The Victorian Church in Decline*; Taylor, *The Secular Age*; A.N. Wilson, *God's Funeral*.

6 Taylor, *The Secular Age*, 363. Taylor's picture is illustrated well by Samuel Butler's Ernest Pontifex in *The Way of All Flesh*. Pontifex's biography was not unfamiliar to many Victorians, which explains the novel's resonance. After a constricted and unhappy upbringing in the home of an Evangelical minister, the young Pontifex is grudgingly ordained, yet his spiritual discontent drives him away from the Evangelical to the Tractarian Movement and eventually into the Broad Church. But one disillusionment follows another until his maturation is complete, and he settles into a role as a

social critic, with little semblance of his Christian faith left intact. His final position seems to be an ill-defined agnostic and scientific materialism in which the very lack of metaphysical or theological strictures actually provides a more comprehensive worldview, though in this case it is important to note that comprehensiveness is gained more by the removal of limitations than by the expanding of old ones, which is to say that the highly defined traditional notions of God in some sense pushed God away as opposed to drawing him near.

7 Calderwood, "The Philosophy of the Infinite," 438.

8 Lightman, *The Origins of Agnosticism.*

9 I look more fully at Mansel's skeptical epistemology in the second chapter, but here I explore some possible traditions in which he might be placed.

10 "The Reformers' challenge of the accepted criteria of religious knowledge raised a most fundamental question: How does one justify the basis of one's knowledge? This problem was to unleash a skeptical crisis not only in theology but also, shortly thereafter, in the sciences and in all other areas of human knowledge." Popkin, *The History of Scepticism,* 15.

11 Ibid., 5.

12 Ibid., 15.

13 Michel de Montaigne, "Apology for Raymond Sebond," 199–282.

14 Popkin, *The History of Scepticism,* 73.

15 Iain Hampsher-Monk, "Burke and the Religious Sources of Conservative Skepticism," 237.

16 This is Mansel's view of Pyrrhonist skepticism, but while he criticizes the idea that the senses deceive in his essay "Philosophy and Theology," in *Letter, Lectures and Reviews, Including the Phrontisterion, or, Oxford in the 19th Century,* his sympathies are clearly closer to this form of skepticism than its dogmatic counterpart: "reason, the highest faculty, is privileged to attain to a knowledge of the real and absolute nature of objects in themselves, and thus to establish a philosophy of realities as the supplement to and corrective of the philosophy of appearances," 344.

17 Locke's emphasis on the essence of Christianity is well known. In *The Reasonableness of Christianity* especially, Locke's epistemology is borne out by an emphasis on these simplified, textual realities, i.e., the life of Jesus, the moral code, and the evidences of his life. To Hampsher-Monk's point, this method placed the more doctrinal elements of Christianity in an uncertain position. Locke, though not denying their reality, wished to focus on the more concrete, visible aspects of the faith: "This is a religion suited to vulgar capacities, and the state of mankind in this world, destined to labor and travail. The writers and wranglers in religion fill it with

niceties, and dress it up with notions, which they make necessary and fundamental parts of it; as if there were no way into the Church, but through the Academy or Lycaeum," 77.

18 Locke, *The Reasonableness of Christianity*, 77.

19 Hampsher-Monk, "Burke and the Religious Sources of Conservative Skepticism," 239.

20 Ibid., 255.

21 Mansel, "Freethinking – Its History and Tendency," in *Letters, Lectures and Reviews*, 334.

22 Jean-Paul Pittion and David Berman, "A New Letter by Berkeley to Browne on Divine Analogy," 376.

23 Peter Browne, *A Letter in Answer to a Book Entitled, Christianity Not Mysterious*, 1703.

24 Toland, *Christianity Not Mysterious*, 79.

25 Ibid., 86.

26 Ibid., 53.

27 Ibid., xxv.

28 Ibid., 32.

29 Daniel Clifford Fouke argues that Toland used the public language of scripture in order to subvert its meaning, a method which conceals his atheism. While this may be true, his stated intention still seems plausible, especially given the similar arguments and concerns that he draws from Locke. Fouke, *Philosophy and Theology in a Burlesque Mode*.

30 Toland, *Christianity Not Mysterious*, 86.

31 Pittion and Berman, "A New Letter by Berkeley to Browne on Divine Analogy," 376.

32 Browne, *A Letter in Answer to a Book Entitled, Christianity Not Mysterious*, 31.

33 Mansel did read Browne and quoted him, but not extensively. Mansel's critique of the human understanding of the infinite and the absolute was derived primarily from William Hamilton in direct response to idealist philosophers in Germany and France. Still, Mansel was fully aware of Browne's arguments, and A.W. Winnett has suggested that Mansel was the first important Anglican theologian to make use of Browne's arguments that fell into disrepute. Winnett, *Peter Browne*.

34 Browne, *A Letter in Answer to a Book Entitled, Christianity Not Mysterious*, 35.

35 Ibid., 38.

36 Browne, *The Procedure, Extent, and Limits of Human Understanding*, 142.

37 Ibid.

38 Ibid., 139.

39 Browne, *Things Divine and Supernatural*, 51.

40 Browne had a place for the illumination of the Spirit in epistemology based upon this basic analogical structure of the world. This, to some degree, marked him off from many of his contemporaries, and for this reason he had a traceable influence on John Wesley and the Methodist movement. Richard Brantley has made this argument in *Locke, Wesley, and the Method of English Romanticism*.

41 Bob Tennant argues that Browne did not understand the scholastic subtleties of analogical reasoning and that he tended to "compare objects, not relations." Tennant, *Conscience, Consciousness and Ethics in Joseph Butler's Philosophy and Ministry*, 84. In part this fault derives from the modern attempt to "graft together scholastic rationalism with post-Cartesian empiricism," a self-defeating task within a philosophical worldview that was hostile to metaphysical systems and schemes.

42 David Berman, *George Berkeley*, 90.

43 Ibid., 98.

44 Ibid., 99.

45 Ibid., 129.

46 Michael Hooker, "Berkeley's Argument from Design," 26.

47 Berman, *George Berkeley*, 107.

48 Winnett remarks that both Browne and Berkeley appealed to the scholastics in this regard. But Browne, perhaps, is less clear in his use of analogy: "Inevitably Browne tends at one moment to stress the element of difference and at another that of resemblance in analogy." Winnett, *Peter Browne*, 140.

49 Berman, *George Berkeley*, 111.

50 Ibid.

51 Pittion and Berman, "A New Letter by Berkeley to Browne on Divine Analogy," 391.

52 Ibid., 166.

53 Ibid., 167.

54 Berman, *George Berkeley*, 130.

55 In Mansel's *A Letter to Goldwin Smith*, he defends Browne against Berkeley, partly on the supposition that Berkeley was unjust to attack a fellow clergyman on such a slight point of difference, and furthermore, he believed that Berkeley misrepresented Browne, when in fact their positions were quite close. Mansel believed that Berkeley had Archbishop King in mind or at least a more incautious version of Browne. In any case, after

quoting from Berkeley and noting the misrepresentation, Mansel notes, "But great and good as Berkeley undoubtedly was, the above language will not appear undeserved to those who have read his satirical attack upon a prelate of his own church, under the cover of a fictitious character," 8.

56 Alan Sell, *John Locke and the Eighteenth-Century Divines*, 270.

57 This is not to say that Browne's thought tended toward atheism, an argument made by Berkeley and seemingly endorsed by Tennant (*Conscience, Consciousness and Ethics in Joseph Butler's Philosophy and Ministry*, 84). Genealogically this does not seem to be the case, but even more, a failure to articulate a satisfactorily comprehensive theological worldview must not always end in the charge of implicit atheism. Browne's position was mostly defensive and, to this degree, perhaps not creative or visionary enough to compel his contemporaries.

58 Mansel's main appeal to Browne was on the issue of analogy and the distinctions between analogous, figurative, and metaphorical language. Perhaps like Browne, Mansel's overall acquaintance with the history of analogy in scholastic theology was only cursory in some sense. In Mansel's eyes Browne was simply repeating the long-held wisdom of the Church, represented in figures like Aquinas and Augustine. But Winnett's claim that Browne lacked the scholastic precision on the topic could just as easily be applied to Mansel. Nonetheless, however much Mansel needed to discuss analogy in relation to his theory of regulative truth, it was not the main focus of his argument, and by and large he seems to have assumed a general theological consensus on the analogical character of theological language.

59 Mansel's published "Bampton Lectures" contain a quote from the *Alciphron* on the opening page: "The objections made to faith are by no means an effect of knowledge, but proceed rather from an ignorance of what knowledge is."

60 Terence Penelhum, "Butler and Human Ignorance."

61 The most recent work on Butler by Tennant (*Conscience, Consciousness and Ethics in Joseph Butler's Philosophy and Ministry*) has made the case that Butler should be read primarily from a theological and pastoral perspective, despite his relevance to philosophical ethics.

62 Joseph Butler, "Upon the Ignorance of Man," 141.

63 Butler, "The Analogy of Religion," 152.

64 Jane Garnett suggests that in the Victorian period Butler suffered by association with Mansel for similar reasons and that Mansel drew only on the negative aspects of Butler's analogy, without stressing his positive vision. Garnett, "Bishop Butler and the Zeitgeist," 70, 71.

65 The majority of twentieth-century scholars who have written on Mansel have not stressed this point, largely due to Mansel's self-acknowledged debts to Immanuel Kant and William Hamilton. Don Cupitt, in an early and insightful article on Mansel's theory of regulative truth, interprets Mansel through the lens of Butler. But in general this represents an exception. Cupitt, "Mansel's Theory of Regulative Truth," 104–26.

66 Butler, "The Analogy of Religion," 153.

67 Ibid., 190.

68 Tennant, *Conscience, Consciousness and Ethics in Joseph Butler's Philosophy and Ministry*, 78.

69 Butler, "The Analogy of Religion," 190.

70 Ibid., 264.

71 Ibid., 266.

72 Ibid.

73 Ibid., 183. Tennant provides this description: "he believed that the laws governing the Creation, physical and spiritual, had a mutually reinforcing quality which naturally carried the person's (free) will in a certain direction, and that the effects of these laws, and their affective mechanisms, could be described probabilistically." Tennant, *Conscience, Consciousness and Ethics in Joseph Butler's Philosophy and Ministry*, 97.

74 Butler, "The Analogy of Religion," 220.

75 Ibid., 215.

76 Ibid., 228.

77 Ibid., 229.

78 Ibid., 231.

79 Ibid., 233.

80 Ibid., 244.

81 Gordon Kendal, "A God Most Particular," 153.

82 Butler, "The Analogy of Religion," 255–8.

83 Ibid., 258.

84 Ibid., 283.

85 Ibid., 284.

86 David Brown, "Butler and Deism," 20.

87 "And therefore neither obscurity, nor seeming inaccuracy of style, nor various readings, nor early disputes about the authors of particular parts, nor any other things of the like kind, though they had been much more considerable in degree that they are, could overthrow the authority of the scripture; unless the prophets, apostles, or our Lord, had promised, that the book, containing the divine revelation, should be secure from those things." Butler, "The Analogy of Religion," 241.

88 Butler, "The Analogy of Religion," 288.

89 Mackinnon, *A Study in Ethical Theory*, 200.

90 Kendal, "A God Most Particular," 160.

91 Butler, "Sermon XIII: Upon the Love of God," 131. This is not true also for the entire created order: "to say, that every thing of grace and beauty throughout the whole of nature, every thing excellent and amiable shared in differently lower degrees by the whole creation, meet in the Author and cause of all things; this an inadequate, and perhaps improper way of speaking of the divine nature. But it is manifest, that absolute rectitude, the perfection of being, must be in all sense, and in every respect, the highest object to the mind." Butler, "Sermon XIV: Upon the Love of God," 137.

92 I will make this case more fully in the second and third chapters on Mansel. In the third lecture of *The Limits of Religious Thought*, Mansel writes, "The analogy, which Bishop Butler has pointed out, between Religion and the constitution and the course of Nature, may be in some degree extended to the constitution and processes of the human mind. The representations of God which Scripture presents to us may be shown to be analogous to those which the laws of our minds require us to form; and therefore such as may naturally be supposed to have emanated from the same author," 19. In the seventh lecture, Mansel attributes all of his conclusions about the analogous character of Christian doctrines to Butler: "The very philosopher whose writings have most contributed to establish the supreme authority of Conscience in man, is also the one who has pointed out most clearly the existence of analogous moral difficulties in nature and in religion, and the true answer to both – the admission that God's government, natural as well as spiritual, is a scheme imperfectly comprehended," 160.

93 Garnett, "Bishop Butler and the Zeitgeist," 67.

94 See chapter 1 for an account of England's reception of German Idealism in the nineteenth century.

95 Mark Pattison, "Present State of Theology in Germany," 216.

96 Lightman, *The Origins of Agnosticism*, 50.

97 Coleridge, *Aids to Reflection and the Confessions of an Inquiring Spirit*, 168.

98 Ibid., 50.

99 Ibid., 103.

100 Ibid., 165.

101 Ibid., 195.

102 Barbeau, "Coleridge, Christology and the Language of Redemption."

103 Coleridge, *Aids to Reflection*, 218.

104 Ibid., 198.

105 Coleridge, *The Confessions of an Inquiring Spirit*, 293.

106 Ibid., 314.

107 Ibid., 311.

108 Ibid., 326.

109 Ibid., 335.

110 Ibid., 336.

111 Ibid., 337.

112 Ibid., 296. It is useful to contrast this statement of Coleridge's with Mansel's, made along similar lines: "But we may avail ourselves of that which satisfies our own peculiar needs, only be accepting it as part and parcel of the one indivisible whole," Mansel, *The Limits of Religious Thought*, 187. In other words, Mansel agrees with Coleridge that the believer is likely to find in scripture those things that meet his or her needs, but, for Mansel, these findings are still inseparable from the whole account of scripture.

113 Coleridge, *Aids to Reflection*, 243.

114 Ibid., 185.

115 Ibid., 237.

116 Ibid., 398.

117 Mansel, "Philosophy and Theology," 340.

118 In *A Second Letter to Goldwin Smith* (1862), Mansel quotes, with a hesitating approval, Coleridge's understanding of metaphor, though mostly in an attempt to speak in Smith's language. Mansel also makes a point of establishing his dissent from Coleridge's main ideas, 70.

119 Mansel began an essay on the topic of Berkeley's philosophy, but unfortunately he died before bringing it to completion. What little survives of the fragment suggests a strong affinity with the Bishop's thinking, though he foreshadows an ultimate disagreement, most likely relating to Berkeley's idiosyncratic denial of matter. Mansel agreed with Berkeley, against Reid, that consciousness is the basic fact of existence. Mansel, *Letter, Lectures and Reviews*, 387.

120 Hampsher-Monk, "Burke and the Religious Sources of Conservative Skepticism," 237.

121 Maurice Cowling, *Religion and Public Doctrine in Modern England.*

CHAPTER THREE

1 Lewis, *The Screwtape Letters*, 20.

2 Williams, *Anglican Identities*, 81.

3 Mansel, "Philosophy and Theology," 343.

4 Swanston, *Ideas of Order*, 65.

5 Mansel, *A Second Letter to Goldwin Smith*, 48.

6 Wellek in *Immanuel Kant in England* argues that early English interpretations of Kant confused the psychological for the epistemological aspects of
Kant's thought. Edmund Husserl's *Logical Investigations* provides one of
the best critiques of the psychological interpretation and its reduction to
empiricism: "It therefore fails to see that, having no insightful justification
for our mediate assumptions, no justification, therefore, for the relevant
proof-procedures from the immediately evident general principles that
they follow, its whole psychological theory, its whole mediately known
doctrine of empiricism, is without rational foundation, is, in fact, a mere
assumption, no more than a common prejudice," 116. Though it seems
that Husserl's criticisms apply more to Mill and, before him, Hume.
Mansel was clearly not a pure empiricist, though his theological foundations would not have satisfied Husserl either.

7 Mansel, *Limits of Religious Thought*, 21.

8 Lightman, *The Origins of Agnosticism*, 50.

9 Hamilton, "The Philosophy of the Unconditioned," 20.

10 Ibid., 91.

11 Mansel, *Limits of Religious Thought*, 49.

12 Ibid.

13 Ibid., 69.

14 Mansel, *Prolegomena Logica*, 133.

15 Locke, *The Reasonableness of Christianity*, 76.

16 Kant, *Critique of Pure Reason*, book II, chapter II, section 9:1.

17 Ibid.

18 Mansel, "The Philosophy of Kant," 174.

19 Ibid.

20 Ibid., 175.

21 Ibid., 172.

22 Mansel on Kant: "The moral reason is thus a source of absolute and
unchangeable realities; while the Speculative reason is concerned only with
phenomena, or things modified by the constitution of the human mind. As
a corollary to this theory, it follows that the law of human morality must
be regarded as the measure and adequate representative of the moral
nature of God. Applying these principles to the criticism of Revealed
Religion, the philosopher maintains that no code of laws claiming divine
authority can have any religious values, except as approved by the moral
reason." Mansel, *The Limits of Religious Thought*, 142.

23 Frederick Denison Maurice, *What Is Revelation?*, 163.

24 Ibid., 143.

25 Swanston, *Ideas of Order*, 209.

26 Mansel, *Limits of Religious Thought*, 61.

27 Ibid., 63.

28 Mansel, *Prolegomena Logica*, 129. To this end, he would depart from Reid and the Scottish School, whose fundamental belief was in the existence of matter.

29 Mansel, *An Examination of Maurice*, 15.

30 Butler, "The Analogy of Religion," 293.

31 J.B. Mozley, "Mansel's Bampton Lectures," 104.

32 Mansel, *Limits of Religious Thought*, 103.

33 Gavin Hyman, *The Predicament of Postmodern Theology: Radical Orthodoxy or Nihilist Textualism?*, 47.

34 This would seem to correlate with Lightman's theory concerning the assimilation of Mansel's ideas into English agnosticism, though it should be noted that Lightman does not argue that Mansel's ideas contained any necessary push in this direction, though they were convenient. In part, Spencer and Huxley used Mansel as an orthodox smokescreen behind which they could advance their more radical attacks against Christian revelation. Lightman, *Origins of Agnosticism*, 84.

35 Mansel, *Limits of Religious Thought*, 109.

36 Ibid., 52.

37 Ibid., 93.

38 Cupitt, "What Was Mansel Trying To Do?," 545.

39 Mansel, *A Letter to Goldwin Smith*, 11, 12.

40 It should be noted that Mansel's view of scriptural mediation did not preclude the results of the physical sciences; he only maintained that these empirical truths could not attain a priori validity, and they could not be used to validate arguments against the existence of God and the character of revelation. This is for the same reason that philosophical arguments concerning the infinite and the absolute cannot be used against scripture, namely, because of the limitations of human thought. Mansel, *Prolegomena Logica*; "The Limits of Demonstrative Science Considered," 99; *An Examination of The Rev. F.D. Maurice's Strictures on the Bampton Lectures of 1858 by the Lecturer*, 21.

41 Mozley, "Mansel's Bampton Lectures," 375.

42 John Henry Newman, "John Henry Newman to Charles Meynell," 335.

43 Mansel, *A Letter to Goldwin Smith*, 47.

44 Spinoza, "Theological Political Treatise," 92.

45 Ibid., 85.

46 Ibid., 90.

47 Ibid., 92.

48 It is also possible that Mansel's position was confused with Feuerbach's, but in *Prolegomena Logica* (257) he makes this distinction: "The history of mankind in general, as well as the consciousness of each individual, alike testify that religion is not a function of thought; and that the attempt to make it so, if consistently carried out, necessarily leads, firstly to Anthropomorphism, and ultimately to Atheism." He agrees with Feuerbach that we can only think in finite terms, but this does not mean that we must measure God by these standards. Rather, his mistake is that he thought of religion as a positive act of thinking.

49 Maurice, *Sequel to the Inquiry, What Is Revelation?*, 207.

50 Ibid., 206.

51 Ibid., 209.

52 In the preface to the second edition of *The Patriarchs and Lawgivers of the Old Testament*, Maurice expresses his concern that Mansel's ideas have begun to gain some influence in England: "The notion of a revelation that tells us things which are not in themselves true, but which it is right for us to believe and to act upon as if they were true, has, I fear, penetrated very deeply into the heart of our English schools, and of our English world. It may be traced among person who are apparently most unlike each other who live to oppose and confute each other. Those who speak most of the old Catholic creeds seem to love them because they have been handed down to us, not because they utter the Name in which we are living, and moving and having our being, the name of the Father," v.

53 Mansel, *An Examination*, 106.

54 Ibid.

55 Jeremy Morris's *F.D. Maurice and the Crisis of Christian Authority*, makes a spirited defence of Maurice's commitment to the basic structure and narrative of scripture: "Yet, on the other hand, he was very much a biblical theologian, fully committed to the narrative of creation, fall, and redemption that constituted the doctrinal core of traditional Christian belief. The seeming ambiguity of his treatment of sin illustrates the point perfectly. He could be read as implying that sin was something of an illusion, affecting at most superficially the permanent, underlying union of humanity with God. Yet his language about sin was also intense and vehement, and shot through with a sense of shock and tragedy at the human rejection of God," 191.

56 Mansel criticized Maurice's position on eternal punishment and the atonement. In both cases, he suggested that Maurice's theology did not permit

him to admit that God might be capable of anger and that his inability deformed Maurice's account of God's judgment. Mansel, *An Examination*, 44, 88.

57 Butler, "The Analogy of Religion," 233.

58 Mansel, *An Examination*, 88.

59 Mansel, *Prolegomena Logica*, 32.

60 Mansel, "Freethinking – Its History and Tendencies," 313.

61 Mansel's argument is not unlike David Burrell's in his controversial book *Aquinas: God and Action*. Burrell, for example, writes of Aquinas, "While it may be true to assert that God is wise, therefore, the manner in which we express that fact will fail to exhibit God's manner of being wise. In fact our mode of expression will give a false impression because we cannot say anything about God's wisdom without thereby showing it to be an accident of a subject. Thus even acceptable predicates will fall short of describing God." Burrell, *Aquinas*, 25. Burrell argues that Aquinas' discussion of compositeness, simplicity and limitlessness in God is an attempt to speak linguistically about God and not substantively, 16. This is similar, I would argue, to how Mansel uses "logical essence" in the preceding quote.

62 Mill, *An Examination of Sir William Hamilton's Philosophy*, 46. Mill suggested that if the absolute and infinite are employed this way, one would need to follow Hegel and his reconciliation of opposites and contradictions through the process of dialectic.

63 Hamilton criticized the notion of the absolute in philosophers such as Cousins and Schelling. For Schelling, according to Hamilton, the absolute could be comprehended through the intellectual intuition. But for Hamilton, this represents the annihilation of consciousness and its most basic laws.

64 Mansel, *Philosophy of the Conditioned*, 90, 91.

65 Burrell, *Aquinas*, 16.

66 "Now since our intellect knows God from creatures, it knows Him as far as creatures represent Him, and is like Him, so far as it possesses some perfection: yet not so far as to represent Him as something of the same species or genus, but as the excelling source of whose form the effects fall short, although they derive some kind of likeness thereto, even as the forms of inferior bodies represent the power of the sun ... Therefore, the aforesaid names signify the divine substance, but in an imperfect manner, even as creatures represent it imperfectly." Aquinas, *Summa Theologica*, part 1, question 13, article 2.

67 Mansel, *Philosophy of the Conditioned*, 88.

68 Mansel, *A Letter to Goldwin Smith*, 34.

69 Mansel, *The Limits of Religious Thought*, 223.

70 Mansel, *A Letter to Goldwin Smith*, 32.

71 Ibid., 33.

72 Mansel, *Limits of Religious Thought*, 127.

73 Ibid., 183.

74 In this way, Mansel follows Butler in arguing that scripture's difficulties
    form part of the Christian's moral and intellectual trial on earth: "It is rea-
    sonable to believe that, in matters of belief as well as of practice, God has
    not thought fit to annihilate the free will of man; but has permitted specu-
    lative difficulties to exist as the trial and the discipline of sharp and subtle
    intellects, as He has permitted moral temptations to form the trial and the
    discipline of strong and eager passions." Mansel, *The Limits of Religious
    Thought*, 178.

75 While analogy does not receive a long treatment by Mansel, and his refer-
    ences to the scholastic are slight, it seems Pusey consulted him on fine
    points of scholastic philosophy. In a letter, for example, in 1867, Mansel
    replies to Pusey's question about the role of substance and materiality in
    Eucharistic theology. Mansel references Suárez, Scotus, and *The Sentences*
    but laments that he cannot find the exact reference for the discussion: "I
    was looking in Scotus and *The Sentences* but I was unable to find it this
    morning." Mansel, "Letter to E.B. Pusey."

76 The recent trend is to downplay the apparent conflict between Barth and
    Aquinas on analogy. David Burrell, Eugene Rogers, and Timothy Furry are
    a few examples of theologians who argue that both Barth and Aquinas are
    primarily driven by the priority of revelation, scripture, and theological
    knowledge through the incarnation of Christ.

77 R.W. Dale, *Christian Doctrine*, 238.

78 Butler, *The Analogy*, 214.

79 Mill, *An Examination of Sir William Hamilton's Philosophy*, 90.

80 Ibid., 103.

81 Mansel, *The Philosophy of the Conditioned*, 147.

82 Mansel, *The Limits of Religious Thought*, 148. Though it should be noted
    that Mansel believed the human moral sense to be an *a priori* form given
    before experience. However, characteristic of his method, Mansel denied
    the moral sense any real positive content but rather argued that morality
    builds experientially upon the *a priori* moral sense and accrues a particu-
    lar character in the course of living. "Its nature, like that of the tree, can-
    not be changed by the soil in which it is planted, though its growth may
    be advanced or stunted by this or other accidental circumstances." Mansel,
    Metaphysics or the Philosophy of Consciousness, Phenomenal or Real, 260.

83 Mansel, *The Limits of Religious Thought*, 146. In some sense Mansel and
    Mill were both moral empiricists in opposition to Kant. Mill argued that
    "moral feelings are not innate, but acquired" (Mill, *Utilitarianism*, 27),
    and for Mill, the content of moral ends and goals must await deliberation
    within the empirical circumstances of experience. Furthermore, Mill
    defended utilitarian morality against the charge of being godless: "If it
    be meant that utilitarianism does not recognize the revealed will of God
    as the supreme law of morals, I answer, that a utilitarian who believes in
    the perfect goodness and wisdom of God necessarily believes that what-
    ever God has thought fit to reveal on the subject of moral, must fulfill the
    requirements of utility in a supreme degree," Mill, *Utilitarianism*, 20. Mill
    even upholds the golden rule. There may have been a large area of overlap
    between Mansel and Mill regarding the actual contents of morality –
    Mansel certainly did not believe that Old Testament violence was a sanc-
    tion for human violence – but it was Mill's insistence that God's character
    must be fitted to human conceptions of morality that Mansel could not
    tolerate. In some sense, Mill's invocation of God is a supreme instance
    of utility; that is, God is useful if he fits into the general model of utilitar-
    ian philosophy.
84 See Mackinnon's *A Study in Ethical Theory* for a well-articulated contrast
    between the ethical thinking of Kant and Butler. Mackinnon demonstrates
    the weaknesses of Kant's universal account and argues for a more particu-
    laristic approach as seen in Butler.
85 Christopher Miles Coope's article on this debate between Mansel and Mill
    points out that, in at least this instance, Mansel's more subtle and varied
    construal of human morality is closer to contemporary understanding.
    Coope, "Good-bye to the Problem of Evil, Hello to the Problem of
    Veracity," 379.
86 Mansel, *The Philosophy of the Conditioned*, 168.
87 Ibid., 165.
88 Mill, *An Examination of Sir William Hamilton's Philosophy*, 104.
89 Mansel, *Limits of Religious Thought*, 29.
90 See Christopher Seitz's essay "Canon and Conquest," 292. Seitz argues
    that difficult portions of the scripture like the Canaanite invasion can be
    read within a canonical comprehensive of the Bible that presents a coher-
    ent and unified picture of God's character – just and loving, merciful and
    severe.
91 Maurice, *Theological Essays*, 112.
92 Ibid., 113.
93 Torben Christensen, *The Divine Order*, 212.

 94 Mansel, *An Examination of The Rev. F. D. Maurice's Strictures*, 45.
 95 Maurice, *What Is Revelation?*, 183.
 96 Mansel, *Limits of Religious Thought*, 71.
 97 Ibid., 10.
 98 Maurice, *What Is Revelation?*, 203.
 99 Ibid., 203.
100 Mansel, *Limits of Religious Thought*, 44, 45.
101 Taylor, *A Secular Age*, 387.
102 Mansel, *Free Thinking*, 333.
103 Williams, "General Introductions," xxv.
104 In a letter to E.B. Pusey announcing Mansel's sudden death in 1871, Henry Parry Liddon praises Mansel's role in the establishment of the "positive truth" but immediately qualifies his commendation with the caveat "whether he was right or wrong in his use of the Hamiltonian philosophy in his Bampton Lectures." Hamilton, in this case, represented the skeptical aspects of Mansel's work that made even his closest allies uncomfortable. H.P. Liddon to E.B. Pusey, 2 August 1871 (Oxford: Pusey House Library).
105 Williams, "General Introductions," xxx.
106 Ibid.
107 Ibid.

CHAPTER FOUR

 1 Wolff helpfully places *The Limits of Religious Thought* within the context of other notable works in 1859 as they appear in a list of twenty-five prominent journals: "Tennyson's *Idylls of the King* was reviewed in twenty-two of our twenty-five periodicals; Fitzgerald's *Rubaiyat*, on the other hand, was reviewed by only one. Darwin's *Origin* was noticed at least in twenty-two periodicals and *Adam Bede* was, for a mere novel, exceptionally widely noticed, scoring twenty out of twenty-five. Mill's *On Liberty* comes next with sixteen out of twenty-five possible reviews, then the Mansel–Maurice controversy with fourteen." Of course, Wolff's representative list does not favour theological reviews. Wolff, "Victorian Reviewers and Cultural Responsibility," 273.
 2 Clement Webb's *A Study of English Thought in England from 1850* provides the now usual summary of Mansel's ideas: "It is by a singular irony of fate that the ingenious champion of the ancient creeds who would fain have put the aspiring human reason helpless under the feet of a wholly transcendent revelation has his niche in the history of philosophy as the

immediate forerunner of Herbert Spencer, the most ambitious projector of a system of pure naturalism that the nineteenth century knew," 92.

3 Collingwood in an essay on F.H. Bradley, for example, makes this striking statement: "My suggestion is that Bradley's *Appearance and Reality* is in the first instance a polemic against Mansel. It is from Mansel that Bradley borrows the antithesis of Appearance and Reality; it is against the project of dividing the one from the other that his book is directed, and that project is the task assigned by Mansel to metaphysics in his famous Encyclopaedia Britannica article, which everyone was reading when Bradley was young." Collingwood, "The Metaphysics of F.H. Bradley," 236. There are other interesting correspondences with Mansel's work. While this is only speculative, the Scottish-Canadian theologian William Robinson Clark, in his book *Witnesses to Christ*, provides a number of arguments in the fifth chapter that are virtually identical to Mansel's views on human consciousness, personality, and human knowledge of the infinite and absolute. Clark does not refer to Mansel, but he was a student at Magdalen College in the mid-1860s when Mansel held the Waynflete Chair of Metaphysics. Clark, *Witnesses to Christ: A Contribution to Christian Apologetics.*

4 The following is a list of titles by Henry Mansel that I refer to throughout the chapter: *Essays and Reviews*; *The Spirit a Divine Person*; *The Witness of the Church to the Promise of Christ's Coming*; "The Conflict and Defeat in Eden"; Mansel and Sidney Gedge, "Revelation: iii"; "Personal Responsibility of Man"; "It is Finished"; "St Matthew's Gospel."

5 R.H. Hutton, *Essays on Some of the Modern Guides to English Thought in Matters of Faith*, 326.

6 Charles Meynell, "The Limits of our Thought," 105.

7 Ibid., 106. The words of a writer in *Eclectic Review* are most telling: "The true ally of Christianity, its faithful expositor and its staunchest defender, we shall find, not in a philosophy which curbs and fetters, enfeebles and enslaves, which treads down the human faculties and casts on them suspicion and contempt, but in one elevating, inspiring, and stimulative in tendency, – a philosophy which sees God in man's powers, and honours them because it honours him." Calderwood, "The Philosophy of the Infinite," 457.

8 Mansel's posthumously published lectures on the Gnostic heresies make repeated parallels between early Christian heresies and modern philosophical and biblical criticism. "There are not wanting teachers at the present time who tell us, in the spirit of the Gnostics of old, that dogmas and historical facts are no part of the Christian religion; that there is a spiritual

sense in which these things may be understood which is superior to the letter; that we may be Christian in spirit without troubling ourselves about the facts of Christ's earthly life, or the supernatural doctrines connected with His person." Mansel, *The Gnostic Heresies of the First and Second Centuries*, 78.

9 William Abraham, *Canon and Criterion in Christian Theology*.

10 Ibid., 27.

11 Ibid., 208.

12 Ibid., 27.

13 Ibid., 22.

14 Ibid., 21.

15 In *The Quarterly Review* an article on Mansel appeared in 1885. The author here makes the following reference to Mansel's sermons: "Mansel on being appointed 'Select Preacher,' viz. from October 1860 till June 1862, availed himself of the opportunity to give breadth and symmetry to his philosophical system by enlarging on certain departments of his great subject which he had before but slightly treated. His sermons at this time bear the following titles: – 'Faith and Sight,' – 'Faith and Reason,' – 'Moral Sense in Theology,' – and 'Man's Relation to God.'" There is, however, no record of these sermons being published. Anon, "Dean Mansel," *The Quarterly Review*, 159.

16 Mansel, "Freethinking – It's History and Tendencies."

17 Ibid., 306.

18 Ibid., 298.

19 Ibid., 321. This is an account that has large support today. See Henning Graf Reventlow's *The Authority of the Bible and the Rise of the Modern World*.

20 Mansel, "Freethinking – It's History and Tendencies," 336.

21 Ibid., 307.

22 Mansel, *The Witness of the Church*, 7.

23 Ibid., 8.

24 Ibid., 9.

25 Mansel, *The Gnostic Heresies*, 8.

26 Mansel, *The Witness of the Church*, 17.

27 Barth, *On Religion*, 83.

28 Ibid., 71. The actual historical character of humanity's "belief in man" may have looked different for both writers: Mansel was a high churchman for whom established religious practices were indispensable. The comparison here is more related to the recurring or oscillating waves of unbelief that characterize human history.

29 Mansel, "Revelation: iii," 9.

30 Ibid.

31 Mansel, *The Witness of the Church*, 14.

32 Mansel, *Labourers in the Vineyard*, 420.

33 Peter Harrison, *The Bible, Protestantism, and the Rise of Natural Science*, 4.

34 Ibid., 204.

35 Ibid., 269.

36 Michael Buckley's *The Origins of Modern Atheism* is one of the paradigmatic examples of this approach: "Atheism is the secret of that religious reflection which justifies the sacred and its access to the sacred primarily through its own transmogrification into another form of human knowledge and practice, as though the only alternative to fideism were such an alienation, as though religion had to become philosophy to remain religion. The unique character of religious knowledge does not survive this reduction," 359. In other words, Christian apologists contributed to the rise of atheism by speaking philosophically about God and ignoring the central confessional aspects of Christian theology. The merit of Buckley's position is that he wrests the history of modern philosophy into a theological context by rejecting the notion that "Atheism is taken as if it were simply a matter of retrieving the philosophical positions of the past, rather than a profound and current rejection of the meaning and reality of Jesus Christ," 47. Though Buckley attributes modern atheism to the inadvertent intention of Christians, he relates this inadvertence to central theological claims.

37 Reventlow, *The Authority of the Bible and the Rise of the Modern World*, 349.

38 Ibid.

39 Brad Gregory's *The Unintended Reformation* is perhaps the latest example of this method.

40 Lightman, *Origins of Agnosticism*, 84.

41 Mansel noted Spencer's *First Principles* and made the following comment: "Because a certain person deduces certain consequences from a certain book, therefore his deduction must needs be legitimate: and of course if two persons deduce contradictory consequences from the same book, therefore both deductions are legitimate. According to this canon, every heresy which has ever claimed the authority of the Bible must needs be found in the Bible ... I have not read Mr Spencer's book on First Principles, which I believe is only printed for his own subscribers; but from what I know of it indirectly, and from what I know directly of the author's other writings, I believe his teaching to be the contradictory, not

the complement of mine ... The acknowledgment, that that which is absolute and infinite is beyond the boundaries of positive thought, and is
known only as a negation, may, like any other proposition, lead to very
different conclusions, according the premise with which it is combined
in reasoning." Mansel, *A Second Letter to Goldwin Smith*, 53–5.

42 Mansel, "Letter to Pusey: 1866."

43 In John Maynard Keynes's *Essays on Biography* he quotes this unpub-
lished note by the English economist Alfred Marshall: "About the year
1867 (while mainly occupied with teaching Mathematics at Cambridge),
Mansel's Bampton Lectures came into my hands and caused me to think
that man's own possibilities were the most important subject for his study.
So I gave myself for a time to the study of Metaphysics; but soon passed
to what seemed to be the more progressive study of Psychology. Its fascinating inquiries into the possibilities of the higher and more rapid development of human faculties brought me into touch with the question: how
far do the conditions of life of the British (and other) working classes generally suffice for fullness of life?" Keynes, *Essays in Biography*, 138. The
comment is somewhat elusive, but Marshall's contribution to economics,
to some degree, concurs with this observation: namely, the study of human
behaviour.

44 Mansel, *Metaphysics*, 284.

45 Ibid., 292.

46 Ibid., 67.

47 Ibid., 346.

48 Milbank, *The Word Made Strange*, 32.

49 "This self-personality, like all other simple and immediate presentations, is
indefinable; but it is so, because it is superior to definition. It can be anal-
ysed into no simpler elements, for it is itself the simplest of all: it can be
made no clearer by description or comparison, for it is revealed to us in
all the clearness of an original intuition." Mansel, *Prolegomena*, 129.

50 "The Cartesian cogito, ergo sum, is so far from being, as its opponents
have maintained, an illogical reasoning from a premise to its conclusion,
that its only fault consists in assuming the appearance of a reasoning at all.
My consciousness does not prove my existence, because it is my existence.
Descartes does not intend, as Reid imagined, to reason from the existence
of thought to the existence of a mind or subject of thought: he intends to
state wherein personal existence consists; and he rightly places it in consciousness." Mansel, *Metaphysics or the Philosophy of Consciousness*, 356.

51 This claim is one of the more striking parallels between Mansel's conception of reason and religious faith and that of J.H. Newman: "After all man

is not a reasoning animal; he is a seeing, feeling, contemplating, acting animal. He is influenced by what is direct and precise ... life is not long enough for a religion of inferences ... Resolve to believe nothing and you must prove your proofs and analyze your elements, sinking farther and farther, and finding in the lowest depth a lower deep, till you come to the broad bosom of skepticism." Newman, *An Essay in Aid of a Grammar of Assent*, 72.

52 Mansel, *The Limits of Religious Thought*, 12, 13.
53 R.V. Sampson, "The Limits of Religious Thought," 68.
54 Gordon Lewis Phillips, *Seeing and Believing*, 60.
55 Mansel, *The Limits of Religious Thought*, 75.
56 Mansel, *The Limits of Religious Thought*, 76.
57 Mansel, *The Limits of Religious Thought*, 77.
58 Mansel does not lean as heavily on the sense of dependence as does Friedrich Schleiermacher, but they use the term in a similar manner: "Now this is just what is principally meant by the formula which says that to feel oneself absolutely dependent and to be conscious of being in relation with God are one and the same thing; and the reason is that absolute dependence is the fundamental relation which must include all others in itself ... In this sense it can indeed be said that God is given to us in feeling in an original way." Friedrich Schleiermacher, *The Christian Faith*, 17. Dependence for both authors is a fundamental reality of being human, but for Mansel, this dependence is not the absolute field of experience; he would most likely describe personality in these terms, a concept with similar though different theological implications.
59 Mansel, *Limits of Religious Thought*, 78.
60 Ibid., 96.
61 Ibid., 164.
62 Ibid., 186.
63 Michael Polyani, *The Study of Man*.
64 Ibid., 26.
65 Mansel, *Limits of Religious Thought*, 178.
66 Henri de Lubac, *Drama of Atheistic Humanism*, 31.
67 Stephen Sykes, *The Identity of Christianity*, 6, 7.
68 Sykes, *The Identity of Christianity*, 7.
69 Mansel, *Limits of Religious Thought*, 175.
70 In note xvii in Lecture VIII, Mansel writes, "I do not mean by these remarks to deny the possibility of any progress whatever in Christian Theology, such, for instance, as may result from the better interpretation of Holy Writ, or the refutation of unauthorized inferences therefrom." He

then quotes Butler from the *Analogy*: "As it is owned the whole scheme of Scripture is not yet understood." These comments come on the heels of Mansel's characteristic denouncement of progress in theology: "We can test the progress of knowledge, only by comparing its successive representations with the objects which they profess to represent: and as the object in this case is inaccessible to human faculties, we have no criterion by which to distinguish between progress and mere fluctuation. The so-called progress of theology is in truth only an advance in those conceptions of man's moral and religious duties which form the basis of natural religion; – and advance which is regulative and not speculative; which is primarily and properly a knowledge, not of God's nature, but of man's obligations … a closer study of the laws of the finite." *Limits of Religious Thought*, 179.

71 R.W. Matthews, *The Religious Philosophy of Dean Mansel*, 20.

72 F.W. Dockrill, "The Doctrine of Regulative Truth and Mansel's Intentions," 77–88.

73 Mansel, *Limits of Religious Thought*, 99, 100.

74 Milbank, *The Word Made Strange*, 19.

75 Mansel, "Essay on Miracles," 28.

76 In a curious letter to Pusey, Mansel excitedly relays his recent hunch based upon the poem *The Botanic Garden* by Erasmus Darwin: "I have just lighted on a remarkable passage in Darwin's Botanic Garden (ref on back of letter) in which the author (the grandfather, I believe, of the recent Darwin) suggests the possibility of man being able to force and to change the direction of the winds by chemical interference. I do not venture to speculate on the scientific value of the conjecture but it is worth looking at, as a proof, coming from a scientific authority of the last century, that the results of science may be supposed to lead, not to necessity but to contingency, in the recurrence of material phenomena – at least as regards those phenomena with which the physical welfare of mankind is most immediately connected." Mansel, "Letter to E.B. Pusey."

77 Mansel, *Limits of Religious Thought*, 110.

78 Mansel, "It is Finished," 427.

79 Ibid.

80 "If we put the case, that for the present, it was intended, revelation should be no more than a small light, in the midst of a world greatly overspread, notwithstanding it, with ignorance and darkness: that certain glimmerings of this light should extend, and be directed, to remote distances, in such a manner as that those who really partook of it, should not discern from whence it originally came: that some in a nearer situation to it, should

have its light obscured, and, in different ways and degrees, intercepted: and that others should be placed within its clearer influence, and be much more enlivened, cheered and directed by it; but yet that even to these it should be no more than a light shining in a dark place: all this would be perfectly uniform and of a piece with the conduct of providence, in the distribution of its other blessings." Butler, "The Analogy of Religion," 26.

81 Mansel, "It Is Finished," 427.

82 Ibid.

83 Mansel, *Higher Vocation*, 437.

84 Mansel, *The Witness of the Church*, 9.

85 Ibid., 16.

86 Ibid.

87 Ibid., 11.

88 Mansel, "Revelation: iii," 9.

89 Henry Sidgwick, "To H.G. Dakyns from Douglas, Isles of Man, June 9, 1862."

90 Mansel, "A Commentary on Matthew."

91 Mansel, *The Spirit a Divine Person*, 9.

92 Ibid., 4, 5.

93 Ibid., 6. Mansel's commentary on chapter 24 of Matthew's Gospel, as an isolated example, contains a variety of examples of this method. The whole of chapter 24 is taken as a prophecy in the immediate context of the first century and yet it is expanded into the age of the Church, 135–47.

94 Ibid., 8.

95 Ibid.

96 Ibid., 10. Again, Newman's consideration of Darwin's work triggered an almost identical reply. In speaking of the Genesis account and Darwin's account of human origins, Newman writes in *The Grammar of Assent*, "the two cannot stand together; one or other of them is untrue. But whatever means I might be led to take, for making, if possible the antagonism tolerable, I conceive I should never give up my certitude in that truth which on sufficient grounds I determined to come from heaven. If I so believed, I should not pretend to argue, or to defend myself to others; but I should be patient; I should look for better days; but I should still believe," 195.

97 In a footnote Hannah acknowledges this coincidence: "I am happy to find that the argument of this discourse is supported by an excellent sermon of Mr Mansel's, which I had not seen when my own was preached: The Spirit a Divine Person, to be worshipped and glorified; one of the Oxford Lenten Sermons for 1863." John Hannah, *The Relation*, 320.

98 Hannah, *The Relation*, 300, 301.

99 Ibid., 188.

100 Ibid., 84–98.

101 Ibid., 108.

102 See Hannah's fourth lecture in the Bampton series for an extensive application of the double sense of scripture.

103 Lindbeck, *The Nature of Doctrine*, 117. I do not wish to simply cast
Mansel as a proto postliberal in Lindbeck's manner, however, the similarities are obvious, despite largely dissimilar methods of philosophical and
theological reasoning. The following statement by Lindbeck, though,
could have been pulled from the "Bampton Lectures": "The primary focus
is not on God's being in itself, for that is not what the text is about, but on
how life is to be lived and reality construed in the light of God's character
as an agent as this is depicted in the stories of Israel and of Jesus."
Lindbeck, *The Nature of Doctrine*, 121.

104 Mansel, *The Limits of Religious Thought*, 136.

105 Ibid., 134.

106 Hannah, *The Relation*, 125.

107 Mansel, *The Witness of the Church*, 8.

108 Mansel, "It Is Finished," 429.

109 Mansel, "The Conflict and Defeat in Eden," 28.

110 This inclination comes out forcefully, though indirectly, in his essay on
spiritualism. Consider the following sarcastic remarks concerning one spi-
ritualist leader: "Mr Howitt, on the other hand, who regards all spiritual
manifestations, ghosts included, as the results of one and the same universal principle, agrees with Stilling and Swedenborg in holding that 'the
animated spirit, the divine spark in man, is inseparably united with an
ethereal or luminous body.' Hence arises a question – Is this ethereal or
luminous body visible or invisible to mortal eyes? If visible, what is the
need of incarnating hands out of vital atmospheres; and why are hands
alone, and not whole human figures, visible at Mr Home's séances? If invisible, how comes it that the old-fashioned ghost managed to make himself
seen from head to foot; and not himself only, but likewise the ghost of
a dress, which, with a due regard to modesty, he used to put on?" 272.
While the spiritualism here has little to do with traditional mysticism, it is
the general threat to the particular personality of God that Mansel ultimately bases his critique upon, 287. Mansel, *Letter, Lectures and Reviews*,
255–92.

111 Mansel, *The Limits of Religious Thought*, 160.

112 See the section on Coleridge in chapter 2.

113 Benjamin Jowett, "On the Interpretation of Scripture," 511.

114 Jowett, "On the Interpretation of Scripture," 481, 498, 516.

115 Hannah makes this point particularly well: "The earlier moral lessons, for
     instance, will no longer be thought to be the mere vehicles of an unrelen-
     ting sternness, fitted for the world's childhood, but unworthy of its matu-
     rity. We shall no longer look on that old Jewish zeal, which bore fruit in
     hatred for evil as well as love for good, as though it could yield no prece-
     dent for Christian conduct, no pattern meet for Christian men. The same
     is true of every portion of that ancient record. To the devout and enlighte-
     ned Christian intelligence, the words of those elder Scriptures can never
     become like the narrow cottage which is abandoned to decay and desola-
     tion when its inmates have left it for an ampler home. Still less are they
     like the dead husk which may be cast away when the fruit has been
     secured, or like the dead body which may be buried when the spirit has
     departed. Rather they are still and forever alive with the abiding presence
     of the indwelling Spirit." Hannah, *The Relation*, 118.

116 Mansel, *The Spirit a Divine Person*, 18.

117 Mozley, "Mansel's Bampton Lectures," 376.

118 Mansel, "St Matthew's Gospel," 136.

119 Hannah, *The Relation*, 134.

120 Lindbeck, *The Nature of Doctrine*, 134.

121 Ibid., 130.

122 Ibid.

123 Ibid., 134.

124 Mansel, *The Limits of Religious Thought*, 175.

125 Lindbeck, *The Nature of Doctrine*, 131, 135.

126 Vladimir Lossky, *In the Image and Likeness of God*, 113.

127 Ibid., 120.

128 Ibid., 129.

129 Williams, *Wrestling With Angels*, 18.

CHAPTER FIVE

1 Burrows, "Dean Mansel as a Christian Philosopher," 3, 4.

2 Ibid., 26.

3 Burrows wrote: "The destructive portion of Mansel's work has certainly
   had a considerable effect. So-called Rational Religion, at least in its technical sense, no longer takes a prominent place amongst us," 8.

4 While Spencer did make wide use of Mansel's arguments, he is clear about
   the limitations they imply for his own purposes. In some sense, Spencer
   argues that Mansel's skepticism is dishonest in not recognizing the further

incognizability of even revealed claims, 92. For Spencer, the unknowable is
real in some sense, and history gradually reveals its full extent: "Through
all its successive phases the disappearance of those positive dogmas by
which the mystery was made unmysterious, has formed the essential
change delineated in religious history. And so Religion has ever been
approximating toward that complete recognition of this mystery which
is its goal." Spencer, *First Principles*, 91.

5 Gouldstone, *The Rise and Decline of Anglican Idealism in the Nineteenth
   Century*, 10.
6 Ibid., 18.
7 W.J. Mander, *British Idealism*, 138.
8 Michael Ramsay, *From Gore to Temple*, 10.
9 Gouldstone, *The Rise and Decline of Anglican Idealism in the Nineteenth
   Century*, 38.
10 Mansel, *Second Letter to Goldwin Smith*, 28.
11 Ibid., 28.
12 David Hume, *An Enquiry Concerning Human Understanding*, 150.
13 Mansel, *A Second Letter to Goldwin Smith*, 20.
14 Taylor, *Hegel*, 493.
15 Williams, *Wrestling With Angels*, 37.
16 G.W.F. Hegel, *The Phenomenology of Mind*, 51.
17 Williams, *Wrestling With Angels*, 48.
18 Ibid., 48.
19 Mansel, *Metaphysics*, 313.
20 Ibid., 306.
21 Ibid., 313.
22 Ibid., 312.
23 Ibid., 322.
24 Ibid., 314.
25 Ibid., 322.
26 Gouldstone, *The Rise and Decline of Anglican Idealism in the Nineteenth
   Century*, 24, 25.
27 Mansel, "The Phrontisterion, or Oxford in the 19th Century," 403.
28 Gouldstone, *The Rise and Decline of Anglican Idealism in the Nineteenth
   Century*, 25.
29 Richard Rorty regards the idealism of Hegel and the later idealists as the
   end, in some measure, of a philosophical commitment to common reasoning
   and verification. He writes, "Hegel had also shown that there can be a kind
   of rationality without argumentation, a rationality which works outside the
   bounds of what Kuhn calls a 'disciplinary matrix,' in an ecstasy of spiritual

freedom." Rorty, "Nineteenth-century Idealism and Twentieth-Century Textualism," 155–73. To some extent this is true of Green and Bradley, though neither author conceals the fact that their notions of the absolute rely, in some measure, on some kind of religious or philosophical faith.

30 Green, *Prolegomena to Ethics*, 40.

31 Ibid., 42.

32 T.H. Green, *Works of Thomas Hill Green*, 173. According to Green, Kant held "that there could be, but that such mere conception or thought did not amount to knowledge. Hence, according to him, though you could think such objects as a cosmos (the totality of conditions), freedom (*causa sui*), God (the self-conscious subject of the physical and moral worlds), and though you might be sure that there were such objects (which he held to be the case at least with regard to freedom), you could not know them, because from the nature of the case they were not presentable as intuitions, i.e. as distinct in space or time," 173.

33 Ibid., 169.

34 Ibid., 175.

35 Ibid., 190.

36 Mander, *British Idealism*, 278.

37 Green, *Prolegomena to Ethics*, 40.

38 Ibid., 71.

39 Ibid., 196.

40 Ibid., 198.

41 Ibid., 199.

42 Maria Dimova suggests that Green's idealism places him somewhere in between these two schools in a manner that is quite particular to his era in England. "Continental philosophy has inherited one important insight from German Idealism: the discovery that experience is formed through the meanings invested in it by human consciousness. This insight is essentially missing in British empiricist thought. British moral and political thought as represented by Mill's liberalism and utilitarianism, undertakes an inquiry into the human personality. A similar reorientation took place much later on the Continent. This breakthrough, against the background of the dominant objectivistic and universalistic spirit of German Idealism, was performed by the school of twentieth-century existentialism. Being influenced by German philosophical thought, and having inherited the spirit of Mill's liberalism, by the end of the nineteenth century, Green had developed philosophical approaches as mature as those of twentieth-century phenomenology." Dimova, "T.H. Green as a Phenomenologist: Linking British Idealism and Continental Phenomenology," 87.

43 Mathew Arnold, *St Paul and Protestantism*, 111.

44 Gouldstone, *The Rise and Decline of Anglican Idealism in the Nineteenth Century*, 52.

45 Green, "The Conversion of Paul" in *The Works of Thomas Hill Green: Volume III*, 188.

46 Green, "Justification by Faith," in The *Works of Thomas Hill Green: Volume III*, 193.

47 See the section on Maurice and Mansel in chapter 2. Mansel did not adhere to any particular atonement theory, though he insisted that the Old Testament, the ceremonial and moral law in particular, must be allowed to inform Christ's own work on the cross.

48 Green, "Justification by Faith," 199.

49 Ibid., 195.

50 Green, "Essay on Christian Dogma," in *Works of Thomas Hill Green: Volume III*, 177.

51 Ibid., 175.

52 Ibid., 184.

53 Dimova argues, as others have, that this aspect of Green's thought, shorn of the theological element, secures him a place in the genealogy of British liberalism: "According to Green, the pursuit of the moral ideal is the pursuit of self-fulfillment. In this sense the moral ideal is not an abstract concept which is the same for all – quite the reverse, everybody should be able to find the right object of her, or his own self-realisation. By developing this view Green made a major contribution to British liberalism." Dimova, "T.H. Green as a Phenomenologist," 84.

54 Green, "Fragment of an Address on Romans x. 8 'The Word in Nigh Thee,'" in *Works of Thomas Hill Green: Volume III*, 228.

55 Green, *Works of Thomas Hill Green*, 276.

56 See chapter one. Spencer and Green, of course, had very different philosophical influences, but the result of their respective skepticisms, while not obvious to Victorian theologians, had a highly similar effect on the status of Christian doctrines and scriptural claims: particular claims about God's activity in the world eventually dissolve into temporal or historical moments in a greater process toward incomprehensibility.

57 Green, *Works of Thomas Hill Green*, 262.

58 Collingwood, "The Metaphysics of Bradley," 236. Collingwood's claim is supported by W.J. Mander in his recent study of British idealism. See *British Idealism*, 116, note 118.

59 Collingwood, "The Metaphysics of F.H. Bradley," 239.

60 Bradley, *Appearance and Reality: A Metaphysical Essay*, 87.

61 Ibid., 156.

62 Ibid., 123.

63 Ibid.

64 Ibid., 169.

65 Ibid., 170.

66 Stephen Carr writes, "Bradley's philosophy is fideistic to this extent then, that it requires a faith in certain notions of truth and goodness as a presupposition of its metaphysical project. These notions are integrated, by Bradley, into a form of religious life." Carr, "F.H. Bradley and Religious Faith," *Religious Studies* 28, no. 3, 258.

67 Bradley, *Appearance and Reality*, 200.

68 Ibid., 98.

69 Bradley, "On God and the Absolute," in *Essays on Truth and Reality*, 37.

70 Bradley, *Appearance and Reality*, 391.

71 Bradley, "On God and the Absolute," 432.

72 Mander, *British Idealism*, 400.

73 Bradley, "On God and the Absolute," 443.

74 Ibid., 437.

75 Ibid., 443.

76 Ibid., 446.

77 Collingwood, "The Metaphysics of F.H. Bradley," 251. While Bradley was severely criticized by Russell and Moore, Collingwood suggests that the turn to realism in philosophy had its roots in Bradley's affirmation that all that we perceive is in some way real.

78 Collingwood, "The Metaphysics of F.H. Bradley," 246.

79 Ramsay, *From Gore to Temple*, 129.

80 Talbot refers directly to Westcott for his historical schematic that describes the Greek and Jewish aspects of Christ's fulfillment in history, 157. Further, both Gore and Lyttleton refer to Westcott for their arguments concerning the narrowing of theology in traditional renderings of the atonement, 304, 333. Both of these themes are integral to the overall scope of the volume.

81 S.C. Carpenter, *Church and People 1789–1889*, 536.

82 The relationship between the two men is unknown, but Westcott's close friend J.B. Lightfoot edited Mansel's posthumously published lectures on the Gnostic heresies.

83 Westcott, *The Gospel of the Resurrection*, 21.

84 "Indeed, the clearest conception which we can form of a person is the special limitation of a self-moving power. The power must be self-moving because a person is necessarily endowed with a will which is a spring of

motion. It must be limited, because, as far as our experience reaches, a will can only make itself felt in and through an organism with which it is connected." Westcott, *The Gospel of the Resurrection*, 143.

85 It should also be noted that Westcott's defense of miracles uses the same language that Mansel used in his 1862 essay on miracles: "But on the other hand it is distinctly laid down that in the case of a miracle a new force is introduced, or rather, as the source of all force is one, that the force which usually acts freely in a particular way now acts freely in another. That is, to continue to use popular language, the law is not suspended, but its natural results are controlled. The law produces its full effect, but a new power supervenes, and the final result represents the combined effect of the two forces." Westcott, *The Gospel of the Resurrection*, 40.

86 Graham A. Patrick argues that Westcott's historic optimism or belief in progress was attributable in some respects to F.D. Maurice. Though Westcott expressed some concern about Maurice, he certainly read Maurice, and even more, close friends such as Hort were open admirers. There is not much evidence that Westcott had read Green or considered Hegel deeply, yet ideas of progress were certainly part of the intellectual fabric of the era. Graham Patrick, *The Miner's Bishop: Brooke Foss Westcott*, 107.

87 Westcott, *The Gospel of the Resurrection*, 239.

88 Westcott, "Christianity as the Absolute Religion" in *Essays in the History of Religious Thought in the West*, 348.

89 Westcott, "Christianity as the Absolute Religion," 353.

90 Westcott, *The Gospel of the Resurrection*, 241.

91 Westcott, *Christus Consummator*, 13.

92 Westcott, *Christus Consummator*, 109.

93 Ibid., 142.

94 Ibid., 134.

95 Illingworth, "The Incarnation in Relation to Development," in *Lux Mundi: A Series of Studies in the Religion of the Incarnation*, 5th ed., 183.

96 Illingworth, "The Incarnation in Relation to Development," 198.

97 Rorty, "Nineteenth-Century Idealism and Twentieth-Century Textualism," 141.

98 Mander, *British Idealism*, 402.

99 Hermann Lotze, *Outlines of the Philosophy of Religion*, 67.

100 Ibid., 69.

101 Illingworth, *Personality, Human and Divine*, 27, 244, 245.

102 Ibid., 74.

103 Lotze, *Outlines of the Philosophy of Religion*, 149.

104 Illingworth writes, "The belief in the Incarnation, while it intensified and emphasized the notion of divine personality, necessitated a further intellectual analysis of what that notion meant, and issued in the doctrine of the Trinity in Unity." Illingworth, *Personality, Human and Divine*, 66.

105 Mander suggests that Personalism was a way of retaining the idealist structure of metaphysics while making space for traditional forms of piety. With respect to Clement Webb, Mander writes, "he nevertheless argues strongly for a 'personal God.' This restricts our metaphysics in more than one direction; extreme immanence and extreme transcendence alike he argues would destroy personal relations (such as prayer or worship) between human and divine, because on neither scheme is there scope for reciprocation from God to us. Only theism can really grasp the personality of God." Mander, *British Idealism*, 408.

106 Anon., "Illingworth's Bampton Lectures," *The Church Quarterly Review*, 203.

107 Patrick, *The Miner's Bishop*, 6.

108 Talbot agrees with Westcott that these two histories could not produce a revelation but they both served to prepare the way ("Preparation for Christ in History," 135). It should also be noted that this particular scheme of preparation for the Incarnation has clear roots, certainly for Westcott, in Maurice's *The Kingdom of Christ*.

109 Talbot, "Preparation for Christ in History," in *Lux Mundi*, 135.

110 Ibid., 165.

111 Ibid.

112 Ibid., 174.

113 Holland, "Faith," in *Lux Mundi*, 17.

114 Ibid., 24.

115 Ibid., 43.

116 See the section on Coleridge in chapter 2.

117 Holland, *The Optimism of Butler's Analogy*, 23.

118 Ibid., 24.

119 See Gore's essay on inspiration in the *Lux Mundi* (346) as well as his Bampton lectures on the incarnation, 169.

120 Gore, "The Holy Spirit and Inspiration," in *Lux Mundi*, 350.

121 Seitz, *Figured Out*, 55.

122 Gore, "The Holy Spirit and Inspiration," 329.

123 Avis, "Charles Gore and Modernism: A Half-Centenary Exercise in 'Corporate Believing,'" 269, 272.

124 Gore, "The Holy Spirit and Inspiration," 359. Mansel, it seems, believed in the omniscience of Christ, though it only appears in a brief statement in his commentary on Matthew: "The cup of suffering and death which He

was about to drink to the dregs, every feature of that suffering being already present to his omniscient vision." Mansel, *The Limits of Religious Thought*, 160.

125 The article "Theology and Criticism" in *Church Quarterly Review* (April 1890) is anonymous, but Ramsay claims that its was well known that Stone was the author. Ramsay, *From Gore to Temple*, 8, 9.

126 Gore, "The Holy Spirit and Inspiration," 345.

127 Stone, "Theology and Criticism," 215.

128 Ibid., 216.

129 Gore, *The Incarnation of the Son of God*, 115.

130 Mansel, *A Second Letter to Goldwin Smith*, 32.

131 "Man has fallen from that image ... man's nature is but an imperfect likeness of God's, and man's moral judgments but an imperfect criterion of god's actions." Mansel, *A Second Letter to Goldwin Smith*, 50.

132 Butler, "The Analogy of Religion," 257–60.

133 Ibid., 259.

134 Lyttelton, "The Atonement," 276.

135 Stone, "Theology and Criticism," 231.

136 Lyttelton, "The Atonement," 292.

137 Ibid., 309.

138 Ibid., 304.

139 "The doctrine of Atonement, more than any of the great truths of Christianity, has been misconceived and misrepresented, and has therefore not only been rejected itself, but has sometimes been the cause of the rejection of the whole Christian system. The truth of the vicarious sacrifice has been isolated till it has almost become untrue, and, mysterious as it undoubtedly is, it has been so stated as to be not only mysterious, but contrary to reason and even to conscience." Lyttelton, "The Atonement," 307.

140 Ibid., 307.

141 Moore, "The Influence of Calvinism on Modern Unbelief," 507.

142 Ibid., 517.

143 Ibid., 518.

144 Though Mozley was critical of Mansel's lectures, his own study of Augustine and predestination applies Mansel's hermeneutical style. There, Mozley argues that Augustine gives precedence to certain scriptural realities over others and does not allow conflicting statement about God's act of election to remain in juxtaposition. Mozley, *A Treatise on the Augustinian Doctrine of Predestination*, 173.

145 Copleston, *A History of Philosophy III*, 283.

146 Taylor, *A Secular Age*, 409.
147 Mander, *British Idealism*, 546.
148 Gouldstone, *Anglican Idealism*, 180.
149 Ibid., 185.
150 See Avis, "Charles Gore and Modernism."
151 Gore, *Belief in God*, 29.
152 Ibid., 29. Gore goes on to speak in particular about the collapse of faith
      among young people in England: "Certainly, on the whole, it has left the
      youth of the country widely and deeply alienated from the Church and
      from organized religion." Gore, *Belief in God*, 29.
153 Gore, "The Holy Spirit and the Church," 853.
154 Gore, *Belief in God*, 44.
155 Ibid., 45.
156 Ibid., 58.
157 Ibid., 122.
158 Ibid., 148.
159 Ibid., 8.
160 Ibid., 28.
161 Mill, *An Examination of Sir William Hamilton's Philosophy*, 104.
162 Much as in the *Lux Mundi* essay, Gore still spoke about the Old
      Testament depictions of God's character as imperfect and immature:
      "The limitations and the imperfections of the Old Testament conception of
      divine love, which are conspicuous in its earlier stages, are here quite obli-
      terated. The love of God is active and universal." Gore, *Belief in God*, 118.
163 Ibid., 92.
164 Ramsay, *From Gore to Temple*, 133.
165 Edwyn Hoskyns, "The Christ of the Synoptic Gospels," 177.
166 Hoskyns, "The World," in *Cambridge Sermons*, 98.
167 Hoskyns, *Cambridge Sermons*, 89–150.
168 Ibid., 91.
169 Ibid., 103.
170 Ibid., 122.
171 Ibid., 128.
172 Ibid., 147.
173 See Introduction.
174 Webster, *Holy Scripture*, 88.
175 *Jude the Obscure* and *Two in a Tower* are examples of Hardy's pessimistic
      view of history and fate.
176 "And yet it is not lawful for the Church to ordain any thing that is
      contrary to God's Word written, neither may it so expound one place of

Scripture, that it be repugnant to another," *Book of Common Prayer: Canada 1962*, Article XX.

CHAPTER SIX

1 Cupitt, *The Old Creed and the New*, 135.
2 Bernard Reardon, *Religious Thought in the Victorian Age: A Survey from Coleridge to Gore*, v.
3 I will not discuss L.E. Elliot-Binns's book in what follows. His history was intended as a sequel to Storr's book and in many ways continues with the same theme. The theology that Mansel stood for ignored modern scientific and moral concerns and for that reason risked driving the Church into further irrelevance. L.E. Elliot-Binns, *English Thought 1860–1900*, 10, 11, 17, 18.
4 Vernon Storr, *The Development of English Theology in the Nineteenth Century, 1800–1860*, 3.
5 Ibid., 363.
6 Ibid., 5.
7 Ibid., 8.
8 Ibid., 422.
9 S.C. Carpenter, *Church and People, 1789–1889*, 480.
10 Ibid., 479.
11 Webb, *God and Personality*. In this work Webb is deeply appreciative of Green and Bradley's idealistic metaphysics, but he follows Hermann Lotze in insisting that the absolute must be conceived as a personal reality, in the light of the demands of religious consciousness, 260.
12 Webb, *God and Personality*, 218. In this particular book, Webb also demonstrates his indebtedness to great figures of Catholic Modernism like George Tyrell and Baron Von Hugel.
13 Ibid., 242.
14 Webb, *A Study of Religious Thought in England from 1850*, 88.
15 Ibid., 91.
16 Ibid., 89, 92.
17 Ibid., 149.
18 Ibid., 168.
19 To be sure, Gore was far more cautious in his general assessment of historical progress than Webb, though both men allowed the war to shake, but in the end not significantly alter, their philosophical frameworks.
20 Webb, *A Study of Religious Thought in England from 1850*, 179.
21 Ibid., 182.

22 See chapter 3 of this document, 68–96. Mansel's understanding of the typological expansion of scripture, centered around the person of Christ, was an attempt to present the narrative of scripture as the encompassing framework within which Christians interpret and understand God's presence within the world.

23 Elliot-Binns' history very much confirms this portrait. *English Thought 1860–1900*, 17, 18.

24 Reardon, *Religious Thought in the Victorian Age*, 223. Unlike the previous authors, Reardon, despite having some sympathies for Maurice, nevertheless suggests that "Maurice did not get to grips with Mansel's arguments in that he did not understand the principles on which they were advanced." The conflict was an example "of the plain man's impatience with the philosopher." Reardon, *Religious Thought in the Victorian Age*, 242.

25 Ibid., 224.

26 Bevan was an ancient historian and philosopher who spent the majority of his life in London. His influences were wide ranging: he was a well-known linguist who ascribed to a form of philosophical pragmatism and was a long-time member of the *London Society for the Study of Religion*, founded by Baron Von Hugel.

27 Bevan, *Symbolism and Belief*, 24.

28 Ibid., 26.

29 Ibid., 335.

30 Mansel spoke also of natural moral sense and innate feeling of dependence upon something greater as human realities that are satisfied in Christian revelation. But as in the case of personality, Bevan suggests that "Mansel cannot have meant that a man could no more help believing in a personal God than he could help believing in his own existence: he must have meant that, for himself and many other people, belief in God's existence was a conviction which something in themselves made it impossible for them to question." Bevan, *Symbolism and Belief*, 329.

31 Ibid., 334, 335.

32 Bevan seems to recognize this to be the case: "How does this differ from the Pragmatic view? It differs because in religious faith there is an enduring reference all through to a Reality believed to exist in absolute independence. The worth of the conception does not lie only in its effects in experience, but in the measure of its correspondence with that Reality." Bevan, *Symbolism and Belief*, 335. Yet for Mansel this reality is bound up inseparably with a particular history embodied in the scriptures, represented in the history of Israel, the life of Christ, and his death and return.

This is not untrue for Bevan, but he cannot, like any modern he claims, follow Mansel fully in his "scripturalism."

33 Ibid., 384.

34 Bevan, in a Manselian fashion, is critical of the notion of a *nunc stans* as presented by various figures like Maurice, Bosanquet, and Inge. His argument is simply that, while this particular speculation may be true of God, there is no way for the human mind to determine one way or another: "It seems to me also to theorize about the psychology of God in a way which it is absurd for human beings to do." Bevan, *Symbolism and Belief*, 96, 97.

35 Ibid., 328.

36 Freeman, *The Role of Reason in Religion*, 106. In an earlier article on the same topic Freeman compares the seemingly disparate views of Mansel and Whitehead and suggests a fundamental affinity between the two men: Whitehead's notion of "imaginative rationalization" was an attempt not to move beyond the elements of experience but to simply imagine the differences and relations within experience in cases where direct observation is not possible. In this sense, Freeman suggests, Mansel would have no quarrel with Whitehead's conception of relations. Kenneth Freeman, "Mansel's Religious Positivism," 96.

37 Ibid., 104.

38 Ibid., 107.

39 Thomas Altizer, *The Gospel of Christian Atheism*, 75.

40 Freeman, *The Role of Reason in Religion*, 108.

41 Of Kant, Tom Sparrow writes, "Givenness is equiprimordial with being; being just is however it manifests itself to whomever thinks it. It is absurd to believe, after Kant, that it can be otherwise." Sparrow, *The End of Phenomenology: Metaphysics and the New Realism*, 81.

42 Finitism, for Freeman, is "attractive," and Mansel showed that is at least "possible." Freeman, *The Role of Reason in Religion*, 44.

43 Ibid., 108.

44 Ibid., 5–7.

45 Ibid., 102.

46 Ibid.

47 Ibid., 2.

48 Cupitt, "Mansel's Theory of Regulative Truth," 116.

49 Ibid., 117.

50 Ibid., 119.

51 Ibid., 110.

52 Ibid., 114.

53 Ibid., 115.

54 Cupitt, "What Was Mansel Trying To Do?," 545.

55 Cupitt, "Mansel and Maurice on our Knowledge of God," 311.

56 Cupitt, "A Reply to Rowan Williams," 26.

57 Cupitt, *Christ and the Hiddenness of God*, 90.

58 See chapter 5 for my discussion on T.H. Green.

59 Cupitt, *Christ and the Hiddenness of God*, 202.

60 Ibid., 205.

61 Ibid.

62 Ibid., 212.

63 In *The Leap of Reason* Cupitt credits the religious wars of the seventeenth century for creating an atmosphere of skepticism about metaphysics. This atmosphere led to scientific exploration and a growing interest in the material world conceived apart from dangerous metaphysical notions that might lead to violence and discord. Cupitt, *The Leap of Reason*, 10.

64 Cupitt, *The Leap of Reason*, 68.

65 Ibid., 66.

66 Ibid., 56.

67 Steven Shakespeare comments on this general shift in understanding Kant's categories of understanding: "Kant wanted to hold on to the necessity of our shared conceptual apparatus, and so preserve the objectivity of knowledge, but it was not long before his views were radicalized by Nietzsche and others, who drew attention to the contingent, fictional character of our structures of knowledge and truth." Shakespeare, "A Hiding to Nothing," 104.

68 Cupitt, *Taking Leave of God*, 166.

69 I argued that Bevan abstracted religious symbolism from a concrete scriptural framework, but Bevan was not a nonrealist in Cupitt's terms. He in fact believed that Christian faith, in its commonly accepted forms, was still the most viable and fitting form of religious faith.

70 Cupitt, *The Sea of Faith*, 17.

71 Ibid., 16.

72 Cupitt, *The World to Come*, 154.

73 Ibid., 159. Cupitt writes that the old order of eternal rewards "has lost moral authority and in many cases has even become highly objectionable, and it belongs to a past when people lived within narrow myths that have now died."

74 Hyman, "Disinterestedness: The Idol of Modernity," 50.

75 Shakespeare, "A Hiding to Nothing," 105.

76 Cupitt, *The Long Legged Fly*, 106.

77 Ibid., 7.

78 Ibid., 10.

79 This is not to say that Maurice's theology inevitably issues in something like Cupitt's theology. Rather, the press for an immanent encounter with God that is less troubled by the tension of natural and supernatural reality, which characterizes Maurice's thought, for Cupitt is resolved by eliminating the supernatural reality of God entirely.

80 Shakespeare, "A Hiding to Nothing," 109.

81 Ibid., 111.

82 Cupitt, *The Last Philosophy*, 82.

83 Ibid., 81.

84 Cupitt, *Solar Ethics*, 26.

85 Ibid., 66.

86 Ibid., 65, 66.

87 Collingwood, "The Metaphysics of Bradley," 236.

88 John Caputo, *The Weakness of God*, 9.

89 Ibid., 11.

90 See Caputo's *On Religion* for a description of the impossible and its quasi-theological role within the life of faith: "the name of God is the name of the chance for something absolutely new, for a new birth, for the expectation, the hope." Caputo, *On Religion*, 11.

91 Caputo refers to traditional theologies of the Church as strong theologies: "I love the strong theologies that I know the way I love great novels, but I maintain an ironic distance from them occasioned not only by the fact that they are invariable in league with power but also by my conviction that the event that is astir in the name of God cannot be contained by the historical contingency of the names I have inherited in my tradition." Caputo, *The Weakness of God*, 9.

92 Gavin Hyman for instance thinks that this distinction is imperative for understanding Cupitt, although in some way Cupitt never really escapes the modernist trappings of the desire to create an all-encompassing metaphysics. But it could be argued that postmodern religious arguments, for example Caputo's, represent a metaphysical rendering of the world all the same. Hyman, *The Predicament of Postmodern Theology*, 58.

93 Williams, "Religious Realism: On Not Quite Agreeing With Don Cupitt," 230.

94 Ibid.

95 Cupitt, *The Sea of Faith*, 19.

96 Ibid., 31.

97 In a letter to novelist and devotional writer Elizabeth Sewell where Mansel is providing feedback on her brother William's recent book, he writes, "I

cannot pray to the great substance which lies behind the phenomena of the universe. I may just as well pray to the laws of gravitation … on my part prayer implies power but a power who I can influence, a power who can grant my prayer." A letter to Miss Sewell, MS d. 32 (Oxford: Bodleian Library), 1868.

98 Mansel, *The Limits of Religious Thought*, 187.

99 Ibid., 186.

100 Ibid.

101 Gordon Lewis Phillips was, at the time, the rector of Northolt, but, perhaps more notably, he was a student and intimate of Austin Farrer. Philip Curtis, *A Hawk Among Sparrows: A Biography of Austin Farrer*. Curtis references Phillips's own account of conversations between himself and Farrer, 85.

102 Phillips, *Seeing and Believing*, 8.

103 Ibid., 61.

104 Ibid., 63.

105 Phillips understood Mansel's work as preparatory of Austin Farrer's theology of scriptural images: "His lectures seem to be an early edition of the more recent Bampton Lectures for the year 1948, *The Glass of Vision*, by Dr Austin Farrer." Phillips, *Seeing and Believing*, 60. The statement is surprising because Farrer and Mansel have occupied different positions within the history of Anglican theology, and yet the claim is not without warrant. In *The Glass of Vision* Farrer makes arguments that sound highly resonant of Mansel's account of scriptural language: "the images are supernaturally formed, and supernaturally made intelligible to faith. Faith discerns not the images, but what the images signify: and yet we cannot discern it except through the images." Farrer, *The Glass of Vision*, 110. Yet as critics have mentioned, there tends to be in Farrer's understanding of inspiration and providence a deliberate confusion between God's agency and human creative powers. Brian Hebblethwaite suggests that "Farrer says almost nothing about miracle except these few remarks about the Gospel miracles as exceptions to his general idea of providence, and even here he rejects ideas of violation and reverts to the doctrine of the enhancement of natural powers which appeared in *A Glass of Vision*, where the distinction between providence and miracle was lacking." Hebblethwaite, "Austin Farrer's Concept of Divine Providence," 548.

106 Phillips, *Seeing and Believing*, 80.

107 Ibid., 78. He refers here to the conversion of "Psichari or a de Foucauld or in a St Therese."

108 Ibid., 78.

109 Ibid., 73.
110 Ibid., 73.
111 Ibid., 74.
112 Phillips, for example, perceives no real difference between Mansel and
    Maurice: they simply argued toward the same end using different
    methods. Phillips, *Seeing and Believing*, 65.
113 *Doctrine in the Church of England: The Report of the Commission on
    Christian Doctrine Appointed by the Archbishops of Canterbury and York
    in 1922*, 28.
114 Ibid., 29.
115 Ibid., 31.
116 Ibid., 29. Again, such a statement could be taken in a variety of manners.
    The language is strongly reminiscent of Coleridge: spiritual communion
    is the essential aspect of the biblical records, and certain portions of the
    Bible are related more intensely to this central aspect than other.
117 Williams, *Anglican Identities*, 81.
118 *Doctrine in the Church of England*, 11.
119 William L. Countryman, "Anglicanism's Entangled Sense of Authority," 4.
120 Sykes, *The Integrity of Anglicanism*, 8.
121 Stephen Ross White, *Authority and Anglicanism*, 56.
122 Ibid., 59.
123 Ibid., 63. White writes, "Can we still believe that God acts in the autocra-
    tic and interventionist way which our prayers seem to suggest and to
    require of him? And if, as I believe, the answer to this question is 'no,'
    then we are faced with a yawning gap between what we say and what we
    actually believe."
124 Ibid., 128.
125 Gouldstone, "Evangelicals and Contemporary Anglican Theology," 119.
    Gouldstone makes these comments with direct reference to Cupitt.
126 Sykes, *The Integrity of Anglicanism*, 99.
127 Radner, "The Scriptural Community," 90.
128 Ibid., 103.
129 Ibid., 105.

CONCLUSION

1 Levering, "Participation and Exegesis," 598.
2 Levering, "Readings on the Rock," 727.
3 See chapter 5 of this book, 136–83, for a discussion of scripture's role
  in historic Anglicanism.

4 Mansel, *Limits of Religious Thought*, 4, 5. Mansel rejects the one possible meaning of dogmatism: "I do not include under the name of Dogmatism the mere enunciation of religious truths, as resting upon authority and not upon reasoning," 2.

5 Ibid., 3.

6 Ibid., 6.

7 My introduction looks at Mansel's criticism of Kant more closely. Mansel's greatest criticism of Kant was that his philosophical system reduced prayer to a therapeutic activity that had no communicative relation to a real, personal God who can listen and respond. *Limits of Religious Thought*, 15.

8 Mansel provides the example of Samuel Wilberforce's *Doctrine of the Incarnation*. Wilberforce argues that Christ assumed an abstract humanity in the Incarnation not a "new person" but a "substratum, in which personality has its existence." Mansel's response is that this theory "requires a realist theory of the nature of universal notions." But surely, he argues, such a theory should be necessary for belief in the reality of the Incarnation. Mansel, *Limits of Religious Thought*, 9, 10.

9 Mansel quotes Butler in this regard, who cannot rule out the question of "whether God could have saved the world by other means that the death of Christ." In this way, as I have argued earlier, Mansel made arguments, much like Athanasius and other Church fathers, about the fittingness of God's actions in Christ, even if they were not necessitated by some internal or external factor in God's character. Mansel, *Limits of Religious Thought*, 194.

10 Ibid., 14.

11 Ibid., 6.

12 Pickstock, "Theology and Post-modernity," 67.

13 Benjamin Sargent, "John Milbank and Hermeneutics," 253. Sargent criticizes Milbank's treatment of two biblical texts – Colossians 1:24 and 2 Corinthians 1:3–12 – and his argument that the Church participates in a "continuing atonement." Sargent suggests that Milbank oversteps bounds of the text and ignores the historical-critical scholarship on the topic. Sargent, "John Milbank and Hermeneutics," 258.

14 Milbank, *Theology and Social Theory*, 387.

15 Ibid., 387.

16 Milbank writes, "Thus Christians are seen as living within certain fixed narratives which function as *schemas*, which can organize endlessly different cultural contents," Milbank, *Theology and Social Theory*, 388.

17 Lindbeck, *The Nature of Doctrine*, 118.

18 Ibid., 106.

19 Ibid., 117.

20 Milbank, *Theology and Social Theory*, 389.

21 Ibid., 390.

22 Ibid., 401. Milbank goes on: "Without attachment to a particular persuasion – which we can never prove to be either true, or non-violent – we would have no real means to discriminate peace and truth from their opposites."

23 Ibid., 427.

24 Ibid., 442.

25 Hans Boersma has highlighted this aspect of Milbank's thought and questioned his resistance to the idea of redemptive violence, which appears so nakedly in the pages of scripture. Yet for Boersma it is not Milbank's ontology of peace that is the problem: "Recognition of the need for pedagogic or redemptive coercion and violence does not at all require Milbank to abandon his participationist ontology of peace – divine violence, after all, does not have primacy but is used in the interest of eschatological absolute peace." Hans Boersma, "Being Reconciled," 202. Maybe it is true that Milbank could simply absorb the notion of redemptive violence into his ontology of peace, but such an inclusion would surely require some alterations to his larger commitments.

26 Boersma, "Being Reconciled," 199.

27 Milbank, *Being Reconciled*, 40.

28 Ibid., 77.

29 Ibid., 100.

30 Ibid.

31 Ibid., 196.

32 Milbank, *Theology and Social Theory*, 440.

33 Ibid., 442.

34 Cupitt himself has argued that radical orthodoxy is just another extension of his nonrealist position in that it offers no arguments for the worldview it advances; rather, Milbank, Pickstock, Loughlin simply narrate "God into being" in a thoroughly skeptical postmodern fashion. In this sense, Milbank's and Cupitt's respective theological visions stand as competitive "alternatives" to what Milbank calls modern nihilism. Cupitt, "My Postmodern Witch," 9. Cupitt goes on to claim, "They have made the required noises; but they have not delivered clear arguments for the realism they seem to profess. They are indeed a group of my own former pupils, and they are perhaps all of them teaching a version of 'active non realism.'"

35 In Mansel's lectures on Gnosticism one almost expects his section on Clement of Alexandria to be critical with respect to the speculative character of Clement's theology. But on the contrary, though aspects of Clement's style may not have been to Mansel's taste, he speaks glowingly of Clement's overall method: "Yet, however highly Clement may rate the knowledge which he attributes to his true Gnostic, several features are worthy of notice by which it is distinguished from that knowledge claimed for themselves by the Gnostic heretics. First, it is not a special gift of nature, but a habit painfully acquired by preparation and discipline. Secondly, it is not a mere apprehension of speculative theories, but a practical principle, embracing action and love. Thirdly, it is founded on faith; the matter and substance of its doctrine is that which is revealed through Christ; its pre-eminence consists in the manner and certainty of its apprehension, not in any new and distinct teaching. Fourthly, it is a knowledge imparted as far as is possible, possessed in this life according to man's capacity to receive it; and the limits of that capacity Clement has pointed out in several remarkable passages." Mansel, "The Gnostic Heresies," 271.

36 Nicholas Wolterstorff's essay is among them, though he interestingly notes that "The problem is not that we have absorbed modern enlightened views about ethical and theological matters and are, as such, morally offended by the picture of genocidal slaughter in Israel's … Our problem is rather that we have been formed in our understanding of God by the biblical acclamations of God as just and loving and shaped in our ethical thinking by God's command to do justice and love mercy." Wolterstorff, "Reading Joshua," 236. The point is well taken, though one might still respond that the "modern enlightened" seems unable to cope with potentially contrasting statements about the nature of God's character. Or more to the point, as Christopher Seitz argues in the same volume, the Bible itself contains answers to these concerns, however palatable they may be to various readers.

37 Seitz, "Canon and Conquest," 293.

38 Ibid., 308.

39 Ibid., 315.

40 Gary Anderson, "What about the Canaanites?," 282.

41 Ibid., 282.

42 Seitz, "Canon and Conquest," 293. Seitz writes, "The character of God is inextricably connected with the character of Christian Scripture as a two-fold witness."

43 In chapter 3 I discuss Peter Harrison and William Abraham as two figures who offer comparable accounts of modern secularism.

44 Mansel, *Limits of Religious Thought*, 152.

Bibliography

PRIMARY WORKS BY HENRY MANSEL

Mansel, Henry. "A Commentary on Matthew." In *The Holy Bible, According to the Authorized Version A.D. 1611, with an Explanatory and Critical Commentary and a Revision of the Translation by Bishops and Other Clergy of the Anglican Church*, edited by F.C. Cook. New York: Scribner, 1873.
– *A Letter to Goldwin Smith Concerning the Postscript to His Lectures on the Study of History*. Oxford: Henry Hammans, 1861.
– *An Examination of The Rev. F.D. Maurice's Strictures on the Bampton Lectures of 1858 by the Lecturer*. London: John Murray, 1859.
– *A Second Letter to Goldwin Smith, With An Appendix Containing An Examination of Some Passages in His Work on Rational Religion*. Oxford: Henry Hammans, 1862.
– "Essay on Miracles." In *Aids to Faith: A Series of Theological Essays, By several writers, Being a Reply to "Essays and Reviews,"* edited by William Thomson. New York: D. Appleton and Company, 1862.
– *Essays and Reviews*. Edited by William Thomson. New York: D. Appleton and Company, 1862.
– "Free Thinking – It's History and Tendencies." In *Letters, Lectures and Reviews*. London: John Murray, Albemarle Street, 1873.
– *Higher Vocation: A Sermon Preached by the Dean of St Paul's, Preached in St Paul's Cathedral on Sunday Evening, February 27, 1870*. London: James Paul, 1870.
– "It is Finished: A Sermon Preached by the Very Rev. Dr Mansel, Dean of St Paul's Cathedral on Good Friday Evening, March 26th, 1869." In *Preaching for the Million: Three Sermons*. London: James Paul, 1869.

- *Labourers in the Vineyard: A Sermon Preached by the Dean of St Paul's H.L. Mansel, Preached in St Paul's Cathedral, on Sunday Evening, January 22nd, 1871*. London: James Paul, 1871.
- *Letter, Lectures and Reviews, Including the Phrontisterion, or, Oxford in the 19th Century*. London: John Murray, 1873.
- "Man's Conception of Eternity. An Examination of Mr. Maurice's Theory of a Fixed State out of Time." In *Letters, Lectures and Reviews*. London: John Murray, Albemarle Street, 1873.
- *Metaphysics or the Philosophy of Consciousness, Phenomenal or Real*. 2nd ed. Edinburgh: Adam and Charles Black, 1866.
- "Modern German Philosophy." In *Letters, Lectures and Reviews*. London: John Murray, Albemarle Street, 1873.
- "Modern Spiritualism." In *Letters, Lectures and Reviews*. London: John Murray, Albemarle Street, 1873.
- "On the Idealism of Berkeley." In *Letters, Lectures and Reviews*. London: John Murray, Albemarle Street, 1873.
- "On the Philosophy of Kant." In *Letters, Lectures and Reviews*. London: John Murray, Albemarle Street, 1873.
- "Personal Responsibility of Man, as Individually Dealt with by God." In *Personal Responsibility of Man: Sermons Preached During the Season of Lent, 1868, in Oxford*, edited by Samuel Wilberforce et al. Oxford: James Parker and Co., 1869.
- "Philosophy and Theology." In *Letters, Lectures and Reviews*. London: John Murray, Albemarle Street, 1873.
- *Philosophy of the Conditioned, Comprising Some Remarks on Sir William Hamilton's Philosophy and on Mr J.S. Mill's Examination of that Philosophy*. London: Alexander Strahan Publisher, 1866.
- *Prolegomena Logica: an Inquiry into the Psychological Character of Logical Processes*. Oxford: Graham, 1851.
- "St Matthew's Gospel. Commentary and Critical Notes, Chapter i-xxvi." In Vol. 1, *The Holy Bible According to the Authorized Version A.D. 1611, with an Explanatory and Critical Commentary*, edited by F.C. Cook. London: John Murray, 1878.
- "The Conflict and Defeat in Eden." In *The Conflict of Christ in His Church with Spiritual Wickedness in High Places. Sermons Preached During Lent, 1866, in Oxford*, edited by Samuel Wilberforce. Oxford: James Parker and Co., 1866.
- *The Gnostic Heresies of the First and Second Centuries*. Edited by J.B. Lightfoot. London: John Murray, 1875.– *The Limits of Religious Thought Examined in Eight Lectures*. Oxford: John Murray, 1858.

- *The Limits of Religious Thought Examined in Eight Lectures.* 2nd ed. London: John Murray, 1858.
- *The Limits of Religious Thought Examined in Eight Lectures.* 3rd ed. Boston: Gould and Lincoln, 1859. Reprint, New York: AMS Press Inc., 1973.
- *The Limits of Religious Thought Examined in Eight Lectures.* 4th ed. London: John Murray, 1859.
- *The Limits of Religious Thought Examined in Eight Lectures.* 5th ed. London: John Murray, 1867.
- *The Spirit a Divine Person, to Be Worshipped and Glorified, A Sermon Preached in the Church of the St Mary-The-Virgin, Oxford, on Friday, Feb. 20, 1863.* Oxford and London: John Henry and James Parker, 1863.
- *The Witness of the Church to the Promise of Christ's Coming: A Sermon Preached in the Cathedral Church of Canterbury, on St Peter's Day, 1864.* Oxford and London: John Henry and James Parker, 1864.

Mansel, Henry, and Sidney Gedge. "Revelation: iii." In *Two Sermons Preached in Peterborough Cathedral, On August 30, 1868, the Sunday succeeding the Enterment of the Right Rev. Francis Jeune, D.C.L., Lord Bishop of Peterborough.* Oxford: James Parker and Co., 1868.

UNPUBLISHED LETTERS OF HENRY MANSEL

Bodleian Library. MS. Acland d. 101, fols. 90–1.

Bodleian Library. MS. Autogr. b. 4, fol. 51b.

Bodleian Library. MS. Autogr. d. 32, fols. 26–7.

Bodleian Library. MS. Autogr. d. 33, fols. 32–4.

Bodleian Library. MS. Autogr. d. 34, fols. 64–8.

Bodleian Library. MS. Eng. c. 3998, fols. 61–5, 10.

Bodleian Library. MS. Eng. lett. c. 297, fols. 342–3.

Bodleian Library. MS. Eng. lett. e. 47, fols. 9–10.

Bodleian Library. MS. Eng. lett. e. 132, fols. 136–7.

Bodleian Library. MS. Phillipps-Robinson e. 363, fols. 163–4.

Bodleian Library. MS. Phillipps-Robinson f. 56, fols. 3102.

Bodleian Library. MS. Wilberforce c. 13, fols. 84–5, 90.

Bodleian Library. MS. Wilberforce c. 14, fols. 6–7.

Pusey House. 51/13. H.L. Mansel to E.B. Pusey. 2 April 1860.

Pusey House. 51/14. H.L. Mansel to E.B. Pusey. 14 April 1860.

Pusey House. 51/15. H.L. Mansel to E.B. Pusey. 29 January 1866.

Pusey House. 51/16. H.L. Mansel to E.B. Pusey. 2 February 1866.

Pusey House. 51/17. H.L. Mansel to E.B. Pusey. 29 October 1867.

Pusey House. 51/18. H.L. Mansel to E.B. Pusey. 1867.

Pusey House. 51/19. H.L. Mansel to E.B. Pusey. 29 May 1869.

PRIMARY SOURCES

Abraham, William. *Canon and Criterion in Christian Theology: From the Fathers to Feminism.* Oxford: Clarendon Press, 1998.

Altizer, Thomas. *The Gospel of Christian Atheism.* Philadelphia: The Westminster Press, 1966.

Anderson, Gary. "What about the Canaanites?" In *Divine Evil? The Moral Character of the God of Abraham,* edited by Michael Bergmann, Michael J. Murray, and Michael C. Rea. Oxford: Oxford University Press, 2013.

Anon. "Dean Mansel." *The Quarterly Review* 159 (January 1885).

– "Illingworth's Bampton Lectures," *The Church Quarterly Review* (April 1895).

Aquinas, Thomas. *Summa Theologica.* New York: Benziger Bros, 1947.

Arnold, Matthew. *St Paul and Protestantism.* London: Smith, Elder & Co, 1906.

Artz, Johannes. "Newman in Contact with Kant's Thought." *Journal of Theological Studies* 31, no. 2 (1980): 517–35.

Avis, Paul. "Charles Gore and Modernism: A Half-Centenary Exercise in 'Corporate Believing.'" *Theology* 85 (1982).

Barbeau, Jeffrey W. "Coleridge, Christology and the Language of Redemption." *Anglican Theological Review* 93, no. 2 (Spring 2011): 263–82.

– "The Development of Coleridge's Notion of Human Freedom: The Translation and Re-formation of German Idealism in England." *Journal of Religion* 80, no. 4 (2000): 576–94.

Barth, Karl. *On Religion: The Revelation of God As the Sublimation of Religion.* Translated by Garret Green. London: T & T Clark, 2006.

Berman, David. *George Berkeley Alciphron in Focus.* London: Taylor & Francis, 1993.

Bevan, Edwyn. *Symbolism and Belief.* Boston: Beacon Press, 1957.

Boersma, Hans. "Being Reconciled: Atonement as the Ecclesio-Christological Practice of Forgiveness in John Milbank." In *Radical Orthodoxy and the Reformed Tradition: Creation, Covenant and Participation,* edited by James K. Smith and James Olthius. Grand Rapids: Baker Academic, 2005.

Book of Common Prayer and Administration of the Sacraments and Other Rites and Ceremonies of the Church According to the Use of the Anglican Church of Canada. Toronto: Anglican Book Center, 1962.

Bradley, F.H. *Appearance and Reality: A Metaphysical Essay.* Oxford: Clarendon Press, 1930.

– "On God and the Absolute." In *Essays on Truth and Reality.* Oxford: Clarendon Press, 1914.

Brantley, Richard E. *Locke, Wesley, and the Method of English Romanticism.* Gainesville: University Presses of Florida, 1984.

Brown, David. "Butler and Deism." In *Joseph Butler's Moral and Religious Thought: Tercentenary Essays,* edited by Christopher Cunliffe, 7–28. Oxford: Clarendon Press, 1992.

Browne, Peter. *A Letter in Answer to a Book Entitled, Christianity not mysterious. As also to All those who set up for Reason and Evidence In Opposition to Revelation and Mysteries.* 3rd ed. London: Robert Clavel, 1703.

– *The Procedure, Extent, and Limits of Human Understanding.* London: William Innys, 1728.

– *Things Divine and Supernatural Conceived by Analogy with Things Natural and Human.* London: William Innys and Richard Manby, 1733.

Buckley, Michael. *The Origins of Modern Atheism.* New Haven: Yale University Press, 1987.

Burgon, John. *The Lives of Twelve Good Men.* London: Murray, 1888.

Burrell, David. *Aquinas: God and Action.* London: Routledge & K. Paul, 1979.

Burrows, Montagu. "Dean Mansel as a Christian Philosopher." *Church Quarterly Review,* 1877.

Butler, Joseph. "Sermon XIII: Upon the Love of God." In *The Works of Bishop Butler,* edited by David E. White. Rochester: University of Rochester Press, 2005.

– "The Analogy of Religion." In *The Works of Bishop Butler,* edited by David E. White. Rochester: University of Rochester Press, 2005.

– "Upon the Ignorance of Man." In *The Works of Bishop Butler,* edited by David E. White. Rochester: University of Rochester Press, 2006.

Butler, Samuel. *The Way of All Flesh.* London: Grant Richards, 1903.

Calderwood, Henry. "The Philosophy of the Infinite." *Eclectic Review* (1861).

Caputo, John. *On Religion.* London: Routledge, 2001.

– *The Weakness of God: A Theology of the Event.* Indiana: Indiana University Press, 2006.

Carlyle, Thomas. *On Heroes, Hero-Worship, and the Heroic in History: Six Lectures.* London: John Wiley, 1849.

– "State of German Literature." In *Critical and Miscellaneous Essays, Collected and Published by Thomas Carlyle.* 2 vols. Boston: Houghton, Mifflin and Company, 1881.

Carpenter, S.C. *Church and People, 1789–1889; A History of the Church of England from William Wilberforce to "Lux Mundi."* London: Society for Promoting Christian Knowledge, 1937.

Carr, Stephen. "F.H. Bradley and Religious Faith." *Religious Studies* 28, no. 3 (1992): 258.

Chadwick, Owen. *The Mind of the Oxford Movement.* London: A & C Black, 1960.

– *The Secularization of the European Mind in the Nineteenth Century: The Gifford Lectures in the University of Edinburgh for 1973–4.* Cambridge: Cambridge University Press, 1975.

Christensen, Torben. *The Divine Order: A Study in F.D. Maurice's Theology.* Leiden: E.J. Brill, 1973.

Clark, William Robinson. *Witnesses to Christ: A Contribution to Christian Apologetics.* Chicago: McClurg, 1888.

Cockshut, A.O.J. *Anglican Attitudes: A Study of Victorian Religious Controversies.* London: Collins, 1959.

Coleridge, S.T. *Aids to Reflection and the Confessions of an Inquiring Spirit.* London: G. Bell, 1901.

– *Aids to Reflection in the Formation of a Manly Character: on the Several Grounds of Prudence, Morality, and Religion.* London: Taylor and Hessey, 1825.

– *Biographia Literaria.* London: J. M. Dent and Sons Ltd., 1927.

Collingwood, R.G. "The Metaphysics of F.H. Bradley." In *An Essay on Philosophical Method.* Oxford: Clarendon Press, 2005.

Coope, Christopher Miles. "Good-bye to the Problem of Evil, Hello to the Problem of Veracity." *Religious Studies* 37, no. 4 (2001): 373–96.

Copleston, F.C. *A History of Philosophy III: Modern Philosophy, Bentham to Russell.* New York: Image Books, 1967.

Countryman, L. William. "Anglicanism's Entangled Sense of Authority." In *A Questioning Authority: The Anglican Witness to the World*, edited by Jeremy Morris. London: Third Millennium 5, 2002.

Cowling, Maurice. *Religion and Public Doctrine in Modern England.* Cambridge: Cambridge University Press, 1980.

Cupitt, Don. "A Reply to Rowan Williams." *Modern Theology* 1, no. 1 (1984).

- *Christ and the Hiddenness of God*. London: Lutterworth Press, 1971.
- "My Postmodern Witch." In *Modern Believing* 39, no. 4 (1 October 1998).
- *Solar Ethics*. London: SCM Press, 1995.
- *Taking Leave of God*. London: SCM Press, 1980.
- *The Last Philosophy*. London: SCM Press, 1995.
- *The Leap of Reason*. London: Sheldon Press, 1976.
- *The Long Legged Fly: A Theology of Language and Desire*. London: SCM Press, 1987.
- "Mansel and Maurice on our Knowledge of God." *Theology* 73 (July 1970): 301–11.
- "Mansel's Theory of Regulative Truth." *Journal of Theological Studies* 18 (April 1976): 104–26.
- *The Old Creed and the New*. London: SCM Press, 2006.
- *The Sea of Faith*. London: British Broadcasting Corporation, 1984.
- "What was Mansel Trying to Do?" *Journal of Theological Studies* 22, no. 2 (22 October 1971): 544–7.
- *The World to Come*. London: SCM Press, 1982.

Curtis, Philip. *A Hawk Among Sparrows: A Biography of Austin Farrer*. Eugene: Wipf and Stock, 1985.

Dale, R.W. *Christian Doctrine: A Series of Discourses*. London: Hodder and Stoughton, 1894.

Darwin, Charles. *On the Origin of Species*. London: John Murray, 1859.

Dimova, Maria. "T.H. Green as a Phenomenologist: Linking British Idealism and Continental Phenomenology." *Angelaki: Journal of the Theoretical Humanities* 3, no. 1 (1998): 77–88.

Dockrill, F.W. "The Doctrine of Regulative Truth and Mansel's Intentions." *Journal of Theological Studies* 20 (1974): 453–66.

Doctrine in the Church of England: The Report of the Commission on Christian Doctrine Appointed by the Archbishops of Canterbury and York in 1922. London: Society for Promoting Christian Knowledge, 1938.

Dyson, A.O. "Theological Legacies of the Enlightenment: England and Germany." In *England and Germany: Studies in Theological Diplomacy*, edited by S.W. Sykes. Frankfurt am Main: Lang, 1982.

Eliot, George. *Adam Bede*. Edinburgh: William Blackwood and Sons, 1859.

Elliot-Binns, L.E. *English Thought 1860–1900: The Theological Aspect*. London: Longmans, Green and Co., 1956.

Farrer, Austin. *The Glass of Vision: The Bampton Lectures of 1948*. Westminster: Dacre Press, 1948.

Fitzgerald, Timothy. "Mansel's Agnosticism." *Religious Studies* 26, no. 4 (1990): 525–41.

Fouke, Daniel Clifford. *Philosophy and Theology in a Burlesque Mode: John Toland and "the Way of Paradox."* Amherst: Humanity Books, 2007.

Freeman, Kenneth. "Mansel's Religious Positivism." *Southern Journal of Philosophy* (Summer 1967): 91–102.

– *The Role of Reason in Religion: A Study of Henry Mansel.* The Hague: Martinus Nijhoff, 1969.

Fruman, Norman. *Coleridge, the Damaged Archangel.* New York: G. Braziller, 1971.

Garnett, Jane. "Bishop Butler and the Zeitgeist: Butler and the Development of Christian Moral Philosophy in Victorian Britain." In *Joseph Butler's Moral and Religious Thought: Tercentenary Essays*, edited by Christopher Cunliffe, 63–96. Oxford: Clarendon Press, 1992.

Gore, Charles. *Belief in God.* London: Penguin Books Limited, 1939.

– "The Holy Spirit and the Church." In *The Reconstruction of Belief.* London: John Murray, 1926.

– "The Holy Spirit and Inspiration." In *Lux Mundi: A Series of Studies in the Religion of the Incarnation*, 5th ed., edited by Charles Gore. London: John Murray, 1890.

Gregory, Brad. *The Unintended Reformation: How a Religious Revolution Secularized a Society.* Cambridge: Belknap Press of Harvard University Press, 2012.

Gouldstone, Timothy. "Evangelicals and Contemporary Anglican Theology." *Churchman* 095, no. 2 (1981): 110–22.

– *The Rise and Decline of Anglican Idealism in the Nineteenth Century.* New York: Palgrave Macmillan, 2005.

– *The Role of Reason in Religion: A Study of Henry Mansel.* The Hague: Martinus Nijhoff, 1969.

Green, T.H. "The Conversion of Paul (Extract from the Lectures on the Epistle to the Galatians." In *Works of Thomas Hill Green.* 3 vols. Edited by R.L. Nettleship. London: Longmans Green, 1885–8.

– "Fragment of an Address on Romans x. 8 'The Word in Nigh Thee.'" In *Works of Thomas Hill Green.* 3 vols. Edited by R.L. Nettleship. London: Longmans Green, 1885–8.

– "Essay on Christian Dogma." In *Works of Thomas Hill Green.* 3 vols. Edited by R.L. Nettleship. London: Longmans Green, 1885–8.

– "Justification by Faith (Extract from the Lectures on the Epistle to the Romans." In *Works of Thomas Hill Green.* 3 vols. Edited by R.L. Nettleship. London: Longmans Green, 1885–88.

– *Prolegomena to Ethics*. Edited by A.C. Bradley. Oxford: Clarendon Press, 1883.

Hamilton, William. "Philosophy of Perception." In *Discussions on Philosophy and Literature, Education and University Reform*. New York: Harper, 1861.

– "The Philosophy of the Unconditioned." In *Discussions on Philosophy and Literature, Education and University Reform*. New York: Harper, 1861.

Hampsher-Monk, Iain. "Burke and the Religious Sources of Conservative Skepticism." In *The Skeptical Tradition Around 1800: Skepticism in Philosophy, Science and* Society, edited by Johan Van Der Zande and Richard Popkin, 235–59. Boston: Kluwer Academic Publishers, 1998.

Hannah, John. *The Relation Between the Divine and Human Elements in Holy Scripture: Eight Lectures Preached Before the University of Oxford in the Year MDCCCLXIII on the Foundation of the Late Rev. John Bampton, M.A., Canon of Salisbury*. London: J. Murray, 1863.

Harrison, Peter. *The Bible, Protestantism, and the Rise of Natural Science*. Cambridge: Cambridge University Press, 1998.

Hauerwas, Stanley. "How 'Christian Ethics' Came to Be." In *The Hauerwas Reader*, edited by John Berkman and Michael G. Cartwright, 37–50. Durham: Duke University Press, 2001.

Hays, Richard. *Echoes of Scripture in the Letters of Paul*. New Haven: Yale University Press, 1989.

Hegel, G.W.F. *The Phenomenology of Mind*. Edited by J.B. Baille. New York: Dover Publications, 2003.

Hebblethwaite, Brian. "Austin Farrer's Concept of Divine Providence." *Theology* 73 (1970): 541–51.

Hedley, Douglas. *Coleridge, Philosophy and Religion: Aids to Reflection and the Mirror of the Spirit*. Cambridge: Cambridge University Press, 2000.

Herbert, Christopher. *Victorian Relativity: Radical Thought and Scientific Discovery*. Chicago: University of Chicago Press, 2001.

Holland, Scott. "Faith." In *Lux Mundi: A Series of Studies in the Religion of the Incarnation*, 5th ed, edited by Charles Gore. London: John Murray, 1890.

– *The Optimism of Butler's Analogy*. Oxford, Clarendon Press, 1908.

Hooker, Michael. "Berkeley's Argument from Design." In *Berkeley: Critical and Interpretive Essays*, edited by Colin M. Turbayne, 261–70. Minneapolis: University of Minnesota Press, 1982.

Hoskyns, Edwyn. "The Christ of the Synoptic Gospels." In *Essays Catholic and Critical, By Members of the Anglican Communion*, edited by Edward George Selwyn. New York: The Macmillan Company, 1926.

- "The World." In *Cambridge Sermons*. London: SPCK, 1938.

Hume, David. *An Enquiry Concerning Human Understanding: A Critical Edition*. Edited by Tom Beauchamp. New York: Oxford University Press, 2000.

Husserl, Edmund. *Logical Investigations*. Vol. 1. Translated by J.N. Findlay. New York: Humanities Press, 1970.

Hutton, R.H. *Essays on some of the Modern Guides to English Thought in Matters of Faith*. London: Macmillan and Co., 1891.

Hyman, Gavin. *The Predicament of Postmodern Theology: Radical Orthodoxy or Nihilist Textualism?* Louisville: Westminster John Knox Press, 2001.

- "Disinterestedness: The Idol of Modernity." In *New Directions in Philosophical Theology: Essays in Honor of Don Cupitt*. Lancaster: University of Lancaster, 2002.

Illingworth, J.R. "The Incarnation in Relation to Development." In *Lux Mundi: A Series of Studies in the Religion of the Incarnation*, 5th ed., edited by Charles Gore. London: John Murray, 1890.

Jowett, Benjamin. "On the Interpretation of Scripture." In *Essays and Reviews: The 1860 Text and Its Reading*, edited by Victor Shea and William Whitla. Charlottesville: University Press of Virginia, 2000.

Kant, Immanuel. *Critique of Pure Reason*. Translated by J.M.D. Meiklejohn. New York: Colonial Press, 1899.

- *Religion Within the Limits of Reason Alone*. Translated with an Introduction and Notes by Theodore M. Greene and Hoyt H. Hudson. New York: Harper Torchbooks, 1960.

Kendal, Gordon. "A God Most Particular: Aspects of Incarnation in Butler's Morality." In *Joseph Butler's Moral and Religious Thought: Tercentenary Essays*, edited by Christopher Cunliffe, 141–68. Oxford: Clarendon Press, 1992.

Keynes, John Maynard. *Essays in Biography*. Edited by Geoffrey Keynes. New edition with three additional essays. New York: W.W. Norton and Company, 1951.

Knockles, Peter. *The Oxford Movement: Europe and the Wider World 1830–1930*. Cambridge: Cambridge University Press, 2012.

Know, B.A. "Filling the Oxford Chair of Ecclesiastical History, 1866: the Nomination of H.L. Mansel." *Journal of Religious History* 5 (June 1968): 62–70.

Kuehn, Manfred. *Scottish Common Sense in Germany, 1768–1800: A Contribution to the History of Critical Philosophy*. Montreal and Kingston: McGill-Queen's University Press, 1987.

Levering, Matthew. "Participation and Exegesis: Response to Catherine Pickstock." *Modern Theology* 21, no. 4 (October 2005): 587–601.

– "Readings on the Rock: Typological Exegesis in Contemporary Scholarship." *Modern Theology* 28, no. 4 (October 2012): 701–31.

Lewis, C.S. *The Screwtape Letters.* New York: Time Inc., 1961.

Liddon, Henry Parry. H.P. Lidden to E.B. Pusey, 2 August 1871. Oxford: Pusey House Library.

Lightman, Bernard. *The Origins of Agnosticism: Victorian Unbelief and the Limits of Knowledge.* Baltimore: John Hopkins University Press, 1987.

Lindbeck, George. *The Nature of Doctrine: Religion and Theology in a Postliberal Age.* Louisville: Westminster John Knox Press, 1984.

Locke, John. *Reasonableness of Christianity with A Discourse on Miracles and part of A Third Letter Concerning Toleration.* Edited by I.T. Ramsay. Stanford: Stanford University Press, 1958.

Lossky, Vladimir. *In the Image and Likeness of God.* New York: St Vladimir's Press, 1974.

Lotze, Hermann. *Outlines of the Philosophy of Religion; Dictated Portions of the Lectures of Hermann Lotze.* Edited by George Trumball Ladd. Boston: Ginn, Heath & Co, 1895.

Lubac, Henri de. *Drama of Atheistic Humanism.* Translated by Edith M. Riley. London: Sheed & Ward, 1949.

– *Medieval Exegesis Vol 2: The Four Senses Of Scripture.* Grand Rapids: A & C Black, 2000.

Lyttelton, Arthur. "The Atonement." In *Lux Mundi: A Series of Studies in the Religion of the Incarnation*, 5th ed., edited by Charles Gore. London: John Murray, 1890.

Mackinnon, Donald. *A Study in Ethical Theory.* London: Adam and Charles Black, 1957.

– "Kant's Influence on English Theology." In *Kant and His Influence*, edited by George MacDonald Ross and Tony McWalter. Bristol: Thoemmes Antiquarian Books, 1990.

Mander, W.J. *British Idealism: A History.* Oxford: Oxford University Press, 2011.

Marsh, P.T. *The Victorian Church in Decline: Archbishop Tait and the Church of England, 1868–1882.* London: Routledge and Kegan Paul, 1969.

Maurice, Frederick Denison. *The Patriarchs and Lawgivers of the Old Testament: A Series of Sermons Preached in the Chapel of Lincoln's Inn.* London: Macmillan and Co., 1855.

- *Sequel to the Inquiry, What Is Revelation? in a Series of Letters to a Friend; Containing a Reply to Mr Mansel's "Examination of the Rev. F.D. Maurice's Strictures on the Bampton Lectures of 1858."* Cambridge: Macmillan and Co, 1860.
- *Theological Essays.* London: James Clarke & Co., 1957.
- *What Is Revelation?: A Series of Sermons on the Epiphany, to Which Are Added Letters to a Student of Theology on the Bampton Lectures of Mr Mansel.* New York: AMS Press, 1975.

Matthews, R.W. *The Religious Philosophy of Dean Mansel.* London: Oxford University Press, 1956.

Melnyk, Julie. *Victorian Religion: Faith and Life in Britain.* Westport: Praeger, 2008.

Meynell, Charles. "The Limits of Our Thought." *Rambler* (May 1860): 83–106.

Micheli, Giuseppe. "The Early Reception of Kant's Thought in England." In *Kant and His Influence,* edited by George MacDonald Ross and Tony McWalter. Bristol: Thoemmes Antiquarian Books, 1990.

Milbank, John. *Being Reconciled: Ontology and Pardon.* London: Routledge, 2003.
- *Theology and Social Theory: Beyond Secular Reason.* Oxford: Blackwell Publishing, 2006.
- *The Word Made Strange: Theology, Language, Culture.* Oxford: Blackwell Publishing, 1997.

Mill, J.S. *The Collected Works of John Stuart Mill, Volume 9: An Examination of William Hamilton's Philosophy [1865].* Edited by J.M. Robson. Toronto: University of Toronto Press, 1979.
- *Utilitarianism, Liberty & Representative Government.* London: Dent, 1960.

Montaigne, Michel de. "Apology for Raimond Sebond." In *The Works of Montaigne,* edited by W. Hazlitt, 199–282. London: John Templeman, 1842.

Moore, Aubrey. "The Influence of Calvinism on Modern Unbelief." In *Lectures and Papers on the History of the Reformation in England and on the Continent.* London: Kegan Paul, Trench, Trübner, 1890.

Moorman, John. *A History of the Church of England.* 3rd ed. Harrisburg: Morehouse Publishing, 1980.

Morris, Jeremy. *F.D. Maurice and the Crisis of Christian Authority.* Oxford: Oxford University Press, 2005.

Mozley, J.B. "Mansel's Bampton Lectures." *The Christian Remembrancer* 37 (April 1859): 358–61.

Newman, Francis. *Phases of Faith: Or Passages from the History of My Creed*. London: Trübner, 1881.

Newman, John Henry. *An Essay in Aid of a Grammar of Assent*. Toronto: Longmans, Green and Co., 1947.

– "John Henry Newman to Charles Meynell, May 9, 1960." In *Letters and Diaries: Volume XIX*, edited by Charles Stephen Dessain and Francis J. McGrath. London: T. Nelson, 1961.

Graham Patrick. *The Miner's Bishop: Brooke Foss Westcott*. Peterborough: Epworth Press, 2007.

Pattison, Mark. "Present State of Theology in Germany." In *Essays by the Late Mark Pattison, Sometime Rector of Lincoln College*, edited by Mark Pattison and Henry Nettleship. Oxford: Clarendon Press, 1857.

Penelhum, Terence. "Butler and Human Ignorance." In *Joseph and Religious Thought: Tercentenary Essays*, edited by Christopher Cunliffe, 117–40. Oxford: Clarendon Press, 1993.

Phillips, Gordon Lewis. *Seeing and Believing*. London: Dacre Press, 1953.

Pickstock, Catherine. "Theology and Post-modernity: An Exploration of the Origins of a New Alliance." In *New Directions in Philosophical Theology: Essays in Honor of Don Cupitt*. Lancaster: University of Lancaster, 2002.

Pittion, Jean-Paul, and David Berman. "A New Letter by Berkeley to Browne on Divine Analogy." *Mind* 78, no. 311 (July 1969): 375–92.

Polyani, Michael. *The Study of Man*. Chicago: The University of Chicago Press, 1958.

Popkin, Richard. *The History of Scepticism: From Savonarola to Bayle*. Oxford: Oxford University Press, 2003.

Prickett, Stephen. *Romanticism and Religion: The Tradition of Coleridge and Wordsworth in the Victorian Church*. Cambridge: Cambridge University Press, 1976.

Pusey, E.B. *An Historical Enquiry into the Probable Causes of the Rationalistic Character Lately Predominant in the Theology of Germany*. London: C. & J. Rivington, 1828.

Ramsay, Michael. *From Gore to Temple: The Development of Anglican Theology Between Lux Mundi and the Second World War 1889–1939*. London: Longmans, 1960.

Radner, Ephraim. "The Scriptural Community: Authority in Anglicanism." In *The Fate of Communion: The Agony of Anglicanism and the Future of the Global Church*, edited by Ephraim Radner and Philip Turner, 90–112. Grand Rapids: William B. Eerdmans Publishing Company, 2006.

– *Time and the Word: Figural Reading of the Christian Scriptures*. Grand
   Rapids, MI: William B. Eerdmans Publishing Co, 2016.

Reardon, Bernard. *Religious Thought in the Victorian Age: A Survey from
   Coleridge to Gore*. London: Longman, 1995.

Reventlow, Henning Graf. *The Authority of the Bible and the Rise of the
   Modern World*. Philadelphia: Fortress Press, 1985.

Rorty, Richard. "Nineteenth-century Idealism and Twentieth-Century
   Textualism." *The Monist* 64, no. 2 (April 1981): 155–73.

Ryan, Alan. "Introduction." In *The Collected Works of John Stuart Mill,
   Volume 9: An Examination of William Hamilton's Philosophy [1865]*,
   edited by J.M. Robson. Toronto: University of Toronto Press, 1979.

Sampson, R.V. "The Limits of Religious Thought: The Theological
   Controversy." In *1859: Entering an Age of Crisis*, edited by Philip
   Appleman, William Madden, and Michael Wolff, 63–80. Bloomington:
   Indiana University Press, 1961.

Sargent, Benjamin. "John Milbank and Hermeneutics: The End of the
   Historical Critical Method?" *Heythrop Journal* LIII (2012).

Schleiermacher, Friedrich. *The Christian Faith*. Translated and edited by
   H.R. Mackintosh and J.S. Stewart. London: T&T Clark, 1999.
   Originally published as *Der christliche Glaube. Nach den Grundsätzen
   der evangelischen Kirche im Zusammenhange dargestellt*. Berlin, 1830.

Sell, Alan. *John Locke and the Eighteenth-Century Divines*. Wales:
   University of Wales Press, 1997.

Seitz, Christopher. "Canon and Conquest: The Character of the God of the
   Hebrew Bible." In *Divine Evil?: The Moral Character of the God of
   Abraham*, edited by Michael Bergman, Michael J. Murray, and Michael
   C. Rea. Oxford: Oxford University Press, 2010.

– *Figured Out: Typology and Providence in Christian Scripture*.
   Louisville: Westminster John Knox Press, 2001.

Shakespeare, Steven. "A Hiding to Nothing: Cupitt and Derrida on the
   Mystery Tour." In *New Directions in Philosophical Theology: Essays in
   Honour of Don Cupitt*. Aldershot: Ashgate, 2004.

Sidgwick, Henry. "To H.G. Dakyns from Douglas, Isles of Man, June 9,
   1862." In *Henry Sidgwick, A Memoir*, by A. Sidgwick and E.M.
   Sidgwick. London: MacMillan, 1906.

Sparrow, Tom. *The End of Phenomenology: Metaphysics and the New
   Realism*. Edinburgh: Edinburgh University Press, 2014.

Spencer, Herbert. *First Principles*. Chicago: Rand McNally, 1915.

Spinoza, Benedict de. "Theological Political Treatise." In *The Chief Works
   of Benedict De Spinoza*. Vol. 1. Translated by R.H.M. Elwes. New
   York: Dover Publications, 1951.

Stone, Darwell. "Theology and Criticism." In *Church Quarterly Review* (April 1890).

Storr, Vernon. *The Development of English Theology in the Nineteenth Century, 1800–1860.* London: Longmans, Green and Co., 1913.

Strauss, David Friedrich. *The Life of Jesus, Critically Examined.* Cambridge: Cambridge University Press, 2010.

Strong, Rowan. "Introduction." In *The Oxford History of Anglicanism, Volume III: Partisan Anglicanism and its Global Expansion, 1829–c.1914.* Edited by Rowan Strong. Oxford: Oxford University Press, 2017.

Swanston, Hamish. *Ideas of Order: Anglicans and the Renewal of Theological Method in the Middle Years of the Nineteenth Century.* Assen: Gorcum, 1974.

Sykes, Stephen. *England and Germany: Studies in Theological Diplomacy.* Frankfurt am Main: Lang, 1982.

– *The Identity of Christianity: Theologians and the Essence of Christianity from Schliermacher to Barth.* Philadelphia: Fortress Press, 1984.

– *The Integrity of Anglicanism.* London: Mowbrays, 1979.

Talbot, E.S. "Preparation for Christ in History" In *Lux Mundi: A Series of Studies in the Religion of the Incarnation*, 5th ed., edited by Charles Gore. London: John Murray, 1890.

Taylor, Charles. *Hegel.* New York: Cambridge University Press, 1975.

– *Sources of the Self: The Making of Modern Identity.* Cambridge: Cambridge University Press, 1989.

– *The Secular Age.* Cambridge: The Belknap Press of Harvard University Press, 2007.

Tennant, Bob. *Conscience, Consciousness and Ethics in Joseph Butler's Philosophy and Ministry.* Woodbridge: Boydell Press, 2011.

Tillich, Paul. *The History of Christian Thought: From Its Judaic and Hellenistic Origins to Existentialism.* Edited by Carl Braaten. New York: Simon and Schuster, 1967.

Toland, John. *Christianity Not Mysterious: A Treatise Shewing, That There Is Nothing in the Gospel Contrary to Reason, Nor Above It: And that no Christian Doctrine can be properly call'd A Mystery.* London, 1696. Reprint, *Christianity Not Mysterious.* New York: Garland, 1978.

Turner, Frank. "Victorian Scientific Naturalism and Thomas Carlyle." *Victorian Studies* 18, no. 3 (March 1975): 325–43.

Ward, Humphrey. *Robert Elsmere.* London: T. Nelson, 1907.

Ward, W.R. "Faith and Fallacy: English and German Perspectives in the Nineteenth Century." In *Victorian Faith in Crisis: Essays on Continuity and Change in Nineteenth-Century Religious Belief*, edited by Richard

J. Helmstadter and Bernard V. Lightman. Basingstoke, Hampshire: Macmillan, 1990.

Webb, Clement. *A Study of English Thought in England from 1850.* Oxford: Clarendon Press, 1933.

– *God and Personality: Being the Gifford Lectures Delivered in the University of Aberdeen in the Years 1918 & 1919, First Course.* London: Allen & Unwin, 1918.

Webster, John. *Holy Scripture: A Dogmatic Sketch.* Cambridge: Cambridge University Press, 2003.

Wellek, Rene. *Immanuel Kant in England, 1793–1838.* Princeton: Princeton University Press, 1931.

Westcott, Brooke Foss. *The Gospel of the Resurrection: Thoughts on Its Relation to Reason and History.* London: Macmillan, 1884.

– "Christianity as the Absolute Religion." In *Essays in the History of Religious Thought in the West.* London: Macmillan, 1891.

– *Christus Consummator: Some Aspects of the Work and Person of Christ in Relation to Modern Thought.* London: Macmillan, 1890.

White, Stephen Ross. *Authority and Anglicanism.* London: SCM Press, 1996.

Williams, Rowan. *Anglican Identities.* Cambridge: Cowley Publications, 2003.

– "General Introductions." In *Love's Redeeming Work: The Anglican Quest for Holiness,* compiled by Geoffrey Rowell, Kenneth Stevenson, and Rowan Williams. Oxford: Oxford University Press, 2001.

– "Religious Realism: On Not Quite Agreeing With Don Cupitt." In *Wrestling With Angels: Conversations in Modern Theology.* Grand Rapids: William B. Eerdmans Publishing, 2007.

Wilson, A.N. *God's Funeral.* London: John Murray, 1999.

Winnett, A.W. *Peter Browne: Provost, Bishop, Metaphysician.* London: S.P.C.K., 1974.

Wolff, Michael. "Victorian Reviewers and Cultural Responsibility." In *1859: Entering an Age of Crisis,* edited by Philip Appleman, William Madden, and Michael Wolff. Bloomington: Indiana University Press, 1959.

Wolterstorff, Nicholas. "Reading Joshua." In *Divine Evil? The Moral Character of the God of Abraham,* edited by Michael Bergmann, Michael J. Murray, and Michael C. Rea. Oxford: Oxford University Press, 2010.

Work, Telford. *Living and Active: Scripture in the Economy of Salvation.* Grand Rapids, MI: William B. Eerdmans Publishing Co, 2002.

Index